the
BATTLE of the
BIG HOLE

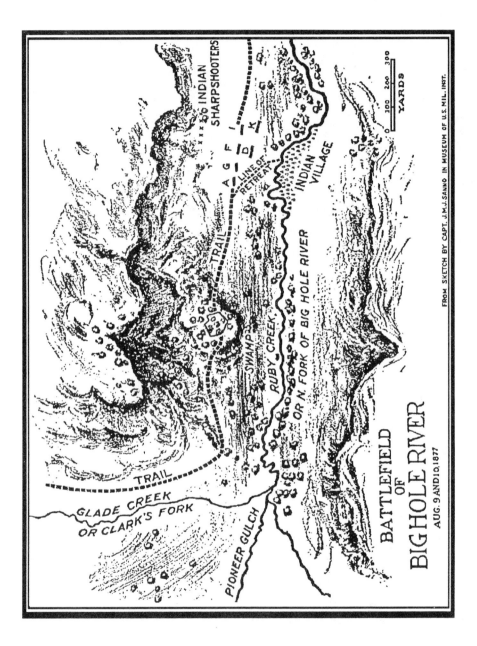

INDIAN SHARPSHOOTERS

Line of retreat

A G F
D
I
K

TRAIL

SWAMP

RUBY CREEK

INDIAN VILLAGE

OR N. FORK OF BIG HOLE RIVER

TRAIL

GLADE CREEK
OR CLARK'S FORK

PIONEER GULCH

100 200 300
YARDS

FROM SKETCH BY CAPT. J.M.J.SANNO IN MUSEUM OF U.S. MIL. INST.

BATTLEFIELD
OF
BIG HOLE RIVER
AUG. 9 AND 10, 1877

the BATTLE of the BIG HOLE

The Story of the Landmark Battle of the 1877 Nez Perce War

AUBREY L. HAINES

TWODOT®

GUILFORD, CONNECTICUT
HELENA, MONTANA
AN IMPRINT OF THE GLOBE PEQUOT PRESS

To buy books in quantity for corporate use
or incentives, call **(800) 962–0973, ext. 4551,**
or e-mail **premiums@GlobePequot.com.**

A · T W O D O T® · B O O K

Frontispiece reproduced from Brady's Northwest *Fights and Fighters* (1909).

Library of Congress Cataloging-in-Publication Data
Haines, Aubrey L.
  Battle of the Big Hole : the story of the landmark battle of the 1877 Nez Perce War / Aubrey L. Haines. — 2nd ed.
     p. cm.
  Includes bibliographical references and index.
  ISBN-13: 978-0-7627-4148-9 (alk. paper)
  ISBN-10: 0-7627-4148-1 (alk. paper)
  1. Big Hole, Battle of the, Mont., 1877 2. Nez Percé Indians—Wars, 1877.
3. Nez Percé Indians—History. 4. Nez Percé Indians—Government relations.
I. Title.
  E83.877.H34 2007
  973.8'3—dc22
                                                            2006023154

Manufactured in the United States of America
First Globe Pequot Edition/First Printing

CONTENTS

ILLUSTRATIONS

MAPS

PREFACE

Colonel John Gibbon's claim to a victory in the Battle of the Big Hole, because his command "slept on the field of battle," ignores the fact that he failed to accomplish his intended purpose of stopping the Nez Perce retreat. Instead, victory slipped from his grasp when the Nez Perces unexpectedly rallied following the dawn attack on their encampment, driving his remaining men into a defensive position where they remained under siege — surviving only because the Nez Perces were unwilling to pay the cost of a direct assault.

On the other hand, the battle was also something less than a victory for the Nez Perces because, like King Pyrrhus of old, they paid more for their success than it was worth. Though forced to abandon their homeland, with loss of much stock and property, the fighting strength of the non-treaty bands was not seriously impaired by the earlier conflicts in Idaho. Before the Big Hole fight the Nez Perces believed they could cross the mountains to the buffalo land and resume life in safety among friends of former days, but after it they understood that every hand was against them, and that their situation was perilous indeed. For them, it was not so much a victory as a reprieve, with despair taking the place of hope.

From a broader perspective, the Battle of the Big Hole, like the military campaign in which it was the central event, was similar to a Greek tragedy — quite devoid of real winners, from any viewpoint.

The battle is, in itself, an interesting set-piece. The locale is nearly the same in appearance as it was a century ago and the areas where the fighting took place have suffered only a minimal disturbance over the intervening years. The historical record is particularly complete, with adequate coverage of all events from the differing viewpoints of the soldiers, civilian volunteers and Nez Perces involved, and there are no great unknowns to trouble interpretation and foster myth. The record is supported by a fortunate artifact recovery based on systematic metal locator searches in which all finds were mapped in place for future reference. And yet, the story latent in what is surely one of the best documented fights of all our struggles with the western Indians has received, at best, only chapter treatment in works concerned with the entire Nez Perce War of 1877.

It has been evident for many years that the available information would justify a book on the battle and its associated events, and I had marked it as a possible future project. And so, when Jock Whitworth called me in the spring of 1989 to ask if I was interested in writing such a book, the answer was an enthusiastic *"Yes!"* But there was more in that acceptance than just the opportunity to turn out a needed book; there was also a personal reason best explained as nostalgia remaining from an earlier association with the old Big Hole National Battlefield. Hopefully, this work profits from those experiences of more than a quarter century ago.

Something needs to be said about the historical basis of the work. Much which has been written previously about the Big Hole battle suffers from over reliance on the reminiscent accounts of aged participants, introducing error and confusion into the record. Of course, each item had to be assessed on its particular merits, but, generally, contemporary sources such as documents, reports, letters, diary entries and news items were given preference.

The contemporary records used were of three types: official military, private (letters and diaries), and news items. Access to records pertinent to the Nez Perce War of 1877, as reproduced by National Archives from file 3464 AGO 1877, was had on microfilm rolls 666-336 through 340. Reports of officers — line, field and staff — were found in *Reports Of The Secretary Of War* (1877), Vol. I. The early records of Fort Missoula, as edited by Capt. A. E. Rothermich, were available in *The Frontier And Midland*, XVI/3 (1930), while reports of Generals Phillip H. Sheridan and William T. Sherman, were published in *Reports Of Inspections Made In The Summer Of 1877* (1878). Muster rolls of the Seventh Infantry and pension records of individual soldiers were provided by Big Hole National Battlefield (obtained from National Archives). Copies of correspondence between military officers and officials of the government of Montana Territory, as edited by Dr. Paul C. Phillips, were available in *The Frontier And Midland,* X/1 (1929), and miscellaneous statistics were obtained from Heitman's *Historical Register And Dictionary Of The United States Army*, 1789-1903, 3 Vols. (1903).

Contemporary records of a private nature included Lt. Charles A. Woodruff's correspondence with his wife, as edited by Edgar Stewart in *The Montana Magazine Of History*, II/4 (1952), and excerpts from the "Diary of Lt. Edward E. Hardin, 7th Infantry, 1874-78," as furnished to the author by Historian Don Rickey, Jr.

The Big Hole battle, and its peripheral events, was reported extensively in the newspapers of Montana Territory, but the most important local coverage was found in *The Weekly Missoulian, The New North-West* (Deer Lodge), *The Madisonian* (Virginia City), *The Helena Daily Herald, The Avant Courier* (Bozeman), *The Butte Miner*, and *The Benton Record*. Duncan McDonald's series of articles in the *New North-West*, in which he presented the Nez Perce view of the war, as obtained from Chief White Bird's people in Canada, was particularly important, as were several items which appeared in *The Nation*.

Reminiscent accounts which were used, though with the degree of reservation which seemed appropriate in each case were similarly grouped, according to origin: soldier, citizen or Nez Perce. Perhaps the most influential, at least in former years, was *The Battle Of The Big Hole*, by G. O. Shields (1889), some of which was plagiarized from Duncan McDonald's article in *The New North-West* (and which is otherwise unduly biased in favor of the military). *Nez Perce Joseph . . . His Pursuit And Capture*, by Gen. O. O. Howard (1881), is a self-serving account with a romantic tinge, and *A Vision Of The "Big Hole,"* by Gen. John Gibbon (1882), though in poetic form, adds some essential facts, while his later article in *Harper's Weekly*, "Battle of the Big Hole," (1895), provides details not in his official report. "Battle of the Big Hole," by Gen. C. A. Woodruff, in *Contributions To The Historical Society Of Montana* (1910), is correct in all but a few minor details. "Battle of the Big Hole," by Cpl. C. W. Loynes, in *Winners Of The West* (March, 1925), is in error in many details while others cannot be substantiated, and "The Outbreak of Chief Joseph," by Pvt. Homer Coon (Coe Collection MS., Yale, n. d.), is also unreliable in many details.

The reminiscent accounts originating with citizen volunteers comprise a large group because of the proximity of the battlefield to their homes and continuity encouraged by reunions and local historical groups. *The Story Of Ajax*, by A. J. Noyes (1914), is an above-average account of peripheral events, while the "Review of the Battle of the Big Hole," by Amos Buck, published in *Contributions To The Historical Society Of Montana* (1910), is, in much of its text, so similar to "The Battle of the Big Hole," by John Catlin, in *Montana State Historian's Report* (1927), that one must have been drawn from the other, with internal evidence indicating that the Catlin manuscript is considerably older, regardless of the date of publication. "The Battle of the Big Hole As I Saw It," told to A. J. Noyes by T. C. Sherrill (n. d.), is mainly believable, though later accounts of Sherrill's are very unreliable. The untitled and undated account of M. F. Sherrill, as told to A. J. Noyes, (Montana Historical Society, SC-739), is also unreliable. "Bitter Indian Battle Near Missoula," by Will Cave, in *Daily Missoulian* (Aug. 7, 1921), is mainly hearsay, except for Cave's boyhood recollections and what he heard from his uncle, Captain Catlin, and "Battle of the Big Hole in August, 1877," by Ella C. Hathaway is also hearsay, except for some rather dubious information she obtained from Tom Sherrill. "The Story of the Nez Perce Indian Campaign During the Summer of 1877," by Henry Buck (1927), published serially in the *Great Falls Tribune* (1944-45), provides a peripheral view of the Nez Perces in the Bitterroot Valley and Gen. Howard's pursuit. *Brother Van*, by Stella W. Brummitt (1919), provides a post-battle view of the battlefield, as does *The Calumet Of The Coteau*, by P. W. Norris (1884).

The Nez Perce accounts are all reminiscent, with the greater number known from *Yellow Wolf, His Own Story*, by L. V. McWhorter (1940), which is, at some points, contradictory, and at others, not in agreement with known facts; and yet, it is a useful, even indispensable work, as is the later (1952) *Hear Me, My Chiefs!*. *The North American Indian*, by E. S. Curtis (Hodge, VIII, 1974), contains three important accounts — Yellow Bull, Tom Hill and W. R. Logan. The article, "An Indian's View of Indian Affairs," by Chief Joseph in *North American Review* (April, 1879), is a memorable glimpse into the mind of that great man.

Among a number of compiled works used, the following were found to be the most useful: *The Flight Of The Nez Perce*, by Mark Brown (1967); *I Will Fight No More Forever*, by Merrill D. Beal (1963); *The Nez Perce Indians And The Opening Of The Northwest*, by Alvin M. Josephy (1965); and *History Of Montana, 1739-1885*, by M. A. Leeson (1885).

Of course, over the years, many people have contributed generously of their time and knowledge, so that what appears in these pages is also the fruition of their efforts. Foremost among them is my long-time friend, Jack R. Williams, whose stewardship of the battlefield put the place together and made it one of the small areas the National Park Service could be proud of. It was his enthusiasm and ability that provided, for what was then an unwanted stepchild of Yellowstone Park, an office, small museum, signs, a self-guiding trail system where points of interest were marked — hats for soldiers, feathers for Nez Perces and Celtic crosses for casualties — with each numbered point explained in a trail guide of his design. Jack also slyly involved me his researches into the area's history, though I really had enough to do at that time as historian for Yellowstone. Now that he is retired, after serving as the second Superintendent of Nez Perce National Park, I can even-up with him by drawing upon his great knowledge of the Nez Perces for the Prologue and Epilogue for this book.

Kermit M. Edmonds, who was a seasonal historian at Big Hole Battlefield for a number of seasons, began the process of marking on the ground those places where battle artifacts were found, and his systematic cataloguing, description and storage became the basis of the area's valuable study collection. Mapping of the three battle areas — Nez Perce encampment, siege area and howitzer site — by field survey methods evolved out of his work. Kermit has remained in contact over the years, contributing to the store of knowledge concerning the battle right down to the present time.

My particular appreciation is due another friend of many years, Stuart W. Conner, whose great interest in the Nez Perce War of 1877 led him to purchase microfilm copies of the pertinent records which are a part of the National Archives. Those he shared with me, thereby making available a mass of records which would have been beyond my reach.

The present Unit Manager, Jock F. Whitworth, who got this project started last year, has been generous in providing copies of important records from Big Hole National Battlefield's research collection — particularly the muster rolls of the Seventh Infantry and the files on officers and enlisted men.

Many librarians and archivists gave of their time assisting me with the tedious newspaper research which was such an important aspect of the project. The staff at the Montana Historical Society, where they put up with me for several weeks last summer, as well as off and on during the Sixties and Seventies, has always been helpful.

My son, Calvin, has been my computer expert, instructing a slow learner in the intricacies of an unfamiliar word processor, and he is the one who has put my efforts into "camera-ready" copy for the printer. There is one more I would like to thank if I could; Betsy, my teen-aged daughter of twenty-five years ago, who was more of a help and inspiration than she ever knew.

Aubrey L. Haines
Tucson, Arizona.

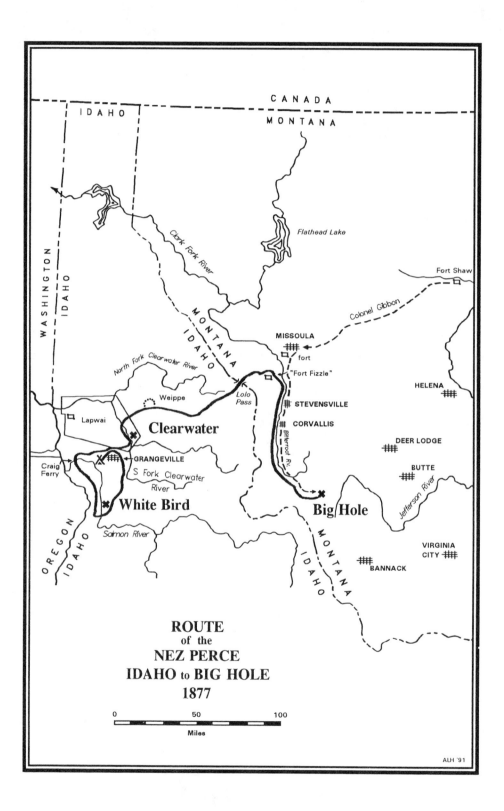

CANADA

MONTANA

IDAHO

WASHINGTON

IDAHO

Clark Fork River

Flathead Lake

Fort Shaw

Colonel Gibbon

MONTANA

IDAHO

MISSOULA

fort

"Fort Fizzle"

North Fork Clearwater River

Weippe

Lolo Pass

HELENA

Lapwai

STEVENSVILLE

CORVALLIS

Clearwater

DEER LODGE

Craig Ferry

GRANGEVILLE

S Fork Clearwater River

Bitterroot Rv.

BUTTE

Jefferson River

White Bird

Big Hole

OREGON

IDAHO

Salmon River

MONTANA

IDAHO

VIRGINIA CITY

BANNACK

ROUTE
of the
NEZ PERCE
IDAHO to BIG HOLE
1877

0   50   100

Miles

ALH '91

PROLOGUE

They were neither yelling demon nor Noble Savage,
They were a people.
A people not yet fused,
Made into a whole nation, but beginning,
As the Gauls began, or the Britons that Caesar found,
As the Greeks began in their time.

They were a people, beginning —
with beliefs,
Ornaments, language, fables, love of children
(You will find that spoken of in all the books)
And a scheme of life that worked.

Stephen Vincent Benet

History can be very unfair.   Especially where it involves a conflict of cultures. A prime example of this is the tragedy of the Nez Perce Indians in the Pacific Northwest, which was due to the fickleness of politics: Federal, church and local.

The problem began innocently enough in 1805-06 when the Lewis and Clark Expedition passed through the country of a people they called *Chopunnish,* who befriended them with food, shelter, horses and guides. These Sahaptin speaking people, who called themselves *Ne-Mee-Poom* (The People) are better known as Nez Perces. That name, from Canadian French for *"Pierced Nose,"* is a misnomer but firmly established.

The Lewis and Clark expedition precipitated the Nez Perces into the trapper/trader era almost simultaneously with the missionary movement. By 1836 when the Reverend H. H. Spalding, a Protestant missionary, settled on the Clearwater River, at the mouth of Lapwai Creek, to *"save the heathens,"* troubles were brewing in the Pacific Northwest. The United States and Great Britain were squabbling over sovereignty, fur trade rivalry was sharp, and animosities between Indian tribes, and between bands within tribes, flared through a concern for their territorial *"rights."* Into that touchy situation came settlers — hungry for land.

In 1845, the expression *"Manifest Destiny"* appeared. It was a term used to describe a *belief* in the inevitability of the territorial expansion of the United States. Those who preached manifest destiny maintained that the United States, through the superiority of its institutions, resources, and rapidly growing population, should rule all of North America. Such reasoning assuaged the consciences of many who might otherwise have looked upon the taking of Indian land as immoral; others used it as a quasi-legal umbrella to cover pillage and murder.

The treaty of 1855 established a reservation for the Nez Perces of about 12,000 square miles (out of an original homeland of nearly 30,000) in Idaho, Oregon and Washington. But discovery of gold in Idaho in 1860 led to another treaty in 1863 reducing the reservation tenfold — to 784,996 acres — with all of it lying in Idaho. A consequence was creation of a rift in the Nez Perce Nation. Chiefs of the five bands living outside the reduced boundaries refused to sign the treaty or acknowledge it was binding on them due to differences varying from the religious to the political. Henceforth these bands were referred to as the non-treaty Nez Perces.

Congress amended, and finally ratified, the 1863 treaty in 1868, entirely disregarding the rightful claims of the non-treaty bands. By 1876, as far as the white settlers were concerned, they were faced with an Indian problem that demanded resolution. In October of that year, Secretary of the Interior Zachary Chandler established a commission to visit the Nez Perces and find ways to solve the difficulties existing between the non-treaties and the settlers.

The recommendations of the commission added up to just one thing — an ultimatum. If the non-treaty Nez Perces did not suppress the Dreamer religion and peacefully settle on the reservation within a reasonable time, military force would be used.

To effect the *"reasonable time"* stipulation, the government, in January of 1877, instructed General Oliver O. Howard to implement the removal of the non-treaty bands to the Lapwai reservation. Agent Monteith notified the chiefs that it was the *"wish and purpose of the government for them to come to the reservation by April 1."* Subsequent meetings by Ollokot (Chief Joseph's brother and emissary) and others, with Monteith in March, and with General Howard at Walla Walla in April, resulted in a final council between Howard and the non-treaty bands to be held at Fort Lapwai beginning May 3.

At the council, Chief Toohoolhoolzote, who was also a Dreamer *"priest,"* was so angrily adamant in his stand against going onto the reservation that General Howard had him confined to the guardhouse. Though Chief Joseph reiterated their past grievances with great eloquence and sincerity, it was immediately apparent from General Howard's reply that he was only there to reaffirm the ultimatum. Unknown to the Indians, Agent Monteith had, on that very day, formally requested General Howard to put the non-treaty bands on the reservation; what they did know was that he had *"shown them the rifle."* The council was a mockery.

Though the chiefs were offended by General Howard's arrogance and the thirty-day deadline he set for them to move themselves, their possessions and their livestock to certain vacant lands upon the reservation, they did agree to examine the lands offered them, and in return, asked that Toohoolhoolzote be released from jail. He was.

Reluctant to begin their move while the rivers were in flood, the Nez Perces had to be prodded. On May 14, General Howard told them they had thirty days and no more, and he began positioning his troops. After seeing one troop of cavalry arrive at Fort Lapwai and learning of the approach of two more, the chiefs recognized that their situation was perilous. Only Toohoolhoolzote desired to fight, so they returned to their various homes to begin the tremendous task of moving. One can perceive the difficulty of accomplishing such an undertaking in that short time *only* by knowing the vastness of the area, the deep and rough canyons to negotiate, the flood-swollen rivers to be crossed — all on foot or horseback.

Joseph's band suffered the greatest loss: of personal possessions left behind, of cattle and horses abandoned or stolen by white settlers, and both possessions and stock lost in the swirling flood waters of Snake River.

By June 2, the approximately 600 people of the non-treaty bands met at Tolo Lake, on the prairie six miles west of Grangeville, Idaho. With twelve days remaining, they set up camp for their last gathering before submitting to reservation life. This was a fatal mistake, for, as the deadline approached, a warlike spirit developed in many and tempers flared easily.

One young man of White Bird's band was shamed for having failed to avenge the death of his father, killed some years earlier by a settler he had befriended. So, Wah-Lit-Its and two cousins went in search of the man but were unable to find him; instead, they went to the home of an elderly white man they hated for his past brutal treatment of Nez Perces and shot him dead. Before the day was over they had killed three more white men and wounded three others living along Salmon River.

News of this created a near panic at the Tolo Lake camp. Joseph and his brother, Ollokot, pleaded for restraint, saying things could be explained to the Army, so that the actions of a few would not condemn the entire group. But others felt differently and for two days twenty-odd Nez Perces took their revenge on white men by killing, looting and burning. By then all the chiefs recognized the need for a safer haven and the bands moved to White Bird Canyon, where they hoped to stop the depredations and explain to the military just what had happened.

However, that was not to be. General Howard, who felt certain Joseph had started the war, sent Captain Perry with two troops of cavalry to protect the settlers, and with him went Arthur Chapman, a white man married to a Umatilla Indian woman, as guide and interpreter. He spoke the Nez Perce language, but was an officious, self-styled expert that the Indians held in contempt. Chapman told Perry the Nez Perces were cowardly scoundrels and could be whipped easily.

That was all the urging Captain Perry needed. Accompanied by eleven citizen volunteers who knew the country, his small force left Grangeville at 9 p.m. on the night of June 16, intending to attack the camp in White Bird Canyon at dawn. About midnight they reached the top of White Bird Hill and were immediately spotted by Nez Perce sentries who sent word down to the village.

Everything was against Captain Perry. The route of attack was long, broad and open. The terrain below afforded the Indians numerous hiding places. The Nez Perce warriors were in widely dispersed groups and ready, but they wanted to talk. A peace party with a white flag was advancing toward the soldiers when Arthur Chapman (whom the Indians recognized by his big, white hat) ruined a chance to avert war by firing two shots at the group.

The troops were doomed from the beginning because the return fire killed Perry's bugler and prevented him from maneuvering his men. The uncontrolled fight was brief. First, the volunteers panicked, then the cavalry became disorganized from a Nez Perce mounted charge, and a general rout back up the hill, nearly to Grangeville, developed. Lieutenant Theller and 33 enlisted men died, but only two Nez Perces were wounded.

Sixty-three rifles and many pistols were recovered by the warriors to augment their armament of bows and miscellaneous firearms. It was a significant victory; 60 to 70 fighters from three non-treaty bands had vanquished a command which included 100 soldiers and 11 citizens under four regular officers.

For the next three weeks General Howard played hide-and-seek with the "hostiles," as he called them. Though encumbered with 3,000 horses, their possessions, their old and blind people, and a preponderance of women and children, the Indians were able to stay two days ahead of the soldiers (even though they had to cross the swollen Salmon River twice). To Howard's dismay upon returning to Grangeville on July 8, he found that his plan to have Captain Whipple escort Chief Looking Glass — a strong advocate of peace — and his band to Grangeville for safekeeping had resulted in an unprovoked attack. The result was that those Nez Perces, though left practically destitute, escaped to join the other bands camped nearby.

Howard also learned that Captain Whipple had lost a citizen scout on July 3, and the following day, Lieutenant Rains and a select group of ten men were attacked and killed near their camp at Cottonwood by a party of warriors under Five Wounds, Rainbow, and Two Moons. No Indians were hurt in those actions.

A reinforcement of 17 volunteers under Captain Randall approaching Cottonwood from Mount Idaho were attacked a mile and a half from the camp. When soldiers came to their rescue, Captain Randall and another lay dead, and three men were wounded. It was in this fight that the first Nez Perce fighter was killed (due to his unmanageable horse). The civilians claimed they were attacked by 136 warriors, but the number was actually much less.

Citizen morale was further damaged when 80 volunteers under Captain McConville were kept pinned down by Ollokot and a small group of warriors, who also managed to recover 40 horses the Army had captured in the attack on the village of Looking Glass.

At this time an embarrassed General Howard decided to end the mess by an attack on the hostile encampment on the South Fork of Clearwater. Gathering his troops he moved down the river. For some unexplained reason, he crossed the river two miles above, so that, on the morning of July 11, the soldiers were on a high plateau, above and across from the Nez Perce encampment — their presence entirely unknown to the Indians.

For the first time the Nez Perces came under cannon fire when Howard unlimbered his artillery and commenced firing on the camp nearly a mile away. The Army's position, on a bluff from which they could not easily descend, was a poor one, so that Chief Toohoolhoolzote with 24 picked warriors was able to prevent Howard's 400 men from descending to the river during two days of fierce fighting.

Many of the Indians appeared to be in a state of panic and took little or no part in the fighting. On the second day the screen of warriors withdrew to the Indian camp and began a very hasty evacuation of the families. The haste and confusion prevented the Nez Perces from taking a portion of their supplies — which may have been to their advantage. When the soldiers reached the camp the temptation to plunder and destroy was too great, and the pursuit was delayed, allowing the fleeing Nez Perces to escape.

The Indians moved down the Clearwater to Kamiah that day, and at dawn of the next, bull boats, made from bent poles covered with buffalo hide tipi covers, were used to ferry the women, children, infirm and their supplies across to the east side. By late afternoon all were safely over and encamped beyond howitzer range of the crossing.

Back scouts kept the people informed as to the whereabouts of the troops by their ingenious message relay system based on blanket waving. This allowed the warriors to prepare a holding action against the cavalry when they came to the crossing. A few random shots across the river sent the troops back to the security of the nearby bluff.

An interesting bit of strategy was employed by the band chiefs the next morning to gain time, and possibly peace. As the camp was being struck in preparation for a move farther east, a young fighter and good talker from Joseph's band was sent to pretend a surrender. Several volunteers thought this man, No Heart, was Chief Joseph. The ruse worked, for General Howard held up the crossing until shortly after noon, when a shot was fired at No Heart. It missed, but that was all the young man needed to be on his way. As a parting gesture of contempt he slapped his bare buttock toward the troops before riding off.

There was discord among the non-treaty bands as they left Kamiah, the legendary *"Home-of-creation"* of the Nez Perce people; some wished to continue the fight in the homeland, some would seek a new home among old friends, the Crows, in Montana, while others wanted to surrender. Ten miles northeast of Kamiah, at Weippe Prairie, the bands halted to decide what to do. In council on the evening of July 15, the decision was made to go to Montana. Joseph did not want to go but was out voted by Looking Glass, Toohoolhoolzote and others. He agreed only reluctantly, intending to return when things quieted down. It was a decision undoubtedly based on his promise to his dying father never to give up their beloved Wallowa Valley. His attitude toward the treaty which deprived him of his land through the operation of the white man's principle of majority rule was explained to C. S. Wood in 1884 by the use of a parable. He said: *"A man comes to me, and says, 'Joseph, I like your horses, and I want to buy them.' I say I do not want to sell them. Then he goes to my neighbor and says, 'Joseph has some good horses, but he will not sell them,' and my neighbor says, 'Pay me and you may have them.' And he does so, and then comes to me, and says, 'Joseph, I have bought your horses.'"* He considered that if he had ever sold his land, that was the way it had happened. Joseph told the others that he would conduct the retreat of the women and children, while they, the fighters, with Looking Glass as war chief, must keep the soldiers away.

When the non-treaty bands arrived at Weippe Prairie, they found Chief Red Heart there with twenty of his people who were returning from a hunting trek to Montana. They knew about the hostilities and were camped there to avoid involvement. Continuing toward the reservation on July 16, those peaceful people were gathered in by General Howard's advance guard near Kamiah, and were roughly handled and imprisoned until the fighting was over.

For some time the Nez Perces had been referring to General Howard as *"General Day-After-Tomorrow"* because he seemed to stay that distance behind them. Reaching Kamiah on the 13th, he halted his advance for over two weeks, sending dispatches to the outside world that victory was imminent. He made plans, but waited for reinforcements, before attempting to carry them out.

There was one exception. On July 17 he sent Colonel Mason with a party of volunteers and friendly Nez Perce scouts to follow the hostiles for two days and find out which way they were going. They found out on the first day's march.

A rear guard of 17 warriors had been left near Weippe Prairie, at the beginning of the Lolo trail, to find out if the Army was going to pursue. Mason's Indian scouts were 400 yards in front of his command when they were fired on by Rainbow's rear guard. With one scout dead and two wounded, Colonel Mason returned *"in haste"* to General Howard. Many Nez Perce thought Rainbow could have turned the encounter into a victory similar to that at White Bird Canyon, but he prudently retired without loss.

For a full week the 700 non-treaty Nez Perces drove the 2,000 horses left to them over the terribly rough Lolo trail, believing they were leaving the war behind them in Idaho; but theirs was not a war to be fought on tribal terms. The war was going to Montana also, and would meet them there.

Chapter 1

WAR COMES TO MONTANA

The Nez Perce War came to Montana Territory in waves of panic and confusion. The first accounts of the murder of settlers on Idaho's Salmon River, followed by news of the defeat of regular troops in White Bird Canyon on June 17, 1877, were quite enough to raise the specter of a general Indian uprising — a particularly unnerving prospect for the residents of the few small towns and many scattered ranches of the territory's western valleys. In addition to a feeling of nakedness before any onslaught from the west (a direct result of an alignment of such defenses as there were to form a barrier against the Sioux menace on the east), the people of western Montana believed local Indians — particularly Flatheads and Pend d'Oreilles — might turn against them.

While no record of the population of Missoula County in June of 1877 has been found, it probably did not differ greatly from the estimate Missoula resident Frank Woody provided an officer at Fort Missoula two years later. He listed 1,875 white residents, distributed as follows: Missoula City, 500; Frenchtown, 180; Stevensville, 150; Corvallis, 100; Skalkaho, 75; rural Bitterroot Valley, 400; Hell Gate and Grass Valleys, 300; mining camps, 160; Flathead Lake country, 20, and Horse Plains, 10. The resident Indians were given as 350 Flatheads of Chief Charlot's band, who had refused to move onto the Jocko Reservation and were living as best they could in the vicinity of Stevensville, and a reservation population of 120 more Flatheads, 1,000 Pend d'Oreilles and 500 Kootenais.[1] Add to those Salish Indians eleven lodges of Nez Perces under Eagle-from-the-Light — probably no more than 50 in number — who, though they spoke a somewhat different language, made their home in the Bitterroot Valley with Charlot's Flatheads in 1877.

Though often termed a *"city"* by residents, Missoula was only *"a nice little place"* in 1877, according to Lieutenant Edward E. Hardin's diary entry for August 3rd.[2] In addition to being the county seat, it did have a hotel (the Kennedy House), bank, newspaper (*The Weekly Missoulian*, published by Chauncey Barbour), a half-dozen stores (several being of brick and stone construction), with work on the building which would later house the Missoula Mercantile progressing well. A grist mill and two saw mills were nearby. The town owed its

---

[1]Letter, Lt. Col. George Gibson to Delos B. Sackett, Inspector General, Headquarters, Division of the Missouri, October 8, 1879. This letter was first published, with other correspondence, by Captain A. E. Rothermich in "Early Days at Fort Missoula" (*The Frontier*, Vol.X, No.1, November, 1929). The article has been reprinted in *Frontier Omnibus*, John W. Hakola, ed., (Missoula: Montana State University Press, 1962), pp. 385-97. See pp. 392 and 395 for the population figures quoted. Further reference to this article will be cited as *Frontier Omnibus*.

[2]Excerpts from the "Diary of Lt. Edward E. Hardin, 7th Infantry, 1874-78" were supplied by Don Rickey, Jr., from a typed copy in his possession.

local importance to fortunate placement transportation-wise. It was on the old Mullan Road (the military route connecting Fort Walla Walla, Washington Territory, with Fort Benton, Montana Territory, at the head of navigation on the Missouri River), and that east-west travel axis insured reasonably good connections with Helena, by then the seat of Territorial Government, and, by way of a spur road off of that *"main stem,"* with the neighboring towns of Deer Lodge and Butte. From Missoula, a road ran south up the Bitterroot Valley to Stevensville (the point of first permanent white settlement in Montana; evidences of that remaining in old Fort Owen and the St. Marys Mission church), and on to Corvallis and Skalkaho. Hamilton had not yet appeared as a town, the rudimentary settlement at that point passing as *"the big corral"*. North from Missoula, or rather, from nearby Frenchtown, there was a road to the Indian agency on the Jocko Reservation.

The Bitterroot Valley settlers, living as they did adjacent to a large Indian population, had earlier felt the need for a military installation capable of insuring peaceful relations. At the urging of their Territorial Delegate to Congress, Lieutenant General Phillip H. Sheridan sent an officer to investigate, and, on February 8, 1876, he reported favorably with regard to the establishment of a small military post *"at or near Hell Gate Pass, in the Missoula valley."* The President, on February 19, 1877, set aside Section 31, Township 13 North, Range 19 West (Helena Land District), for use as a military reservation, and it was so declared in General Order No.4, March 17, 1877, Department of Dakota.[3]

Captain Charles C. Rawn,[4] who was to be the commanding officer of the new post, arrived at Missoula on June 19th. His men — Company "A", Seventh United States Infantry — arrived on the 25th, accompanied by Captain William Logan and "I" Company, detailed to assist with construction. For a time the post had no formal name, though local wags suggested it should be called *"Camp Wright,"* because *"the mere mention"* of the name of Colonel Wright *"was always sufficient to induce good behavior among all the Indians!"* (Prompt hanging of a number of Indians following the Yakima War of 1855, without close inquiry as to the degree of guilt, had got the attention of all tribes in the Pacific Northwest). Perhaps there was merit in the joke as work was barely begun on the post when Rawn's command was drawn into the Nez Perce War.

Word of the disaster which had overtaken Captain David Perry and his command in White Bird Canyon reached the Bitterroot Valley on the evening of June 22 — after traveling by courier to Walla Walla, Washington Territory, the nearest town to the battlefield with a telegraph office, and by the daily mail coach from Deer Lodge, the terminus of that fragile, round-about connection. But, ten days after the fight, enough was known concerning the serious nature of that conflict to cause the Bitterroot settlers to organize for defense and address a letter to Captain Rawn asking for arms and ammunition.

His reply to J. A. Landram, of Stevensville, which appears to have been written the following day, except for the postscript, states:

---

[3]*Frontier Omnibus*, p. 385; cited in Note 1.
[4]Rawn was the senior captain of the 7th Infantry.

This office in receipt this morning of Memorial signed by yourself and thirty-one others and dated June 27th, 1877, respecting formation of Militia Company for home defense against hostile Indians, and requesting use of arms from Government. The Commanding Officer of Post (Capt. C. C. Rawn, 7th Infantry) directs me to say in reply: That it is not in his power to comply directly. At present he has no arms for this purpose and is not allowed to issue or loan the arms in his charge to civilians without special authority. Your communication will however be forwarded at once by mail to General Gibbon commanding military district of Montana at Fort Shaw, M.T. It is respectfully suggested that you apply to the Governor of the Territory as it is thought to be especially the province of that Executive to provide for your organization and equipment.

P.S. — It is understood that the people of Missoula City have just received one hundred stand of arms on the Governor's requisition.[5]

It is not clear why Captain Rawn's reply, obviously written on the 28th, was held up three days unless, before posting, he received word of Governor Benjamin F. Potts' intention to look into the Indian scare; the postscript could be construed that way. It is a fact that two editors, James H. Mills of the Deer Lodge *New North-West* (who was also acting secretary to the governor), and Chauncey Barbour of the *Missoulian*, left Deer Lodge early on the 29th for that purpose. At Missoula they found *"a great many rumors floating in the air, many of which are born of terrified imaginations."* Among the things they chose to believe were these: that three Nez Perce Indians had already visited the Flathead reservation, presumably to subvert those friendlies; that the headmen believed the young men of both the Flatheads and Pend d'Oreilles would join the Nez Perce dissidents, if they had a chance; and, that both Chief Charlot's band of non-treaty Flatheads and Eagle-from-the-Light's small band of Nez Perces were absent from their usual haunts in the Bitterroot Valley. That evening Barbour wrote the Governor, *"it is certain that our Indians are fully advised of all that is transpiring,"* and he added, *"We cannot lull people into security of staying at home to be massacred . . . a military organization was effected here today."*[6] Governor Potts responded by sending the arms to Missoula, as noted by Captain Rawn.

A tentative plan to effectively seal off the valley from the intrusion of dissidents was discussed with Captain Rawn, who was asked to put pickets on the

---

[5]Letter, Lieut. A.B. Johnson, to J.A. Landram, Stevensville, Missoula Co., M.T., [marked as dispatched July 1, 1877]. *Frontier Omnibus*, p. 386; cited in Note 1. A Joint Resolution of Congress, approved July 3, 1876, allowed the Secretary of War to make certain quantities of arms *"superseded and no longer issued to the Army"* available to those Governors *"showing the absolute necessity [of] protection of the citizens and their property against Indian raids."* See Headquarters of the Army, Adjutant General's Office. General Orders No. 61, July 8, 1876. (National Archives, RG-94; Microfilm 666-336).

[6]Letter, Barbour to Potts, July 29, 1877, published by Paul C. Phillips in "The Battle of the Big Hole," *Frontier Omnibus*, pp. 363-84. See pp. 364-5 for the letter from which the quotations were taken. Further reference to this article will also be cited as *Frontier Omnibus*.

three routes entering from the west — the Salmon River trail, the Lolo trail and the Clark Fork River route. But the Captain lacked the means to guard such widely separated portals, even if he suspended all work on the new post. He would only agree to establish a small picket at Lolo Pass, with that depending on settlers providing the horses and riding equipment needed to get his men there. They did not, so even that pass remained unguarded.

Since the conclusion was that the Bitterroot Valley settlers really *were* in danger, Governor Potts, who has been, perhaps unfairly, described as a *"sort of letter-writing, telegram-sending busybody,"* telegraphed President Hayes on June 29th, with the following:

> Settlements in western Montana seriously threatened by Nez Perces Indians from Idaho. Settlers are fleeing their homes in Bitterroot Valley to Missoula for safety. More troops are needed for Missoula. We are organizing and arming people for defense. Flathead and other Indians are seriously disaffected.[7]

This appeal to the highest authority was answered from the Adjutant General's Office, on July 3rd, with only the comment that it had been *"communicated to Lieut.-General Sheridan"* (commanding the Department of Dakota).

Meanwhile, Bitterroot Valley settlers took other measures for their own protection. The volunteer company at Stevensville made a refuge of the old adobe-walled trading post formerly operated by "Major" John Owens. Repair of its fifteen foot walls provided an enclosure of 125 by 250 feet, protected by bastions at two adjacent corners and stout plank gates. A well in the center and available rooms ranged inside the two long walls made *"Fort Brave"* — Fort Owen's local *nom de guerre* — both the safest and most comfortable of the valley's defenses. It was occupied briefly by about twenty families during the first alarm while others crowded into Missoula, yet many of the less timid settlers stayed on their ranches.

The initial tensions were relieved somewhat on August 1st when word was received that Chief Charlot's band of Flatheads had been located in the vicinity of French Gulch, between the Deer Lodge and Big Hole Valleys. According to the man who had talked with the Indians, they had been given a join-us-or-else mandate by hostile Nez Perce, and, not wishing to be involved in the war, they had gathered up their stock and moved out of harm's way. That is *not* what had happened, as will soon be shown, but it eased the concern of the settlers — really a concern rooted in a knowledge that the resident Flathead Indians had nearly as much reason for dissatisfaction as the hostile Nez Perces had. Editor Barbour summed up this feeling:

---

[7]National Archives, RG-94; Microfilm 666-336. Governor Potts was not without military experience. During the Civil War he was a brigadier-general and his Ohioans formed the van of Sherman's march to the sea.

When we remember that the Nez Perces are largely intermarried with the Flatheads and the Pend d'Oreilles and that there are at all timesmore or less of the non-treaty Nez Perces among the Flatheads of the Bitter Root valley, and that they are sympathetic with this tribe in the belief that a great wrong has been perpetrated on them by the government in turning over the Bitter Root valley to settlement and occupation by the whites and ordering them to the Jocko reservation . . . [there is] ample cause for an uprising against the whites.[8]

For the settlers, the relief in knowing that the local Indians were not on *"the warpath"* was soon negated by new rumors. A letter from the leading merchant of Beartown, a mining settlement on Three Mile Creek in Deer Lodge County, contained a statement, *"Indians playing Hell on the Blackfoot — also they are cleaning off the Trayl from Nevada Creek to Sun River . . . it looks suspicious . . ."*[9] which again hinted at a general uprising of Indians in league with the Nez Perces. Adding weight to that were wild tales of Indian conspiracy coming out of Frenchtown. James H. Mills, in his capacity of Secretary to the Governor, rather than as editor, commented on the reliability of information from that source: *"From half those people down there being half-breeds and running with Indians all the time they ought to know whether the Indians referred to mean devilment or not — it will take some time for them to arrange a program if they are going to ally with Joseph."* And he added, for the Governor's benefit, *"This is a matter I did not care to refer to in paper."*[10]

Given a little time, such home-grown rumors would have lost their cogency; instead, there was immediate reinforcement. A local Nez Perce Indian commonly known as *"Poker Joe,"* and sometimes as *"Little Tobacco"* from his below average stature, but whose Indian name was *Wahwookya Wasaaw*, or Lean Elk, arrived from Idaho on July 7th with information which made the next issue of *The Weekly Missoulian* under the heading of *"Startling News From The West."* According to the editor, Joe,

. . . who left some three weeks ago with the band that was camped all spring near Missoula, returned across the Lo Lo trail direct from the Nez Perces country. He was spoken to by the driver of the Bitter Root mail and a passenger, and seen by a number of whites who know him well. He took dinner at the camp of Eneas, a Flathead who was up Lo Lo hunting and fishing, and gave to him news which Eneas delivered in town through an interpreter Sunday. Jo said he had been in a battle

---

[8]"Indian Excitement," in *The Weekly Missoulian*, June 29, 1877. Those who are interested in the details of how the Flathead Indians were duped out of their ancestral homeland in the Bitterroot Valley will find an excellent summary by editor Oliver W. Holmes, "James A. Garfield's Diary of a Trip to Montana in 1872," in *Frontier Omnibus*, pp. 347-354; cited in Note 6.

[9]Letter, Joaquin Abascal to an unidentified friend, July 2, [1877], in *Frontier Omnibus*, p. 365; cited in Note 6.

[10]Letter, J. H. Mills to Gov. Potts, July 5, 1877. *Frontier Omnibus*, pp. 365-6; cited in Note 6. The paper referred to was his Deer Lodge *New North-West*.

with the whites two days before he left; that the whites had killed five Indians — one of them Col-col-see-nee-nah, or Red Owl, Nez Perces chief — three women and one child, and that the Nez Perces had killed 191 whites, having gotten one party of whites in ambush and slaughtered them: that the camp of the Nez Perces had been destroyed, their horses killed, and the Indians were all on foot scattered through the mountains. Jo says the fight occurred the same day the band he was with got home . . . Eneas gives credit to Jo's story. It was told to him as one Indian communicates to another. It finds some corroboration in the fact that Jo left us but a short time before, and came back nearly scared to death. His horse had a jaded appearance from rapid travelling.[11]

In passing the information on to fellow editor, James Mills, Barbour commented: *"To be sure the number of whites killed was exaggerated, but that is a universal Indian failing. There was fighting on the 3rd, 4th, and 5th. Joe was in it 2 days,"* and he speculates that Joe left *"the morning of the 5th."*[12] The dates given would indicate that Joe was involved in some of the skirmishing around Cottonwood House, while the attack on the Indian camp would have been Whipple's wanton destruction of the village of Chief Looking Glass near Kamiah. Chief Red Owl was not killed in that assault, but it did convince him there was no alternative to war. He and his peaceful band of non-treaty Nez Perces were thus added to the hostiles and fought with them to the end. But, for the time, the story of Red Owl's death made the rounds of the Indian camps of Western Montana, where the Chief had many friends.

Spurred by the strange blend of fact and rumor reaching Western Montana, things began to happen. July 8th, Captain Rawn went to the Jocko Reservation, and from there, with Indian Agent Peter Ronan, to St. Ignatius Mission to talk with the Flathead and Pend d'Oreille chiefs. Speaking with Arlee and Andrea through the agency interpreter and Father Van Gorp, Rawn was assured both tribes intended to remain friendly. And though he *"was not disposed to take the word of an Indian in such a matter,"* he thought they meant it because it suited their best interest; they being *"rich in horses and land and most of them live in houses."*[13] An attempt to get the agency police to guard the passes into the Bitterroot Valley was less successful. The Indians wanted uniforms and pay for such service, and Rawn could offer only the uniforms.

The next day Captain Rawn, again with Agent Ronan, went up to Charlot's camp, at Silverthorne Creek, across the valley from Stevensville, to sound him out concerning the loyalty of his band. They received the same assurance as at the

---

[11]Issue of July 13, 1877.

[12]Letter, Chauncey Barbour to J.H. Mills, July 15, 1877. *Frontier Omnibus*, p. 371; cited in Note 6. It is interesting that Mills at first called Poker Joe *"the champion liar of the Lo Lo trail"* in his paper, *The New North-West*, but later had to admit that the telegraph confirmed most of the details.

[13]Capt. Rawn to Acting Asst. Adjutant General, Fort Shaw, M.T., July 16, 1877. *Frontier Omnibus*, pp. 387-8; cited in Note 1.

reservation; that all would remain friendly except, perhaps, a few young men who might evade his watchfulness and join the hostiles. Agent Ronan reported:

> In answer to my question: "Where are your people?" he [Charlot] said: "This broad country is our home — it is usual every year, after my people put in their crops, for them to go to the different camas prairies for the purpose of digging those roots for winter use, and while the squaws and children perform that duty, the young men hunt and fish. When the crops begin to ripen they return to their homes — they are on their way home now, as I am informed by one of my young men, and twenty lodges are encamped near Missoula, the rest will soon follow."[14]

That was the real reason why the Flatheads and Eagle-from-the-Light's people were gone from the valley earlier — which Chief Charlot could have explained at any time, since he had remained at home. Agent Ronan added this, with regard to the old Chief's loyalty:

> In answer to my question, will you join the whites, with your warriors, and make war on the Nez Perces, he stated: "If dangers threaten I will send runners to inform the settlers, and the Captain of the soldiers, and you, the agent. I will do all in my power to defend the whites and their homes, but I cannot send my young men out to make war on the Nez Perces. When my old enemy the Blackfeet came here to redden the valley with my people's blood, the Nez Perces assisted us, and helped to drive them away. So, I cannot send my young men out to fight them, but I will help to protect the white man's home."

The rumors circulating during the first week of July having reached the miners on Salmon River, below present Gibbonsville, in greatly magnified form, three of the men working there, Alex Mitchell, J.B. Mitchell and Luther Johnson, decided to return to the Bitterroot Valley in order to protect their property if need be. They left for home on the morning of July 8, and,

> Near the summit of the Montana-Idaho divide the men met "Poker Joe". Joe was a full-blooded Nez Perce Indian, but for some reason of his own had elected to remain away from his redskin brothers and for a number of years had made his home at Corvallis with a small band of Indians, who likewise, were living away from their tribes . . .
> Joe inquired of the men relative to the whereabouts of his Indian friends, saying that he had been informed on his return from a trip, that the band had left several days previous on a hunting trip into the Big Hole country. He said he was on his way to join them if possible. Perhaps the men had seen them. The men knew that Joe was in the

---

[14]Letter, Agent Peter Ronan to Governor B.F. Potts, July 10, 1877. National Archives, RG-94; Microfilm 666-337.

habit of making frequent trips over the Lolo trail into Idaho to visit his
Nez Perce brethren and remaining there for various lengths of time.
Evidently he had just returned from such a visit. It was noticed that
Joe's horse, an exceptionally fine animal which he usually kept well
groomed, showed signs of hard usage. It looked tired and its
customarily sleek coat was covered with sweat-hardened dust and blood-
dried scratches showed on the legs and body. One rather deep cut was
in evidence across the horses breast as though a bullet had found its
mark or had ricocheted to plow through the flesh. Another thing that
impressed the men was Joe's demeanor. Usually of a light-hearted,
good-natured, easy-come-easy-go disposition, he was, for some reason
or other, hard and sour.[15]

The strange behavior of Lean Elk (Poker Joe's proper name) had been noticed
by others in the Bitterroot Valley; a hurried change of horses at the Indian camp
opposite Corvallis, and a glimpse of him running his horse as he passed a ranch 20
miles above that town — such actions, taken with a an earlier report that Nez
Perces had attempted to trade for ammunition at the Warm Springs store (in Deer
Lodge Valley) — *"though their ammunition belts were full"* [16] — could lead to only
one surmise: that the Indian uprising so feared by residents of Western Montana
was close upon them.

Lean Elk is often portrayed as an innocent victim of circumstances. Camille
Williams says he was accidentally injured while traveling the Lolo Trail on a visit
to Idaho, and, on returning, elected to join the hostiles rather than try to explain
his injury to skeptical Bitterroot neighbors — which might result in punishment as
a participant in the war in Idaho. Territorial Secretary Mills saw him in a different
light: *"I can't think what the mission of Poker Joe is! He is not running away
from a fight — I am inclined to think he is drumming up disaffected Indians. He
travels too fast to be on a pleasure trip."* [17] Regardless, enough of Lean Elk's
information was already in circulation, thanks to *The Weekly Missoulian*, to create
a frenzy of organizing and arming of home defense companies, and the building of
two more strong points.

On July 8 the company at Skalkaho, captained by John B. Catlin, proprietor
of a Stevensville hotel and livery business, and a former major in the Union Army,
began building a *"makeshift fort . . . being merely an embankment of earth thrown*

---

[15]A. C. Mitchell, "The Battle of the Big Hole Fought Sixty Years Ago," in *The Sunday
Missoulian*, August 8, 1937, pp. 1 & 7. The author of this article is not the Alex Mitchell mentioned
as one of the three miners, but a nephew, Alexander Cowan Mitchell, born in 1886 and the son of J.B.
Mitchell.

[16]Letter, J. H. Mills to Gov. Potts, July 8, 1877. *Frontier Omnibus*, pp. 366-67; cited in
Note 6.

[17]Letter, J. H. Mills to Gov. Potts, July 12, 1877. *Frontier Omnibus*, pp. 368-89; cited in
Note 6. Camille Williams (War Singer) was a Nez Perce interpreter and chronicler of tribal lore who
is quoted by L. V. McWhorter, *Hear Me, My Chiefs!* (Caldwell, Idaho: Caxton Printers, 1983), p.
360. Since he was not a contemporary of Lean Elk, his version is only hearsay.

up in a circular shape and about four or five feet high. "[18]   And the Corvallis company, captained by J. L. Humble, began a sod fort on July 10.   It was substantial, being *"66 x 95, eight feet high, with triangular bastions at each corner,"* and walls three feet thick at the bottom and 18 inches at the top.[19] It was completed in 12 days — barely in time, as it turned out.   It, too, received a disparaging appellation; it was called *"Fort Skedaddle,"* (from the fact that the area around Corvallis was settled by Missourians who had to leave their former home in a hurry during the Civil War).   The fort was seen as another place they could *"skedaddle to"* if need be).

The flip side of this frenzy of defensive preparation can be seen in a letter written to the Governor by stockman W.B. Harlan of Stevensville, who warned that Chief Charlot was complaining he might not be able to control his young men if there was any more shooting into the lodges of local Indians by rowdies *"overloaded with ammunition and whiskey."* [20]   This complaint might have originated in the careless firing of the old cannon which had been at Stevensville for many years, where it was formerly used for celebrating the Fourth of July (this was not the mountain howitzer used in the Big Hole battle).

After the preparations for defense were well under way — on July 12 — J. H. Mills, additionally appointed as Adjutant General of the Montana Militia the previous day on the strength of his service in the Civil War, wrote the Governor reminding him he ought to get discretionary authority from the President to call out militia, noting that there was *"no authority to act and incur a dollar of expense in fighting for the United States — If you call for Militia you will have to feed them, and help them a good deal in outfitting and who the deuce is going to pay for it?"* [21] It was sound advice but the Governor didn't act on it in a timely manner, to his great embarrassment later on.

Preparation for the defense of the Bitterroot Valley against an invasion by hostile Nez Perce was not the only reaction to Lean Elk's information.   Agent Ronan reported to Governor Potts from the Jocko reservation:

> On Saturday, July 14, Eagle of the Light . . . came to this agency accompanied by Michelle, head chief of the Pen d'Oreilles, and informed me that eleven lodges of Nez Perces were encamped near St. Mary's Mission, up the Bitter Root — that they are peaceable, have

---

[18]"The Battle of the Big Hole . . .," p. 1; cited in Note 15. Mitchell notes that *"Those who came to look at it decided that they would be far safer in their own homes. It probably deserved its local name of 'Fort Run'."* Mark Brown, *The Flight Of The Nez Perce* (New York: G. P. Putnam's Sons, 1967), p. 217, calls it *"a log stockade, with a cabin inside,"* but Lieutenant Hardin's diary entry for August 5th refers to it as *"a very nice earthwork".*

[19]"Personal," in *The Weekly Missoulian*, July 20, 1877, p.3. In "The Song Of The Bitterroot", a 1986 compilation prepared for the Mitchell family by Leda Mitchell Reed, of Denver, Colorado, there is a very good description of the building of this structure, which she calls *"Fort Corvallis."* See also, Henry Buck, "The Story of the Nez Perce Campaign During the Summer of 1877," 1925. His account appeared serially in the *Great Falls Tribune*, in 9 installments from Dec. 24, 1944, through Feb. 18, 1945.

[20]Letter of July 10. *Frontier Omnibus*, pp. 367-8; cited in Note 6.

never been in the hostile camp and are desirous to keep out of trouble,
and to encamp somewhere out of danger. Michelle said the Chiefs of
the reservation would consent to let them camp here, providing I gave
my permission. After reflection, I told the reservation Chiefs that as
they professed peace and friendship, it was bad policy to throw the
reservation open as a shelter as suspicion could not be avoided . . . [22]

Eagle-From-The-Light was advised to take up the sanctuary matter with
Captain Rawn, which accomplished nothing; those peaceable Nez Perce remained
in the Bitterroot Valley — to be swept up by the hostiles as an increment to their
force.

Eagle-from-the-Light has been described as *"a noble savage who declares he
never accepted a present from the white man, and that he never yielded his title to
any of the land of his people."* [23] He was the second chief of the Nez Perce people
at the time of the Stevens treaty (1855), but lost influence through marrying a
Umatilla woman. He was always peaceable and considered the non-treaty Nez
Perces fools to go to war.

At this same time, an overly belligerent Missoula merchant wrote to Mills,
suggesting there was a *"Splendid chance to strike the Hostiles by way of the Lo Lo
pass with 4 or 500 well armed men."* It was a ridiculous idea, for the Governor
was without authority to call the militia into Federal service, and, if he had been
able to do so, the movement of so large a body of untrained men over a
mountainous trail which subsequently took the Nez Perces five days to travel and
Howard's regulars nine, would have accomplished nothing beyond rendering them
unfit for any useful service in Idaho. But Higgin's letter also indicates some
practical measures were being taken:

> Have advised the Cos above to scout the passes leading into the
> valley   A picket guard will be sent up the Lo Lo by Co "A" Militia,
> and Capt Raun [Rawn]   we will furnish him 4 horses to mount his men
> for that duty tomorrow. The Frenchtown Co "E" will scout the passes
> below. Will advise you promptly of the approach of any Hostile
> force. [24]

Captain Rawn made prompt use of the four horses and equipment furnished
him by the citizens of Missoula. The same day the Nez Perce Indians completed
their council at Weippe Prairie, at which it was decided to go to the buffalo
country east of the mountains rather than continue to fight General Howard's
troops in Idaho, 2nd Lieutenant Francis Woodbridge was sent with four enlisted
men *"to watch the Loo Loo trail from a point where it can be seen six or eight*

---

[21]*Frontier Omnibus*, p. 368; cited in Note 6.

[22]*The Flight Of The Nez Perce*, pp. 218-19; cited in Note 18.

[23]"Local Mention," in *The Weekly Missoulian*, Aug. 3, 1877.

[24]Letter, C. P. Higgins to J. H. Mills, [July 14, 1877], *Frontier Omnibus*, pp. 369-70; cited in
Note 6.

miles and report the approach of any large band of Indians from the west side. "[25]
Five days passing without word from the scouting party, Captain Rawn sent 1st
Lieutenant Charles Austin Coolidge with a private and several   civilians to see
what had happened.   Near Lolo Pass (about 40 miles from the post) they met
Woodbridge's scouting party on the 22nd, returning from exploring the trail
another twenty miles into Idaho — without sighting the Nez Perce advance.
Woodbridge was amazingly lucky, for he must have been within a day's march of
the Indians when he turned back.

Since the horses of Lieutenant Coolidge's party were fresh, he returned to
Missoula with the word that no Indians had been found, leaving Woodbridge to
come in as suited his tired animals.   The scouting party stopped for the night on
Lolo Creek below the hot springs, and while they were resting, two men came into
camp.   They were local boys, Pete Matt and Billy Silverthorne, who had been on
their way to the Nez Perce reservation on horse business — which may have included horse-stealing — when the hostiles captured them near Weippe Prairie on
the 17th.   Back at Lolo Hot Springs, they were on home ground and easily made
their escape.

Lieutenant Woodbridge sent a courier to Missoula with word that the Nez
Perces were about to enter the Bitterroot Valley.   As Chauncey Barbour later
described it:

> A courier from his camp reached the post early Monday morning
> [July 23rd] with the news that a white man and a half breed, who said
> the Indians were at Warm Springs [Lolo Hot Springs], had been at his
> camp the night before.   The half-breed was Pete Matte and the white
> man Billy Silverthorne.   The notorious character of Pete Matte and the
> suspicion that would naturally fall on anyone found in such company
> did not warrant implicit confidence in this report; however, the report
> was generally believed.[26]

It appears that Captain Rawn thought enough of Lt. Woodbridge's report to
take immediate steps to protect his new post — the future Fort Missoula — which
was yet merely a collection of tents among the piles of supplies and building
materials.   A corporal of Company I, Seventh United States Infantry, wrote: *"We
at once began to fortify our camp as best we could, by throwing up rifle pits,
cutting away the brush that would shelter the Indians, and piling up sacks of grain*

---

[25]Letter, Capt. Rawn to Acting Asst. Adjutant General, Fort Shaw, M.T., July 16, 1877.
Frontier Omnibus, pp. 388; cited in Note 1.   Mark Brown has Woodbridge leaving Missoula on the
18th, but both Rawn and Higgins agree he left on the 15th (*Flight Of The Nez Perce*, p. 220; cited in
Note 18).

[26]"The Indian War," in *The Weekly Missoulian*, Aug. 3, 1877 (the paper did not print on July
27 because the editor was a member of the local volunteer company).   Actually, both boys were half-
breeds;   Pete was the son of Louis Matt, a French-Irish blacksmith who died at the Jocko Agency in
1877, and Billy was the son of John W. Silverthorne, a legendary discoverer of Montana's gold,
whose marriage to *"one of the fair ones of the land,"* on January 10, 1857, is also said to be
Montana's earliest formal wedding of a white man to an Indian woman.

in such positions as to give protection to the wives and children of officers, and the laundresses of the companies. "[27]

With that accomplished, Captain Rawn *"sent a force Tuesday morning [July 24th] to occupy the Lo Lo trail. "* The number of men and their disposition has gone unrecorded, except that Captain E. A. Kenney, with four other Missoula volunteers, established a vidette on Lolo Creek *"far in advance of any other force, and during the night he arrested an Indian who was attempting to pass his camp. This Indian proved to be John Hill, a Delaware who lived with the Nez Perces.* "[28] His purpose in coming down Lolo Creek from the Indian encampment at Lolo Hot Springs was to find out if the Nez Perces would be allowed to pass through the Bitterroot Valley peaceably.

This is the place to explain a Nez Perce misconception which had much to do with the disaster that befell them in the Big Hole. Like most Indians they did not fully understand the concept of a nationhood which transcended tribal unity and bickering. As Duncan McDonald, the Indian trader on the Jocko Reservation, noted:

> The idea among the Indians, uneducated as they were, was that the people of Montana had no identity with the people of Idaho, and that they were entirely separate and distinct, having nothing to do with each other. If they had to fight they believed it was Idaho people they should fight, not Montanans. Looking Glass therefore gave orders to his warriors that in case they should see any white men, either citizens or soldiers, on the Lo Lo, not to molest them . . . He said: "We are going to the buffalo country. We want to go through the settlements quietly. We do not wish to harm anyone if we can help it. "[29]

---

[27]Charles N. Loynes, "Battle of the Big Hole'," in *Winners Of The West*, March, 1925, p. 7. At that time the garrison consisted of 7 officers and 68 enlisted men. The employment of laundresses to wash the clothing of enlisted men was allowed by Army Regulations until June 18, 1878. They were given quarters and subsistence but were paid by the men for their work. So many of those hard working, respectable women married noncommissioned officers that the NCO quarters at some Army posts were known as *"soapsuds row. "*

[28]See, "The Indian War"; cited in Note 26. John Hill was half Nez Perce, a quarter Delaware and a quarter white. He was the son of *"Delaware Jim, "* an eastern halfbreed living in the Bitterroot Valley with his Nez Perce wife. Mark Brown has confused John with brother Tom Hill (*The Flight Of The Nez Perce*, p. 222; cited in Note 18), but L. V. McWhorter's statement that John Hill was one of the three Indians captured in the *"Fort Fizzle"* fiasco (*Hear Me, My Chiefs!*, 1983, p. 348n), is supported by a letter written by Colonel John Gibbon, Oct. 5, 1878, which states that John Hill was *"released last summer by General Sherman in person from the guard house at Fort Missoula, "* and adds that he was a brother of Tom Hill, that Tom Hill's home was in the Bitterroot Valley, and that Tom *"does not speak English well enough for me to communicate with him. "* (National Archives, RG-94; microfilm 666-340). Tom would not have been a satisfactory messenger to the whites, and he was not captured at that time but went on with the hostiles; on the other hand, John Hill was reported to speak *"fair English. "* Kenney was a Civil War veteran and a former sergeant in the regular army.

[29]"The Nez Perce War of 1877 — The Inside History from Indian Sources," in *The New North-West*, Deer Lodge, M. T., December 27, 1878.

John Hill was sent back to ask the chiefs to come down for a talk, and a courier was sent to Captain Rawn with the news that he did, indeed, have an Indian problem. He acted at once to bottle-up the Nez Perces in Lolo Canyon, but, before discussing that, it is necessary to drop back a few days and consider the matter of some ammunition consigned to Duncan McDonald, the agency trader on the Jocko Reservation.

On July 20, 1st Lieutenant William Lewis English wrote to Agent Ronan, as follows:

> I am directed by Capt. Rawn to say that he has just received information that four thousand rounds of ammunition have just started or are about to start from O'Keefes for the Agency, consigned to McDonald the agency trader. He also has been informed that three Nez Perces Indians have been in waiting in expectation of procuring some of this ammunition.
>
> As there are orders from the Department and the Dist. prohibiting the sale of ammunition to any Indian whatever, Capt. Rawn would like it very much if you would see this ammunition so stored and taken care of that none of it gets into the possession of any Indians whatever.[30]

Captain Rawn's concern was that some or all of the ammunition might get into the hands of Duncan McDonald's Nez Perce in-laws; however, there was some doubt about the legality of his action, since it was based on a Presidential Order of November 23, 1876, prohibiting sale of *"fixed ammunition or metallic cartridges"* to the hostile Sioux. General Howard's *"General Field Order No. 4,"* of July 28th, was an attempt to extend the Presidential Order to cover the theater of the Nez Perce War. The uncertainty was removed August 7, 1877, when President Hayes reaffirmed Grant's earlier order.[31]

The Army's policy of prohibiting sale of arms and ammunition to Indians in a theater of operations tended to work a hardship on non-belligerents also. Northwestern Montana's Blackfeet, though not involved in the Sioux War of 1876, were cut off from the supplies of ammunition essential to a life-style largely dependent on hunting. By the summer of 1877, they were in such a very desperate condition that there was some fear near-starvation might force them into hostility. Agent Ronan worried that they might even attack their former enemies, his relatively well-off reservation Indians, whom he was ill prepared to defend from lack of guns and ammunition.[32]

But such worries were trivial in comparison to the drama then opening at the eastern end of the Lolo trail.

---

[30]*Frontier Omnibus*, p. 388; cited in Note 1.

[31]"Information," in *Helena Daily Herald*, Aug. 8, 1877. For the text of General Howard's order, see National Archives, RG-94; Microfilm 666-337.

[32]Letter, Peter Ronan to Gov. B. F. Potts, July 14, 1877. National Archives, RG-94; Microfilm 666-337.

Chapter 2

HELP! HELP! COME RUNNING!

A dusty courier rode into Missoula at 9 o'clock on the morning of July 25th, with the news that the Nez Perces were indeed encamped on the western edge of the Bitterroot Valley with nothing but an insignificant vidette between them and the settlements. While the town's militia gathered, editor Chauncey Barbour got out a one-page extra headlined with the frantic appeal which provides a title for this chapter; then he closed *The Missoulian's* office and joined the company of volunteers. There would be no more *"news"* from there until August 3rd.

Leaving over half his regulars, under two officers, to guard the post, Captain Rawn gathered his available force — 25 to 32 regulars (the number is variously reported) and 5 officers, *"accompanied by a few friendly Indians and thirty or forty citizens"* — and marched the seven miles to the mouth of Lolo Creek, where he met a few volunteers gathered there, and, with them, moved up the stream.[1] According to Corporal Loynes, they had gone about three miles when they were *"accosted by a number of shots coming in our direction from brush in front."* The answer to those harmless warning shots fired by several mounted Nez Perce scouts, was a *"yell, and the friendly Indians with us giving their war whoop, we pushed forward, the few Indians in front retreating."* The advance was continued for another mile and a half; to the point where the canyon appeared narrowest, and there Captain Rawn began a barricade intended to block the twelve hundred-foot width of the valley floor.[2]

---

[1]Captain Rawn, in a 3 p.m. dispatch to Post Adjutant Burnett, at Fort Shaw, notes *"Am entrenching twenty-five regulars and about fifty volunteers in Lou Lou canyon."* This dispatch was first published, with other correspondence, by Captain A. E. Rothermich in "Early Days at Fort Missoula" (*The Frontier*, Vol. X, No. 1, November, 1929). The article has been reprinted in *Frontier Omnibus*, John W. Hakola, ed., (Missoula: Montana State University Press, 1962), pp. 385 -97. See p. 388 for the dispatch referred to. Further references to this article will be cited as Frontier Omnibus. In a report to the Assistant Adjutant General, Department of Dakota, dated September 30, 1877, the Captain mentions having *"5 commissioned officers and 30 enlisted men."* (*Ibid.*, p. 390), while Colonel John Gibbon's report, compiled from information received from Captain Rawn, states that *"Companys A and I, Seventh Infantry, numbering 5 officers and 32 enlisted men, under command of Captain C. C. Rawn, Seventh Infantry, on the 25th of July, left Missoula and marched to LoLo Pass, 14 miles [that pass, where Rawn did not go, is nearer 40 miles], carrying four days rations and 100 rounds of ammunition per man, accompanied by a party of from 100 to 150 citizen volunteers."* (*Report Of The Secretary Of War, 1877*, Vol.I, p. 521). Editor Barbour indicates that the effective force with Captain Rawn at the barricade did not reach 125 until the following day.

[2]Measured on August 25, 1990, as 1,150 feet on a transect passing through a broken concrete pier (probably the SW of four set by W. W. White, 1934-37) to mark the location of the Fort Fizzle redoubt. See the archaeological report by Bill Bradt, January 1, 1972; Ref. 1650, Lolo National Forest library, Missoula, Montana. This point is, by the present Lolo Pass road (U.S. 12), 4.6 miles

The barricade hastily constructed to prevent the Nez Perces from moving down Lolo Creek consisted of a line of rifle pits protected by a breastwork of logs on the western, or upstream side. This barricade began on the north bank of Lolo Creek, which, at that point, ran close against the precipitous and heavily timbered south wall of the canyon, running northward up to the mouth of a small gulch. Trees felled to clear the field of fire were used to construct the breastwork; first a base-log was laid, then short pieces cut from larger limbs were placed across these lower logs, and a *"headlog"* was seated on the spacers. This allowed a man in a rifle pit to push his gun barrel through the slot between the logs and fire at approaching enemies from a protected position. Statements obtained from old timers who remembered the breastwork before it was destroyed by a forest fire indicate that earth from the rifle pits was banked on the outside.

One amusing story concerning the weakness of this barricade, which was never put to the ultimate test of battle, has come down to us in a story which indicates its vulnerability to rifle fire from the sparsely-timbered ridges forming the north wall of the canyon:

> It is related that one of the citizen volunteers, after he had labored arduously to prepare what he considered to be a place of relative security and shelter from anything the Reds had to offer, looked with pride at the results of his efforts and then climbed a short way up the hillside to give it all a better "once over." He returned with a look of genuine disgust on his face. "Hell", he spat out, along with a barrage of tobacco juice, "I can see plumb to the bottom of my pit."[3]

According to editor Barbour, Captain Kenney and his four men met the Nez Perce chiefs that same afternoon, *"and was surrounded by a formidable force of painted savages. He told them that he had no authority to treat with them, but appointed a council for the next day at three o'clock in the afternoon."* That is confirmed by Duncan McDonald and accepted by Mark Brown, but historian Josephy has a different version of this first meeting. He says that several Nez Perce chiefs — Looking Glass, White Bird and Joseph — came down under a flag of truce and *"parleyed with the officer [Rawn] and delegates of the volunteer companies."*[4] If the Nez Perces did get close enough to the half completed

---

west of its junction with the Missoula-Hamilton highway (U.S. 93).; but the location of the barricade is given variously in available accounts as from four to eight miles above the mouth of Lolo Creek. The account by Charles N. Loynes quoted here appeared as "Battle of the 'Big Hole'," in *Winners Of The West*, March, 1925, p. 7.

[3]A. C. Mitchell, "The Battle of the Big Hole Fought Sixty Years Ago," in *The Sunday Missoulian*, Aug. 8, 1937. The author is the son of Alex Mitchell, who was both a volunteer at *"Fort Fizzle"* and a participant in the later Big Hole fight.

[4]Alvin M. Josephy, Jr., *The Nez Perce Indians And The Opening Of The Northwest* (New Haven and London: Yale University Press, 1966), p. 568. This receives some support in James Chaffin's 1939 reminiscence, in which he recalled Captain Rawn and the volunteer officers, *"Catlin, Humbles, Morgan"* meeting with the Indians; however, Jimmy was near death at the time he was interviewed by Hugh Peyton and his chronology is unreliable (see, typescript in the Big Hole National

barricade to liken it to a corral, as Josephy claims, it would have had to be at this much-disputed meeting on the 25th. However, there is yet another version, in which *"That evening, Captain Rawn, accompanied by William Baker, Amos Buck and Cole B. Sanders, proceeded up to the flat [Woodman's where the Indians were camped] with a flag of truce, fashioned by tying a white hankerchief to a gun barrel asking an interview with Chief Joseph."* [5] Whichever it was, the desire of the Nez Perces to pass through the settlements peaceably was definitely made known.

Governor Benjamin F. Potts arrived in Missoula at three o'clock on the morning of the 26th, and he came *"after having fruitlessly endeavored to obtain authority to put volunteers in the field."* He confided to editor Barbour his opinion, *"that it would be madness to attack the Nez Perces with an inadequate force,"* and probably to Captain Rawn also, on his visit to the barricade that forenoon. [6] In that the Governor was right, but *not* in tune with the unreal viewpoint of the officer in overall charge of the *"pursuit and capture"* of the hostiles. Three days before General Howard was able even to *start* his command on its long trek over the Lolo trail, he sent a dispatch to Montana asking *"cannot troops at Missoula or vicinity detain Joseph till I can strike his rear. The two companies there with a little help from volunteers ample considering present condition of hostile Indians!"* [7]

Captain Rawn met the chiefs in council that afternoon [Thursday, 26th], as arranged by Captain Kenney the previous day. Rawn provided no clear record of this council but editor Barbour did. He wrote:

> Looking Glass and White Bird were at this council. It appears that the Indians were as anxious for delay as were the whites; and without arriving at anything definite a council was arranged for the next day, when, the Indians were told, Gov. Potts would be present. At the conclusion of this council a fine-looking Indian was seen approaching, and the Indians at the council involuntarily exclaimed among themselves "Joseph." He rode into the council, and when he was informed of its result he waved his hand in token of assent. Delaware Jim, who acted

---

Battlefield library). McDonald's account, "The Nez Perce War of 1877 — The Inside History from Indian Sources," — appeared serially in the issues of *The New North-West*, Deer Lodge, M. T., July 26, 1878 to March 28, 1879; events at Fort Fizzle are covered in the issue of December 27, 1878. Brown's comments are contained in his *Flight Of The Nez Perce* (New York: G. P. Putnam's Sons, 1967), pp. 222-23.

[5]Henry Buck, "The Story of the Nez Perce Indian Campaign During the Summer of 1877," 1925, (MS, p. 10); also published serially in the *Great Falls Tribune*, in nine installments from Dec. 24, 1944, through Feb. 11, 1945.

[6]"The Indian War," in *The Weekly Missoulian*, Aug. 3, 1877.

[7]Kamiah, July 27, 1877 (National Archives, RG-94; Microfilm 666-338). The Montana press proved it had a memory like an elephant by later twisting those words against Howard as his lame chase of the Nez Perces dragged on. *The Butte Miner* started it — *"One of Howard's late dispatches reads, Quote: 'I have asked to have the troops at Missoula retain Joseph until I can strike his rear.' Now, can't some one hold Joseph until Howard gets in at least one good kick on the rear of that pesky*

as interpreter, said it was Joseph. This noted chief was either present with the Indians, or it was a ruse to surprise the people with an idea of Indian strength. During the council, about seventy-five warriors marshalled within easy range and caused some solicitude that there might be a repetition of the Canby affair.[8]

Governor Potts visited the barricade again on Friday, the 27th. According to editor Barbour's account, Captain Rawn was undecided, in the light of his experience of the previous day, whether to go up and meet with the Indians or not, *"but finally concluded to go up in force, and took with him 100 mounted volunteers, who halted on a knoll over half a mile below the Indian camp."* A Nez Perce speaking Flathead Indian went forward to make the arrangements, with the result that Captain Rawn and Chief Looking Glass met between the lines — each with his own interpreter and unarmed. Barbour wrote of this meeting:

> . . . Looking Glass proffered to surrender all the ammunition of the camp as a guarantee that the Indians intended to go through the country peaceably. When told that nothing but an unconditional surrender would be accepted, he asked for another meeting at nine o'clock the next day to give him time to consult with the other chiefs. Capt. Rawn told him that any further communication must be made under a flag of truce at the fortified camp.[9]

Barbour's account also clarifies the circumstances surrounding the capture of two Nez Perce men as Rawn's force moved up Lolo Creek to the council on the 27th. He indicates that the left flank of the mounted men was protected by a screen of skirmishers moving up the south side of the stream, and,

> . . . as they neared the Nez Perces camp, Lt. Tom Andrews, of the Missoula volunteers, jumped up two Indians who leveled their rifles on him and told him to "hold on". He threw his needle gun into position and told them to hold on. They surrendered and were brought over to the force, where they were held till the close of the council. They were guarding in an open space on the south side of the river about 150 horses which could have been easily driven off if it had been deemed proper. The two Nez Perces captured talked freely with the men, and said that the Nez Perces did not want to fight. One of them spoke fair

---

savage?" — and it ricocheted through the Deer Lodge *New North-West* (Sept. 7) and the Bozeman *Avant Courier* (Sept. 21), with some editorial revision at each bounce!

[8]"The Indian War"; cited in Note 6. See also, "The Story of the Nez Perce Indian Campaign . . .," p. 11 (cited in Note 5), for an explanation of the demands made on the Indians — essentially, an unconditional surrender, which the military termed *"dismount and disarm."* Delaware Jim, who was quite often referred to by his *"white"* name of Jim Simonds, was reputed to have served John C. Fremont as a hunter. He had been an on-and-off employee of Major Owen during his long residence in Bitterroot Valley. See, George F. Weisel, ed., *Men And Trade On The Northwest Frontier As Shown By The Fort Owen Ledger* (Missoula: Montana State University Press, 1955), pp. 117-19.

English. He had but three shots in his belt, and if the other had any they must have been concealed about his person.[10]

In a dispatch sent off at 6:00 p.m., following this final meeting, Captain Rawn informed the Post Adjutant at Fort Shaw:

> Had a talk with Joseph and Looking Glass this afternoon and told them they had to surrender arms and ammunition or fight. They are to consider tonight. I think that for want of ammunition or Charlo's threat, they are wavering. Charlo has sent them word, that if they come into the Bitter-root he will fight them. He has already sent me some of his warriors.[11]

There is a hint in Captain Rawn's official report of September 30, 1877, to the Assistant Adjutant General, Department of Dakota, that he really had serious doubts concerning the outcome on the 28th. His statement, *"Nothing satisfactory having resulted from the conference, I returned to the breastwork expecting to be attacked,"*[12] indicates a lack of confidence in diplomacy as a means of making the Nez Perces *"disarm and dismount,"* Instead, he decided to try what can only be considered a questionable, if not impossible, tactic.

Upon his return from the meeting with Chief Looking Glass, Captain Rawn told Governor Potts that he had men enough to prevent the Nez Perces from passing the barricade (a count at that time showed 216 effectives, including Charlot's Flatheads). So, they formed a plan by which Governor Potts would return to Missoula, gather all available reinforcements and make a flanking movement southward over the ridges into the Indian camp.[13]

---

[9]"The Indian War"; cited in Note 6.

[10]Corporal Loynes mentions this capture in his account in *Winners Of The West* (cited in Note 2), but he puts the number of Indians taken as four in that version; later, in a letter to McWhorter, he makes it *"three or four."* See, L. V. McWhorter, Hear Me, My Chiefs! (Caldwell, Idaho: The Caxton Printers, Ltd., 1983), pp. 347-48. Barbour's statement that one captive spoke *"fair English"* is confirmed by Loynes, who calls him John Hill, thus providing an explanation for Hill's incarceration in the Fort Missoula guardhouse after having been released by Capt. Kenney the night of the 24th as a messenger to the Nez Perce chiefs. The other man with John Hill probably was *"Honan or Kannah, an aged and venerable man,"* as McWhorter says, p.348n. While Loynes is likely right about the manner in which the prisoners were held at the barricade, he is mistaken about their escape from the guard tent *"one dark rainy night, while guarded by a drummer boy."* The Missoula garrison didn't have a drummer boy; but General Sherman *did* release John Hill, and possibly Honan also, when he visited the post in August (National Archives, RG-94; Microfilm 666-339).

[11]*Frontier Omnibus*, p. 388; cited in Note 1.

[12]*Ibid.*, p. 390.

[13]"The Indian War"; cited in Note 6. Leeson, who got his information from the Deer Lodge *New North-West* of Aug. 10, 1877, has it the other way around, with the Governor organizing a force to keep the Nez Perces from breaking to the north, over the low, rolling hills into the valley between Frenchtown and Missoula. See, M. A. Leeson, ed., *History Of Montana*, 1739-1885 (Chicago: Warner, Beers & Co., 1885), pp. 137-38.

At Missoula, Governor Potts prepared a proclamation calling out the militia of Missoula and Deer Lodge Counties, with an accompanying letter to Adjutant Mills, and got them on the way to Deer Lodge. The proclamation left Missoula in the strongbox of the evening coach to Helena, with the letter in the mail sack, but, at Bear Mouth, where the Deer Lodge coach was met, the strongbox could not be opened. The result was that only the letter reached Deer Lodge, where it arrived at 10 o'clock on the morning of the 28th; but *"the note from the Governor was evidence that assistance was needed and that he desired every fighting man at Missoula. At once began the most intense excitement . . . "*[14]

More will be said later concerning the train of events set in motion by the Governor's proclamation; for now, it is enough to take a quick look at that *"intense excitement"* — through the eyes of Alva J. Noyes, better known to old-timers as *"Ajax,"* who was then a resident of the mining town of Butte. He did not think it necessary to respond when the *"people of Missoula began calling for help"* (Barbour's editorial appeal), though, *"The boys even went so far as to intimate that I was afraid to go."* Then,

> There came a day, July 28th . . . [when] I saw a crowd on Main street between Broadway and Granite. Some one was on a dry goods box making a speech. On getting nearer, I saw that it was W.A. Clark. He had just arrived from Deer Lodge, having made the trip from that place to Butte — 42 miles — in three and a half hours, without change of horse. His talk was fiery and enthusing. He would, if they wished, lead them against Chief Joseph and his tribe. This was no time to hesitate, the call had come from Missoula for help. Who would go?
>
> There was no such thing as waiting. We must go to Deer Lodge as fast as we could get transportation. I went to my place of business, turned it over to a boy, then went home for gun and saddle. When I told grandmother what I had done, she began to cry and said: "You are just big fool enough to go and get killed."[15]

The Butte men were too late to be of any help in the Fort Fizzle affair; in fact, they never made it to Missoula. While going down the Deer Lodge River the next day they met a backwash of refugees from the Bitterroot Valley, and returning Deer Lodge volunteers, and decided to go back to town.

Picking up events at Lolo Creek on the 28th, the Nez Perces had something else in mind than fighting their way through Captain Rawn's barricade. They saw an advantage in evasion, rather than force of arms. They had used some of the time gained by parleying to scout out a route which would allow them to by-pass the barricade, their presumption being that the soldiers were their real enemy, so that they had only to pass Rawn's barricade and the Bitterroot Valley settlers — their former friends — would allow them to go on in peace. This idea was un-

---

[14]*Ibid.*, p. 138.
[15]Alva J. Noyes, *The Story Of Ajax* (New York: Buffalo Head Press, 1966), pp. 28-29 [reprinted from the edition of 1914].

doubtedly promoted by Chief Looking Glass, but a general acceptance is indicated by the fact that both Yellow Wolf and Chief Joseph seem to have rationalized the presumption into a *"treaty."*[16]

There has been some speculation that friendly Flathead Indians showed the Nez Perces how to pass around Rawn's right flank, but Chief Peopeo Tholekt's statement to L. V. McWhorter when asked about that was, *"It is all lie about them helping us in any way. They did not show us how to get around that corral barricade. Some Nez Perces well knew that country."*[17] By going up a shallow draw a half-mile west of Captain Rawn's line, they were able get upon the ridge to the north of his defenses, and, from there, follow down the drainage of Sleeman Creek to its junction with the Lolo two miles behind the barricade. Starting early — A. C. Mitchell puts the whole movement between the hours of 9 A.M. and 2 P.M. — a screen of warriors occupied positions on the upper slope to protect the route used by the families (given as 800 yards from the barricade).

Two accounts, a reminiscence of Captain John L. Humble, of the Corvallis volunteers, and another from Corporal Loynes, one of Rawn's regulars, will illustrate the differing views of this maneuver.

CAPTAIN HUMBLE:

Captain Rawn promised me he would not fight. He had given me charge of the pickets who were standing out along a ridge leading up north from the creek. The Indians asked if they could have that ridge the next morning, and I told them, "Yes!" They said they did not want to fight the citizens and would go through the valley and molest nothing.

I moved the pickets below, and the Indians, early in the morning, started the climb. I told Captain Rawn that they were coming, and to keep his men quiet and nobody would get hurt. People had come up from Missoula a time or two and wanted the Captain to fight. They thought it would be fun.

We stayed there until the Indians were well gone, before breaking camp. I did not tell my men we had made an agreement with the Indians.[18]

CORPORAL LOYNES:

Chief Joseph must get by us, for he knew General Howard's command was coming up in his rear, in this he might be successful, but

---

[16]L. V. McWhorter, *Yellow Wolf* (Caldwell, Idaho: The Caxton Printers, Ltd., 1986), p. 131., *"Their Lolo peace treaty was a lie!"*; and, Chief Joseph, "An Indian's Views of Indian Affairs," in *North American Review*, 128 (April, 1879), p. 426, *"We then made a treaty with these soldiers."*

[17]*Hear Me, My Chiefs!*, p. 353n; cited in Note 10.

[18]*Ibid.*, p. 351n. Captain Rawn's orders were: *"The Lieutenant General [Sheridan] directs that Nez-perces entering Montana must be disarmed and, if mounted, dismounted and held prisoners."* (National Archives, RG-94; Microfilm 666-337).

only at a great cost to himself, so during the night we made preparations to receive him, believing he would try to force his way through on the following morning. Before the first streak of daylight, every man was on the alert, with rifles ready, to meet the expected attack. At last daylight came, and with it an occasional shot, just enough to keep our attention. We were beginning to get somewhat impatient, and were preparing to throw out a skirmish line to feel them, when, on a high rocky point to our right, were seen six or eight Indians working their Winchesters right into us. Volunteers were called for, and fourteen sprang forward, led by 1st Lieut. Coolidge (now brigadier general Coolidge, retired), and started up the steep mountain side to drive them off. We had gotten quite well up, when they vanished out of sight.

We then discovered that during the night Joseph had moved his whole camp up the steep mountain side, had passed around us, and was then making rapid time to get to the Bitter Root Valley, and at the same time had left a number of his warriors to keep our attention, and delay us as long as possible.[19]

That there was some shooting is attested by Amos Buck, a volunteer of the Stevensville company, who later wrote, *"A few stray shots from the Indians, spent bullets, found their way into our camp, but no one was hurt,"* and Henry Buck has August K. Gird, for whom Girds Creek near Stevensville was named, firing one shot in return.[20]

But it is *The Missoulian*'s editor, Chauncey Barbour, serving as one of the Missoula Volunteers, who has left the best record of the events of the 28th.

At half past eight o'clock Saturday morning news was brought into Captain Rawn's camp that the Indians had thrown their lodges and were packing up to move. At ten o'clock the men in the camp saw Indians filing by on the ridges above camp. At half past eleven Lt. Tom Andrews [of the Missoula volunteers] was detailed with a force of 45 mounted men to guard the trail below camp and arrest stragglers [Rawn: "to prevent desertions"]. This force was divided into two squads, one to go ahead and observe the enemy. Three of the men of the lower squad ran into the rear guard of the Indian force. As soon as Looking

---

[19]*Winners Of The West*; cited in Note 2. Loynes repeated this account in nearly the same detail in his letter to L. V. McWhorter, November 12, 1943, adding the statement, *"All the friendly Indians at this time had left us, also most of the citizens."* His account differs from those of the other white participants, particularly in the number of days the barricade was occupied (one instead of three), and in the extent of desertion by the volunteers (all but a dozen gone by the morning of the 28th). This latter statement is a misinterpretation of Captain Rawn's official report, where he says, *"At the mouth of the Lolo and before reaching it all the Volunteers had left me but a dozen or 20 Missoula men and I was obliged to return to this post."* (*Secretary Of War, 1877*, Vol.I, p. 548)

[20]Amos Buck, "Review of the Battle of the Big Hole," a speech delivered at Hamilton, Montana, on the 31st anniversary of the battle, August 9, 1908 (Published in *Contributions To The Historical Society Of Montana*, Vol. 7, 1910, p. 120. See also, "The Story of the Nez Perce Campaign of 1877," p. 13; cited in Note 5.

Glass saw them, he waved his hat, and came up and exchanged friendly greetings.

The Indians came down to within half a mile of Captain Rawn's camp before they took to the ridge, and they came off of the ridge on to the Lo Lo about a mile below camp, crossing the Lo Lo and proceeding directly up the Bitter Root. At a quarter past twelve, Capt Rawn gave orders for the entire force to move down the Lo Lo. The force moved in military order, with a skirmish line at the sides and in front.

Lieut. W. J. Stephens, of the Missoula volunteers, was detailed with a force of fifty men to skirmish along the right bank of the Lo Lo. He soon struck the trail of the Indians, and pursued them to near the spot where they camped for the night [J. P. McClain's ranch, about where the Carlton-Florence school later stood]. The greater part of the force with Lieut. Stephens were from Bitter Root and were disposed to let Mr. Looking Glass and his people go in peace. Lieut. Stephens returned to town. Captain Rawn, after detailing Lieut. Stephens to skirmish along the right bank of the Lo Lo [and promising to support him] came directly to the post.

An incident that occurred after the Indians commenced moving may help to a better understanding of the disposition of these Indians. Amos, a Nez Perces who has lived about Missoula for years, came to the breastworks and proffered to surrender the eight lodges under his charge. He was taken into custody, and it has since been learned that the Nez Perces forcibly prevented his eight lodges from coming in.[21]

Thus, the sad result of Agent Peter Ronan's refusal to allow the little band of Eagle-from-the-Light sanctuary on the Jocko Reservation was to leave those noncombatants where they could be swept up by the hostiles. Amos was still in the Fort Missoula guardhouse March 10, 1879, when Lieut. Colonel John R. Brooks, the new post commander, wrote a letter to district headquarters at Fort Shaw asking what he should do about Amos and two other Indian prisoners. The answer, on April 4th, was that *"the Lieutenant General [Sheridan] thinks that 'Amos' who was supposed to have been one of General Howard's scouts should be at once released. "*[22] Thereafter he just disappeared from the official records.

While Captain Rawn nowhere admits to striking a deal with the Nez Perces — his orders precluded such a thing — the Bitterroot volunteers thought he had. His account of the parley on the 27th is followed by a statement which appears to refer to the parley, but is only accurate in the context of the next day's events: *"In the meantime that portion of the volunteers, some 100 or more, representing Bitter-root Valley, hearing that the Nez Perces promised to pass peaceably through it,*

---

[21]"The Indian War"; cited in Note 6. George Amos was also known as *"Thunder Eyes."* He was not a headman but was attempting to find sanctuary for Eagle-from-the-Light's people.

[22]National Archives, RG-94; Microfilm 666-339.

determined that no act of hostility on their part should provoke the Indians to a
contrary measure, and without leave, left in squads of from one to a dozen. "[23]

L.V. McWhorter provides an explanation of where at least some of the
Missoula men disappeared to on the 28th (leaving Captain Rawn with *"but a dozen
or 20"*). Speaking of Lieut. Andrews' lower squad, he says:

> Hurrying ahead, they formed their line of battle directly across the
> enemy's line of march. When the Nez Perce vanguard came in sight,
> and their challenging war whoop woke the morning echoes, the
> guardians of the Bitterroot Valley fled without firing a shot. Sam Scott,
> one of the contingent, said when later narrating the incident, "I don't
> know what I did with my gun. Somehow I lost it. I remember using
> my hat to whip my horse to a swifter pace. Although he was a fast
> runner, I thought that I was never on a slower mount. The Indians did
> not fire on us, nor did they appear to hasten their gait. Perhaps they
> thought we were staging a free riding exhibition for their amusement. "[24]

An approximate tally of Captain Rawn's command on the morning of the
28th — 45 volunteers with Andrews and 50 with Stephens, 30 regulars and their 5
officers, and 20 Flathead Indians — a total of 150, subtracted from the 216 on hand
the evening before, would indicate that the volunteers who decamped without leave
"in squads of from one to a dozen," as Rawn put it, numbered about 66.

Before leaving Captain Rawn's useless fortification, soon to be named *"Fort
Fizzle,"* a mention of its last defenders is in order. After the wild rout of Andrews
lower squad, before Captain Rawn's skirmish line reached the mouth of Sleeman
Creek and while the main column of Nez Perces was crossing the trail, the
company of volunteers from Phillipsburg, under Captain McLean, marched up to
the Indian cavalcade, and *"actually passed through the heart of the Nez Perces, mi-
nus a knowledge of them being the Indians they came to annihilate. "* The
snickering editor of the Deer Lodge *New North-West* says that Captain Rawn put
them into the abandoned rifle pits, and so, *"kept them free from danger, and
literally denied them a chance of becoming better acquainted with the refugees
from Idaho. "*[25] That was just as well, as the Phillipsburg men were armed with
muzzleloading Civil War muskets.

Editor Barbour later made a point of noting emphatically that of the 58 armed
men who answered his call for help and reached Missoula that Saturday, *"only
twenty — the Phillipsburg company — were ever at Rawn's barricade. "* He listed
the others as 20 from Deer Lodge, 10 from Beartown, 5 from Bear Mouth and 3
from Elk, all of them absorbed into the Governor's plan of defense or offense,
whichever it was, in the Missoula area.[26]

---

[23]"The Indian War", cited in Note 6. As shown, Bitterroot volunteers were still with Rawn on
the 28th (the skirmishers with Lt. Stephens); also, the count of 216 effectives present at the barricade
on the evening of the 27th had to include most of the Bitterroot men.

[24]Yellow Wolf, p. 108n; cited in Note 16.

[25] See, *A History Of Montana*, 1739-1885, p. 141; cited in Note 13.

[26] "War Notes," in *Helena Daily Herald*, Aug. 6, 1877.

Picking up events at Missoula on the 28th, the arrangement Governor Potts was able to make was evidently quite rudimentary. With Missoula's volunteers at the barricade on Lolo Creek, he had only the small company at Frenchtown and twenty-eight mounted men who had come from Deer Lodge Valley in response to Editor Barbour's appeal for help. Most of those were sent to guard the bridge over Bitterroot River, three miles below the mouth of O'Brien Creek. That left less than the proverbial corporal's guard to protect the town's environs, unless the 32 men of Stewart's Deer Lodge company, who had marched 90 miles in a little more than twenty-five hours — and thus were of little immediate use for anything — are considered.

Duncan McDonald rode into Missoula that morning to find the town practically deserted,

> . . . with a lone man standing guard at the town end of the bridge which was barred by a log chain stretched across it. McDonald, riding up, inquired why the chain, and was told that it was to hold back the Nez Perces who were expected to come through town. Pointing to the river, above and below the bridge, McDonald exclaimed, derisively, "There! There! See the Indian's bridges! They can cross anywhere, but if they choose to pass on this bridge, your chain will hold them about thirty seconds. You had better show a spirit of hospitality by taking it down!"[27]

McDonald's description of Commander-in-Chief Pott's frazzled nerves, as the volunteers straggled into Missoula from the barricade on Lolo Creek later in the day, is equally ludicrous: *"I was standing in the doorway [of the hotel], and at the cry, 'Nez Perce outriders!' the Governor nearly upset me in his hurry to get inside."* The dust cloud which had caused that alarm was made by a pack train, according to Will Cave:

> My step-father, Alfred Cave, had a train of pack mules. Rawn had engaged 12 of these to carry supplies from Fort Missoula to the camp [Fort Fizzle] . . . the mules were in charge of "Walla Walla" Johnson. Early in the afternoon, Johnson and the loaded mules, having left the fort, were on the road going around the Cold Spring ranch, when "One Armed" John Pickens saw the outfit. He was not a young man and his eyesight was not the best. He jumped at the conclusion that they were Indians coming [and] did not tarry to ascertain to the contrary, but mounted a saddle horse, rode across the flat as fast as his horse could travel, coming into town and excitedly announcing that the Indians were right upon us. Two other boys and myself were swimming in the river near the Higgins Avenue bridge . . . there sure was enough "hurrying in hot haste" about the burg for awhile. Every old

---

[27]*Hear Me, My Chiefs!*, p. 355; cited in Note 10.

shotgun and pistol was brought out, while people prepared to occupy the brick and stone buildings.[28]

There was panic enough at Missoula to send settlers scurrying eastward with their families on the 29th. A soldier of Captain George L. Browning's Company G, of the 7th Infantry, which was being hurried toward Missoula from Fort Ellis in Hugh Kirkendall's wagons, noted that at New Chicago *"wagons packed with families and effects passed us hastening to places of safety,"* and,

> . . . to our great mortification, at 11 A.M., a man reached us reporting the escape of the Indians; and the volunteers soon returning by the score, stating cessation of danger, we slackened up a little in mercy to our animals. Such serious charges for the responsibility of the mistake were constantly heard that we almost feared that some great blunder had been made, and when we met the Governor and Secretary returning to Deer Lodge we concluded we might not be needed.[29]

The reaction to the successful passage of the Nez Perce into the Bitterroot Valley was immediate and vigorous. There were hot heads among the Deer Lodge volunteers, and even some at Missoula, who felt they had been cheated out of a fight. Among the latter was editor Chauncey Barbour, who probably spoke for many concerning future use of the militia when he counseled the governor, *"You don't want any military, or any one to hold your men chafing and tell them to 'wait', 'wait' until the hostiles are gone. Take command yourself, and don't let good men be humiliated by imbeciles or cowards . . . Wipe out the disgrace that has been put upon us, and never let any regular officer again command Montana Militia."*[30]

During the following three days Barbour cooled down enough to see the *"Fort Fizzle"* fiasco in an entirely different light. In his letter to Governor Potts immediately after getting out the first issue of *The Weekly Missoulian* to come off the press following his short stint as a volunteer soldier, the editor wrote:

---

[28]Will Cave, "Most Bitter Indian Battle Near Missoula," in *The Sunday Missoulian*, Aug. 7, 1877; Special Features, p. 1.

[29]"Seventh Infantry," in *The Avant Courier*, Bozeman, M. T., August 9, 1877. Mark Brown places the arrival of Company G on the 30th, but Captain Rawn's official report clearly states, *"The garrison was increased by the arrival, on July 29, 1877, from Fort Ellis, of Company G, 7th Infantry."* Their arrival so much in advance of Colonel Gibbon's force from Fort Shaw was due to an earlier order intended to reinforce the post at Missoula. See, Telegram of July 20, District of Montana, entered into the Fort Missoula post returns as received there July 31 (it *"Directs C. O. Fort Ellis, M. T., to send one of his Co. with all the Cavalry he can mount."*) Copy in the Big Hole National Battlefield Library.

[30]Excerpt from a letter, Chauncey Barbour to Gov. Potts, July 31, 1877. This letter appeared first in "The Battle of the Big Hole," edited by Paul C. Phillips for The Frontier, and it was reprinted in Frontier Omnibus, John W. Hakola, ed., (Missoula: Montana State University Press, 1962), pp. 363-84. See p. 375. Worse, as concerns Captain Rawn's reputation, were rumors that he and his officers were intoxicated at the time the Nez Perces by-passed the barricade on Lolo Creek. See, "The Story of the Nez Perce Indian Campaign of 1877," p. 11; cited in Note 5.

Dear Sir,

Was glad to receive your kind and friendly letter. I felt myself in the most trying position in the last issue of my paper, I was ever in in my life. There was so much of unreason and of reckless statement and vituperation that I felt it my duty to stand against the current if it swamped me. And it is gratifying to me to say that I have compelled a sober, second thought, and that scores of good men have taken me by the hand and thanked me for what they are pleased to term the able manner in which I have performed an intelligent duty. You, who have ever stood our fast friend, did not escape in the general detraction, and I thought it best justice to call attention to the important service you had rendered us in the crisis through which we passed. If you had taken command of the militia and precipitated hostilities you would have merited our unmixed condemnation. It is best as it was, and our people now with one accord congratulate themselves that our welfare was in the hands of discreet men. There were some reckless spirits among us and from Deer Lodge county, who had nothing to lose, who would have precipitated a fight even at the expense of seeing this county ravaged. They could conveniently place themselves in a place of safety if required; but those with their wives and little ones and all they had in the world would have to stay and suffer. I am thankful that my publication day was not last Sunday [29th]: I was then prepared to call Capt Rawn a coward and incompetent to command a force of men who were at the front . . .[31]

Merely as an example of the *"reckless statement and vituperation"* of which Barbour complained, the *Helena Independent* of July 30 ran this from its Deer Lodge correspondent: *"It is stated that when turned by the Deer Lodgers, the Indians stampeded square over Rawn's rifle pits, but not a shot was fired."* That probably was a misinterpretation of Governor Potts poorly worded news release of the 29th, while yet badly shaken: *"Joseph and his band passed Capt. Rawn's entrenchment yesterday late in the afternoon, and although they passed within gunshot not a gun was fired at them."* That criticism, had a larger mark than Captain Rawn and his regulars. The Bitterroot volunteers received a goodly share of blame on account of their forbearance — for *"permitting"* the Nez Perce to camp unopposed in the valley. The following letter, written by rancher W.B. Harlan, to Editor James Mills of the *New North-West* on August 4th, shows how the Bitterroot people felt:

By the way, I have received letters from friends in Deer Lodge, saying that some of the returned Deer Lodge volunteers were branding the Bitter Rooters as cowards, &c., for allowing the Indians to pass through in peace . . .

---

[31]*Ibid.*, pp. 376-77.

When all the Indians were allowed to pass into Bitter Root without a shot, and all the regulars and outside militia had gone to Missoula, does anyone think we were going to pitch into them alone, when they outnumbered us three to one, and had the advantage of position, and all our families and property were beyond them.

On that Saturday morning Fort Owen held 263 women and children, guarded by two needle guns and two Henry guns, with a dozen muskets and shotguns in the hands of as many men. When we overtook the Indians, Looking Glass met us and told us he would not harm any persons or property in the valley if allowed to pass in peace, and that we could pass through his camp to our homes.

The offer was accepted as we could do nothing else, as our place was between the Indians and our homes.

We were not silly enough to uselessly incite the Indians to devastate our valley, and I do not think our critics would have done otherwise had they and their families and homes been situated as were ours.

If they want Indians for breakfast they are still within reach, and have been ever since the fiasco at Fort Fizzle on the Lo Lo trail."[32]

There *were* those who would have *"Indians for breakfast,"* and they were gathering to have a try at it; but the Nez Perces didn't know that.

---

[32]Published August 10, 1877, p. 3.

Chapter 3

OUR WORDS WERE GOOD[1]

The Nez Perce Indians looked upon the forbearance they had offered the white men at Fort Fizzle as a treaty as truly as though signed and sealed. Thinking in tribal terms, rather than national, their war had been with the Idaho people; there was no need to fight with the Montanans, who had always been their friends. They would go peaceably through this land to the buffalo country along the Yellowstone and Missouri Rivers and live there for a time with their old friends, the Crow Indians; then, later, when the war was forgotten, they would return to their former homes and make a peace. What they did not comprehend was that all the white men were of one mind — that, as James Mills put it, *"The people of Idaho are our people and their butchers would be ours if the circumstances were favorable;"*[2] so that any *"treaty"* made by the volunteers at Fort Fizzle was only a tongue-in-cheek compact, intended to get dangerous Indians out of Bitterroot Valley.

But even that much agreement was at odds with the plans of the military, which had always been to capture the dissident Nez Perces and return them to the reservation. It was a task now assumed to require force of arms, not temporizing, as was apparent in the letter Colonel John Gibbon, commanding the District of Montana, wrote Governor Potts on August 2nd, while he awaited the arrival of his troops at Missoula. He was counting on Montana militia to prevent the *"hostiles"* from leaving the Bitterroot Valley before he could bring all his regulars against them, so he cautioned Potts: *"Please give instruction also to have no negotiations whatever with the Indians, and the men should have no hesitancy in shooting down any armed Indian they meet not known to belong to one of the peaceful tribes."*[3]

The militia referred to by Colonel Gibbon were called out in response to Governor Potts' second *"Proclamation,"* on July 31 (the first, on the 27th, called only the Missoula and Deer Lodge County volunteers, who turned out particularly for the protection of Missoula and adjacent settlements); this *"Call For Three Hundred Volunteers"*[4] had a broader purpose — active participation in the war which the Army was waging with so little success. On the same page of the *Herald* with his Proclamation, the Governor explained, under *"Forward!"*: *"I have called for three hundred mounted volunteers to intercept the Indians as they*

---

[1]From L. V. McWhorter, *Yellow Wolf: His Own Story* (1986), p. 131.

[2]Letter to Governor Potts, July 22, 1877, in "The Battle of the Big Hole," edited by Paul C. Phillips for *The Frontier* (Vol. X, No. 1, 1929). The article has been reprinted in *Frontier Omnibus*, John W. Hakola, ed., (Missoula: Montana State University Press,1962), pp. 363-84. See p.372 for the letter quoted. Further reference to this article will be cited as *Frontier Omnibus*.

[3]Letter, August 2, 1877, *Ibid.*, p. 376. John Gibbon's post war rank was that of colonel; however, he is sometimes addressed courteously as *"general"* in consideration of his Civil War rank.

[4]"Proclamation," in *Helena Daily Herald*, July 31, 1877.

pass out of the Bitter Root . . . The Indian murderers must not pass unmolested. B. F. Potts."

That the movement proposed by the Governor had the approval of regular officers then in the field, and may even have been proposed by them, is quite evident from Captain Rawn's correspondence with James Mills:

> Please inform Gov. Potts that Indians will be some six days, maybe less, in getting to Big Hole Prairie, at present rate of moving. Both Gen'ls Howard and Gibbon desire them delayed, Gen. Gibbon instructed me today to temporize with them for that purpose. I will start tomorrow up the valley with my 50 or 60 men, and endeavor to follow out his wishes until Gens. Howard and Gibbon can get in. In the meanwhile, the bearer, who is well acquainted with the country, states that if the Gov. sends from Deer Lodge, by way of French Gulch, several days will be gained and the Indians headed before reaching Big Hole Prairie, and also meet volunteers from Bannack.[5]

Thus, Governor Potts thought he was acting quite properly in involving the militia in further operations against the hostile Nez Perces, though he was not. But first, an amusing anecdote concerning the hasty organization of the Butte Battalion.

On the fiftieth anniversary of the Big Hole battle, The *Butte Miner* ran an article lamenting the fact that the historical record usually leaves events of a merely *"amusing nature, regardless of how authentic,"* to be handed down from father to son. Such an incident was that preliminary engagement which has been aptly termed *"the battle of Blackfoot Bar";* a bloodless encounter which developed from the distribution of guns to the men of the Big Hole expedition. The firearms available for arming the volunteers were obsolete Springfield rifles of .50 calibre breechloading single-shot, and .53 calibre muzzleloading musket types — from Army ordnance stores. Copper-cased ammunition came with the breechloaders, and paper cartridges (each containing black powder and a minie ball) were furnished for the muzzleloaders. The lucky men got the breechloaders and the others had to make do with the Civil War relics.

> With the distribution of the firearms attended to, orders were issued that the volunteers assemble at a certain designation at daylight the next morning in readiness to start on the overland hike to the Big Hole Basin . . . Nothing was said as to where the volunteers were to spend their time before the order to "march" was given. There were some who retired at once to their blankets intent on getting a night's rest, but there were others who realized getting into a battle with the Indians only happened once in a lifetime and considered it worthy of celebrating. Hours later a row of guns lined the walls of the Blackfoot Bar, one of Deer Lodge's original "filling stations," while several rows of various volunteers faced the bar partaking of the cup that is alleged to

---

[5]Letter, August 1, 1877, in *Frontier Omnibus*, p. 376; cited in Note 2.

cheer and telling each other the proper manner in which to kill Indians. For years afterwards one of the "angels in white" who officiated back of the Blackfoot bar that night said that more Indians were butchered within the four walls of the place than were ever really killed in battle in the whole state of Montana.

At the time it seemed a queer coincidence that the majority of drinks were paid for by the men who had been obliged to arm themselves with the muzzleloaders, but the fact was entirely lost sight of at the moment and it was not until the following day that the strategic plan in connection with the impending battle became common knowledge. While the possessors of the breechloading guns stood entrenched in the Blackfoot Bar, knocking over imaginary Indians by the score the more sober possessors of muzzleloading weapons had substituted their more obsolete rifles for the needle guns and decamped in order to retain possession. Many of them had started out alone, or in small groups, hoping thereby to get mixed up in the prospective battle before the real owners had sobered up enough to realize their loss. In theory the plan proved a great success, but luckily for the volunteers no Indians were encountered . . . the fellows who conceived the idea of making the swap had overlooked the matter of ammunition. The men with the 'stolen' breechloaders carried nothing but muzzleloader charges, while those with muzzleloaders could do nothing with their copper cased cartridges.

Deer Lodge residents had occasion to recall the "Battle of Blackfoot Bar" at the time the present Deer Lodge Hotel was erected. An old stone building stood near where the present hotel entrance is now situated. When the old stone building was being demolished the workmen unearthed about 70 stand of Springfield rifles. They were all that remained of the consignment furnished by the Government in 1877 for the purpose of arming volunteer Indian fighters. They had been stored in the building and as the years went by lost sight of. W. C. Spottswood, then manager of the Bonner Mercantile Co. which owned the building, had them removed to the Bonner Store and placed on exhibition in one of the windows. Incidentally, he notified the Federal war department regarding the guns and sent ordnance headquarters in Washington, D.C., a bill covering their storage. Several weeks elapsed before he received an answer. The ordnance department informed him that inasmuch as the guns had become obsolete the Government had no use for them and the Bonner Co. could keep them in lieu of a storage charge. Mr. Spottswood later distributed the rifles among his friends and patrons of the store and in more than one home one of the old guns is now being kept as a prized relic.[6]

While that account is admittedly shaky history, it does help to explain the unmilitary arrival of the militiamen at French Gulch the following day. According to Alvin Noyes:

> It was but a straggling band of men that rode from the Springs to French Gulch that day, no attempt to keep order. Captain James Talbot, John Downs and I were at the head of the column and, of course, the first into French Gulch. Talbot and Downs wanted a drink of whiskey on account of the cold. Talbot remarked: "It won't do to allow the boys all the whiskey they want, so I will order the saloon keeper not to let them have more than one each." This was agreed to by Downs. As soon as we got to town, they got their drink and the Frenchman got his orders. "Do not give more than one drink to any one man. Do you understand?" The boys kept straggling in until dark, each one to get his one drink. No more! I never could tell just what did happen; either those boys got more than one drink, or the poison was intense, as many a one was pretty noisy before midnight. Guards were out with the horses. A beef was killed in the street, and the men proceeded to get their supper on the end of a sharp stick and cook before a big camp fire. We rolled in any old place, with orders to move at daybreak. When the day did break it was to be one of disappointment. Jake Hootman had arrived about 2 o'clock with word from Gen. Sherman, who was at Fort Ellis, to the effect that the government did not need the Volunteers, and that we were to return home.[7]

Noyes was mistaken in his impression that General of the Army William T. Sherman had put a stop to Governor Potts' use of the militia; Sherman *was* at Fort Ellis and about to tour the new Yellowstone National Park, but he was careful to avoid any interference with the plans of field officers. The order to disband had a different source. On July 13th Governor Potts had sought authority to call out volunteers and encumber Federal and Territorial funds for their pay and upkeep. The reply of Secretary of War George W. McCrary, dated the 18th, stated bluntly, *"Department is not authorized to call out volunteers, or will they . . . "* and went on to explain that it was not thought necessary because General Sheridan had a sufficient force at his command.[8]

The slowness with which that reply had come back through channels had put the Governor in a bad position (he had made necessary expenditures *"on the cuff,"*

---

[6]"Old Timer Recalls First 'Strategic Maneuvers' In Connection With Big Hole," in *The Butte Miner*, August 10, 1927.

[7]Alva J. Noyes, *The Story Of Ajax* (New York: Buffalo Head Press, 1966), p. 31. [Reprinted from the 1914 edition]

[8]"No Authority For Raising Volunteers," in *Helena Daily Herald*, August 1, 1877.

and the $2,000 raised by public subscription was $10,000 short of what was needed). Also, the Governor's status as Commander-in-Chief of the militia suffered. The *Herald* accused him of inventing a new weapon of war — the Proclamation — which, to be fully effective, must be immediately revoked; all for the purpose of *"cheap notoriety."*[9]

Before Major William A. Clark brought the 96 men of his Butte Battalion back from French Gulch, he sent Lieutenant Mel Lowery and several men into the Big Hole to scout for Indians. Of course they found none as they were a few days too early, but they did contact the volunteers out of Bannack. That ended the operation of the Territorial Militia as an independent force. It is an open question whether or not the militia would have been able to hold the Nez Perces in the Bitterroot Valley by blocking the pass into Big Hole Basin, as the strategy called for; they might have been by-passed, or even destroyed needlessly if the War Department had approved of the operation. From that time on volunteers would only be allowed to serve under regular officers.

Actually, at McClain's ranch, their first encampment after passing Rawn's barricade, the Nez Perce Indians almost abandoned that first idea of going to the buffalo country by way of the Big Hole Basin, in favor of traveling north, through the Flathead country to safety in Canada. Three treaty Nez Perces who were returning to Lapwai after serving as scouts for General Nelson A. Miles on the Montana plains, had stopped to visit with kinsmen on the Jocko Reservation before starting for home on the Lolo trail (these were the Indians earlier thought to be hanging around the Agency trader's establishment in the hope of purchasing ammunition). Upon resuming their journey, the three met the non-treaty bands at McClain's, and there, Grizzly Bear Youth told Chief Looking Glass how foolish it was to be at war with the government; he thought the refugees ought to go north, through the Jocko Reservation, to Canada.

> Looking Glass then called a council and told Joseph and others what Grizzly Bear Youth had said. White Bird and Red Owl agreed. They wanted to go by the reserve. Joseph did not say a word. Looking Glass wanted to go by Big Hole and down the Yellowstone to join the Crows, according to agreement, because the Crows had promised them that whenever the Nez Perces fought the whites they would join them. There was a disagreement, but after the quarreling among themselves, they concluded to let Looking Glass have his way.[10]

With their original decision thus confirmed, the Nez Perce bands moved leisurely up the Bitterroot Valley on the old Indian trail west of the river. From their first encampment on July 28, they had moved only 28 miles by the 31st, when C. P. Higgins reported them as camped on the west side of the river,

---

[9]"The New Weapon of War," in *Helena Daily Herald*, August 6, 1877.
[10]Duncan McDonald, "The Nez Perce War of 1877 — The Inside History from Indian Sources," in *The New North-West*, Deer Lodge, M. T., January 10,1879. See also, Mark Brown, *Flight Of The Nez Perces* (New York: G. P. Putnam's Sons, 1967), p. 230.

opposite Stevensville (at Silverthorne Flat). He noted that *"The Indians are taking ammunition from citizens whom they meet and although so far as we know have done no damage are very independent . . . "*[11] Chauncey Barbour was able to add, on that same date, *"The Bitter Root mail carrier brings word that about 75 bucks were raiding Stevensville today. They have gone through some houses and helped themselves to what they wanted. They are probably lawless stragglers, as there are no squaws with them or head men which is evidence that the main force is on the move . . . "*[12]

Amos Buck, who kept a store in Stevensville along with brothers Fred and Henry, later described the experience of the townspeople the day the Indians came shopping.

> They camped just over the river from town and came over to trade. They found all the stores closed, but Chief Looking Glass represented that they had money to pay for what they bought and would do so. Looking Glass represented that his people needed provisions, and if refused sale, would take all they wanted anyway. Whereupon the stores opened their doors and sales commenced.
>
> All ammunition had been stored out of sight as a precautionary measure, and although it was the chief article desired, they did not succeed in getting any. They did buy extensively and paid in gold. While the trading was going on some miscreant, who valued a dollar more than the lives of all the people in the valley, furnished the Indians with whiskey and it made some of them insolent. One young buck went to the back door of the house where Mr. Herman, the blacksmith, lived and was inclined to be rude to his wife, and upon Mr. Herman resenting his conduct, the greatest excitement prevailed. Only the most heroic efforts on the part of their war chief, Looking Glass, were sufficient to prevent the outbreak then and there. He used his whip and harangued them until he succeeded in getting them quieted and out of town.[13]

Brother Henry's longer account names the whiskey vendors as Dave Spooner, barkeep of the Reeves Saloon, and Jerry Fahy, another storekeeper — both put out of business by irate townspeople. He also mentions two near shootings, one involving himself, and credits Flathead Indians with saving his life as well as Mrs.

---

[11]Letter, C. P. Higgins to Gov. Potts, July 31, 1877, in *Frontier Omnibus*, pp. 374-75; cited in Note 2. The word got around Stevensville that the Indians had a 16-year- old white girl in their camp, but there is no proof of that.

[12]Letter, Chauncey Barbour to Gov. Potts, July 31, 1877, in *Frontier Omnibus*, p. 375; cited in Note 2.

[13]Amos Buck, "Review of the Battle of the Big Hole"; a speech delivered at Hamilton, Montana, August 9, 1908, on the 31st Anniversary of the battle, and published in *Contributions To The Historical Society Of Montana*, Vol. 7, (1910), p. 120.

Herman's. He thought Chief Whitebird was the headman who got the drunken Indians out of town.[14]

On August 1st Captain Rawn was able to report, *"Am advised by scout that hostile camp is at Corvallis, 30 miles from here, taking their time . . ."* and it was the refusal of at least one storekeeper of that town to do business with the Nez Perces that caused Colonel Gibbon to call Mr. Young, *"one bright exception"* to the general rule in the Bitterroot Valley because he *"refused to barter for their blood money, closed his store, and dared them to do their worst."* [15]

Perhaps Mr. Young's attitude was a factor in the several incidents of pillage and vandalism which occurred in the upper end of the Bitterroot Valley. According to information Rev. W. A. Hall, of Corvallis, provided *The Weekly Missoulian:*

> Mr. Landrum's house was pillaged about $5.00 worth, and several houses were broken into above this place. M. M. Lockwood's house was broken open and everything demolished except the stove. Joe Blodgett's household goods and a large quantity of provisions were stolen, his harness cut all to pieces and about fifteen head of horses stolen. Alex Stewart had several head of cattle shot by the invaders.[16]

Those were considerable losses, yet the only one of the several incidents of which much has been said was the ransacking of Lockwood's house (and theft of his stock; at least he claimed that the Indians made off with $200 worth). Duncan McDonald attributed those depredations to the unruly young men of Chief Toohoolhoolzote's band, and Chief Looking Glass did attempt to make amends by taking seven horses from the guilty parties, branding them with Lockwood's iron and turning them loose on his property — where they damaged the oats and wheat!

Myron Lockwood, who had other reasons for feeling less than appreciative, later said: *"The red rascals turned into my growing wheat field, branded with my brand, a couple of worn-out, worthless cayuses, sore-backed, spavined [and] scarcely able to walk."* [17] After the war, Lockwood claimed damages totalling $1,600, but they were not allowed because Colonel John Gibbon was unable to certify to the correctness of the claim.

Alvin Josephy, who considers the pillage of Lockwood's cabin a trivial matter — *"some flour, coffee, a few shirts, and several other articles"* — dismisses the other incidents as *"groundless; charges that horses and camping equipment were taken from some homes evaporated when it was revealed that the property had belonged, in the first place, to buffalo-hunting Indians who had left their*

---

[14]Henry Buck, "The Story of the Nez Perce Indian Campaign During the Summer of 1877," pp. 16-18 (manuscript in the Montana Historical Society Library, Helena; this was published serially in *The Great Falls Tribune*, December 24, 1944, to February 11, 1945). Mark Brown has presented the pertinent passages in *The Flight Of The Nez Perce*, pp. 231-32; cited in Note 10.

[15]*Flight Of The Nez Perce*, p. 233; cited in Note 10.

[16]Mark Brown quotes this from the issue of August 17, 1877. See *The Flight Of The Nez Perce*, p. 233; cited in Note 10.

[17]*The Butte Miner*, September 18, 1877.

animals and possessions in the care of white friends earlier in the year. "[18]   The truth probably lies somewhere between the extremes.

On another matter of considerable importance, Josephy claims that some of the settlers *"visited the Indian camp and sold bullets to the warriors,"* and Hugh Peyton's interview with Austin A. *"Quiller"* Wilkerson, tends to confirm that, in at least one case, it might be so. Hugh, who was born and raised in the Bitterroot Valley, interviewed several of the survivors of the Big Hole battle in 1939, when he had the oversight of the battlefield for the National Park Service, and among the afterthoughts that Quiller remembered *"was that Dave Spooner, a French-Canadian, traded $90.00 worth of ammunition for a brown mare while the Indians were opposite Stevensville."* [19]

The second-handed statement of correspondent Thomas A. Sutherland, writing for the San Francisco *Chronicle* and several other papers, that the *"avaricious wretches [of Stevensville] followed after the hostiles for miles with their wagons loaded with all kinds of goods, selling to them to the amount of $900,"*[20] seems less likely, and may even be a warped reference to Dave Spooner's greedy mischief.

Captain Rawn's scouts, John Deschamps and Bob Irvine, two volunteers who spoke Nez Perce, rode with the Indians as far as Skalkaho, and, though the Captain appears to have lost touch with them after August 1st, they were able to gather valuable information which later appeared in the Deer Lodge *New North-West.*[21] Those spies credited the Indians with having 250 guns, many being Winchesters and cavalry carbines, sufficient ammunition, and a horse herd of 1,500 to 2,000 animals, some of which were *"American horses and very valuable,"* though *"the horses they ride are very much jaded."* A disquieting note was their report of *"20 or 30 Snakes and Bannocks"* with them — which tended to feed a latent fear that the Nez Perce had, indeed, found allies among those tribes. Henry Buck, who watched from a bastion of Fort Owen as the Indian cavalcade passed by, noted that it took an hour and a quarter for all to pass, and he thought the horse herd could be as large as 3,000 animals. Presumably, Rawn and Gibbon had all that information, for Chauncey Barbour wrote Governor Potts, on the 3rd, that *"A half breed who arrived last night reports the hostiles 50 miles above here [Missoula] on the east side of Bitter Root."*[22] There *was* communication with the upper end of the valley, and the letter was kept open so long that it missed the mail on the 4th, and a P.S.

---

[18] Alvin M. Josephy, Jr., *The Nez Perce And The Opening Of The Northwest* (New Haven and London: Yale University Press, 1965), p. 576.

[19] Oral History Notes — Interview with *"Quiller"* Wilkerson, recorded by Yellowstone Assistant Chief Ranger Hugh Peyton in 1939. Typescript forwarded to the Superintendent, Big Hole National Battlefield, by the Superintendent, Coulee Dam National Recreation Area, May 8, 1985, from the effects of Hugh Peyton following his death. See p. 2. It is interesting that both Wilkerson and Henry Buck name Dave Spooner as a miscreant.

[20] Mark Brown, *Flight Of The Nez Perce*, pp. 132-33 (cited in Note 10), quotes from the San Francisco *Chronicle*, August 27, 1877.

[21] August 10, 1877. Mark Brown indicates editor James Mills had a report by the 5th (see, *The Flight Of The Nez Perce*, pp. 234-35; cited in Note 10).

[22] *Frontier Omnibus*, pp. 376-77; cited in Note 2.

added on the morning of the 5th was able to place the Indians *"at Rosse's Hole, 90 miles from here."*

In seven days of elapsed time the Nez Perces had averaged a little less than twelve miles per day — not bad for a cavalcade as encumbered and travel worn as they undoubtedly were. However, there were those who were not pleased with the progress. According to Yellow Wolf, in the upper end of the valley,

> . . . there was something — a feeling some of us could not understand. One morning a young man who had medicine power rode about camp, calling loudly to the people, "My brothers, my sisters, I am telling you! In a dream last night I saw myself killed. I will be killed soon! I do not care. I am willing to die. But first, I will kill some soldiers. I shall not turn back from the death. We are all going to die!" . . . [and then] Lone Bird, a brave fighter, also rode about one camp wanting more hurry. His voice reached all the people as he warned, "My shaking heart tells me trouble and death will overtake us if we make no hurry through this land! I must speak what is revealed to me. Let us begone to the buffalo country!"[23]

Death was, indeed, overtaking the Nez Perces as they moved leisurely up the Bitterroot Valley and over the Continental Divide toward that beautiful meadow on the North Fork of Big Hole River. It followed them in the form of soldiers of the Seventh United States Infantry carried in Hugh Kirkendall's mule wagons, and mounted citizen volunteers still anxious to have *"Indians for breakfast."*

Upon receiving telegraphic notice, July 21st, that the non-treaty Nez Perce Indians had left their Idaho homeland and were moving eastward over the Lolo trail with the intention of entering Montana Territory, Colonel John Gibbon replied to Assistant Adjutant General R.C. Drum at Chicago:

> Despatch of yesterday received; have ordered one company of infantry from Fort Ellis to Missoula direct. As soon as I can assemble troops here from Camp Baker and Fort Benton, I shall move via Cadotes Pass down the Blackfoot towards Missoula. Shall probably be able to take nearly one hundred men; the troops being all infantry, these movements will necessarily be slow . . .[24]

The available troops (skeleton companies of the Seventh Infantry and the Second Cavalry) were distributed between four posts, Benton, Shaw, Baker and Ellis, which formed a ragged line intended to shield western Montana from the incursions of Siouian people[25] to the east and Piegans to the north. Not only was

---

[23]L. V. McWhorter, *Yellow Wolf: His Own Story* (Caldwell, Idaho: The Caxton Printers, Ltd., 1986), pp. 108-09.

[24]National Archives, RG-94; Microfilm 666-337.

[25]While the "Organization of the Army under the Act of March 3, 1889," allowed a maximum strength of 100 and a minimum of 50 privates per infantry company, Congressional efforts to economize military expenditures in subsequent years put a cap of 25,000 men on the enlisted strength of the Army by 1877. "As a result, a ceiling of 37 soldiers per company was imposed on the infantry,

Fort Shaw a long way from Missoula (150 rough miles), but precious time was lost in concentrating the force. Company F, from Fort Benton, and D, from Camp Baker, joined Company K at Fort Shaw, Gibbon's headquarters, on the 27th. By the time they were ready to move out at one o'clock the next afternoon, the Nez Perces had rendered Captain Rawn's barricade in Lolo Canyon useless by passing around it, and the purpose for which Gibbon's reinforcement was being hurried toward Missoula had changed from one of containment on Lolo Creek, to an even more difficult pursuit and capture mission.

The small numbers of effectives available from the scattered posts is a wry commentary on the condition of the Indian fighting army of post-Civil War days. Company D, from Camp Baker, had 26 enlisted men on its muster roll, but was able to supply only twenty effectives (after six men were detailed to look after the company property), and had to be brought up to *"strength"* by the addition of six men from Company E. Company F, from Fort Benton, mustered 31 enlisted men, of which ten were left behind; however, the situation there may have been similar to that of the Fort Shaw garrison, where Company K — a unit of similar size — also could field only 21 effectives because two of the men on the muster roll had deserted, one was on leave and two were sick. So, it was with a total of only 68 men of his Seventh Infantry, that Colonel John Gibbon left Fort Shaw on July 18th, his men in light marching order and their supplies on pack mules.

Second Lieutenant Edward E. Hardin, who had brought Company F in from Fort Benton in the absence of Captain Constant Williams from that post, kept a diary on the march. His entries show it was no picnic:

> July 28th. Left Fort Shaw about 1 and marched to 6.30. Some of the packs did not get in until midnight . . . Some of F Co. fell out during the day . . . Cut up a sheep corral to cook with. Poor water and lots of mosquitos . . .
>
> July 29th. Marched to the Dearborn and nooned. I had to leave one of my mules back, broke down . . .
>
> July 30th. Crossed the Rocky mountains. Marched about 22 miles. Capt. James killed a deer . . . Woodruff and I had lots of lunch . . . trout for supper. Capt. James gave me a place in his shelter tent.
>
> July 31st. Got up stiff and cold. Rained before we left camp. Wore my overcoat until noon. Carried men across creek [on his horse] . . . Marched 28 miles . . .
>
> August 1st. Marched about 14 miles . . .
>
> August 2nd. Left camp at 5. Carrid [sic] the men across the creek on our horses. Had a hard march of 23 miles . . . Rained at night.

---

which usually meant less than 25 men for duty."   Robert M. Utley, *Frontier Regulars* (Lincoln: University of Nebraska Press, 1973), p. 17.

> August 3rd. Left camp at 5 had a rough road . . . Got to the open
> valley — stopped at 10 0'clock — 12 miles. Marched about 6 miles and
> got to Missoula . . . About four miles up the Bitter Root is the camp
> . . .[26]

At the new post near Missoula, Colonel Gibbon combined the companies he
had brought from Fort Shaw (D, F and K) with the one from Fort Ellis (G) and the
two already there (A and I) to form a battalion of 146 men and 15 officers. That
included 19 mounted men — eleven of the Company F men and eight from the
Second Cavalry who had come through from Fort Ellis with Captain Browning.

Anticipating the usefulness of wagon transportation for moving infantry up
the Bitterroot Valley, Captain Rawn had *"ordered Q.M. to hold Kerkendall's
wagons for transporting us."*[27] The pack mules were retained in case the freight
wagons could not get over the Continental Divide, and a 12-pounder mountain
howitzer, mounted on a *"prairie carriage"* and pulled by six mules, was added to
the column. Actually, this gun had left Fort Shaw the same day as Gibbon's
infantry, but went by the Mullan Road in charge of Lieutenant F. M. H.
Kendrick.[28]

Gibbon's command left the post near Missoula at one o'clock on August 4,
with the infantry in the wagons, which allowed them to make 29 miles before
stopping at eleven that night. As the command passed the mouth of Lolo Creek, a
courier by the name of Joe Pardee was sent by the Lolo trail to apprise General
Howard of the plan and ask for the support of 100 cavalry. According to
Lieutenant Hardin, the troops nooned at Corvallis the next day, where they laid
over for three hours — from eleven to two — to rest the teams. Lieutenant Charles
A. Woodruff used the opportunity to write a letter to his wife, Louie. In it he
mentioned that Colonel Gibbon had appointed him adjutant that morning (before
they left Stevensville), and indicated the plan for handling the Nez Perces, once
they were overhauled, remained fluid: *". . . no deffinite [sic] idea of what we*

---

[26]"Diary of Lt. Edward E. Hardin, 7th Infantry, 1874-78," from a typed copy in the possession
of Don Rickey, Jr.

[27]Letter, Rawn to Gibbon, Aug. 2, 1877, in "Early Days at Fort Missoula," edited by Captain
A. E. Rothermich for The *Frontier* (Vol. X, No. 1, 1936). The article has been reprinted in *Frontier
Omnibus*, John W. Hakola, ed., (Missoula: Montana State University Press, 1962), pp. 385-97. See
p. 389 for the letter referred to here. Unfortunately, the number of these contract freight wagons is
not mentioned in the available records, but, it is possible Kirkendall was still operating the same outfit
of *"nine six-mule teams complete, with teamsters included"* with which he hauled government freight
on the Bozeman Trail. See, "Montana Indian War Claims," 42D Congress, 3d Session. House of
Representatives. Ex. Doc. No. 164.

[28]Post Adjutant, Fort Shaw, to Capt. C. C. Rawn, July 29, 1877; Letters Sent, 1877, Fort
Shaw, M.T. A copy of the letter, with other information authenticating the cannon now on display at
the Big Hole battlefield, was included in correspondence between the Chief, Division of History and
Archaeology and the Superintendent of Yellowstone Park, Sept. 19, 1963. Henry Buck is mistaken in
his statement that the old Fort Owen cannon was the one that accompanied Gibbon's command. See,
"The Story of the Nez Perce Indian Campaign . . .," p. 20; cited in Note 14. The Fort Owen cannon
was *"a six pounder howitzer"* which Major John Owen brought into the valley some time in the
1850's, according to M. A. Leeson, *History Of Montana*, 1739-1885 (Chicago: Warner, Beers &
Co., 1885), p. 884.

shall do, for no one knows. I think the General will try and persuade Joseph to surrender, if we get up to them, or detain them until Howard comes up." To that he added two bad guesses, *"Don't worry, I don't think we will have a fight, and we are strong enough to whip them if we did."*[29]

At that place they were approached by the Corvallis company of volunteers under Captain John L. Humble, but Gibbon was obviously not happy to have them and Humble had misgivings about following and picking a fight with Indians who had mainly kept their word; so, he would agree to go only as far as Ross Hole, at which some of his men went home. The more determined followed Gibbon's command to Skalkaho where they sought out Captain Catlin to lead them because of his reputation as a soldier and an Indian fighter.

In his account, the captain writes, *"I finally told them I would be on hand at sunrise on the following day and if we had enough men to make a showing we would try and overtake the soldiers."*[30] That evening Gibbon's regulars camped at seven o'clock after crossing Bitterroot River at a place where the water was so deep it came into the wagon beds. The mode of travel allowed Gibbon's command to cover twice the distance the Nez Perces had travelled each day, so that their lead was rapidly reduced.

On the 6th, the troops nooned at Lockwood's ranch on Rye Creek, the volunteers with Humble and Catlin having caught up with them by that time. Catlin says of this hybrid unit of men put together from his and Humble's enrolled militia companies, *"When we started from home we had not less than seventy-five men but a great many of them had become discouraged and thought we would never locate the Indians and had gone home."*[31] Perhaps the blunt way Colonel Gibbon told them they would be under his orders if they went along, was not agreeable to the frontier independence of some, and that may be the reason for the resentment that smolders in the account Catlin wrote later. But among the 38 who stuck was Myron Lockwood, whose natural dislike of Indians took an even more decided set in that direction at sight of his trampled field and the wreckage of his household goods.

Colonel Gibbon had thought he might have to abandon the wagons at the upper end of the Bitterroot Valley and resort to the pack mules for moving his supplies, but he found:

---

[29]Letter, "Charlie [Woodruff] Corvallis M. T. Bitterroot Valley   Aug. 5th 1877." to "My darling Louie [Fort Shaw]." See, Edgar Stewart, "Letters from the Big Hole," in *The Montana Magazine Of History*, Vol.II, No. 4 (October, 1952), pp.53-54.

[30]John B. Catlin, "The Battle Of The Big Hole," [n.d.]; typed manuscript in the collection of the Montana Historical Society (SC 52), p. 2; also published in *Historian's Annual Report, Society Of Montana Pioneers*, 1927, p. 11. A wagon loaded with hard bread (evidently the mainstay of their ration) caught up with the column beyond Skalkaho. See, Hardin's "Diary," p. 55 [Aug. 5, 1877]; cited in Note 25. The standard field ration of that day consisted of 10 ounces of bacon, 16 ounces of hard bread, 4 ounces of pea meal, 2 ounces of coffee, 4 grains of saccharin, one half ounce of salt, two-fifths ounce of pepper and one half ounce of tobacco; total, 35 ounces per day. However, in this campaign it seems that all they had plenty of was the hard bread.

[31]*Ibid.*

Mr. Joe Blodgett, a man thoroughly acquainted with the country, who assured me he had brought lightly-loaded wagons over the trail all the way from Bannock, and that it was a passable, though difficult road. The road was excellent until we commenced to climb the divide separating us from Ross Hole at the extreme upper end of the Bitter Root Valley. Here the ascent was so steep, rugged and crooked that we were compelled to halt at nightfall and make a dry camp before reaching the summit, having succeeded in making, during the day only 24 miles. The next day, 7th, we were four hours in reaching the summit and succeeded in making only 13 1/2 miles, with still the greater ascent before us for the next day. [32]

Sometime during the day Captain Constant Williams (F company) and Second Lieutenant John T. Van Orsdale (D company) caught up with the column, and that relieved Lieutenant Hardin of the responsibility of commanding F; but only for two days! The bullets that wounded his captain during the ensuing battle returned Hardin to command. The addition of those officers brought the number of commissioned officers up to 17. [33]

While the troops were descending into Ross Hole, Lieutenant James Bradley scouted ahead with his mounted detachment and a party of volunteers who knew the country, in order to determine which way the Nez Perces had gone out of Ross Hole; whether toward the Big Hole basin, or toward the west and back into Idaho. Late in the afternoon he came back to where the troops were camped, at what later became the John Newnes ranch on Camp Creek, with word that the Indians had gone over the divide and were headed east.

Preparations were immediately made to send out a mounted scouting party to locate the Indians, and, if possible, run off their horses, leaving them afoot and unable to escape from Gibbon's slow moving infantry. Of course, such a tactic required more mounted men than Gibbon had — eleven in the mounted detachment from Fort Shaw and eight cavalrymen from Fort Ellis — and it was necessary to use the volunteers, all of whom were mounted, to make up an adequate force. That decision was objected to by Captain Humble, who later described his clash with the colonel this way:

I told Gibbon that if my men felt individually disposed to go forward in accordance with those orders, it would be on the lookout of each; but that I would not order them to do so, as, should a fight occur under such conditions those engaged would be practically certain of de-

[32]"Report of John Gibbon, Col. Seventh Infantry, Commanding, to Assistant Adjutant-General, Department of Dakota . . . Oct. 18, 1877," in *Report Of The Secretary Of War* (Washington: Government Printing Office, 1877), Vol. I, p. 522. This wagon road was at least 13 years old, as the Mitchell-Chaffin wagon train of 1864 entered the Bitterroot Valley *"by the old Trail creek route over the Big Hole mountains. "* See, Kate Mitchell, "Journey Across the Plains in 1864," clipping in the Big Hole National Battlefield Library purported to have come from the *Dillon Examiner*, 1928; however, the item was not located in a cursory search of the files of that newspaper.

truction before the main command could reinforce them . . . It was my opinion then, and is yet, that a half dozen scouts instructed to locate the camp, taking precautions to remain unobserved [and] to return with the required information, were all that was necessary . . .[34]

As a result, Captain Catlin took over command of all the volunteers — about 38 — and Captain Humble went home. Catlin's account, which seems to be accurate in spite of its resentful tone, begins, *"Notwithstanding Gibbons had no use for the citizens, we were invited to join Lieut. Bradley . . ."* and he describes the night march of that detachment of 60 men, as follows:

[We] crossed the divide with Lieut. Bradley in command to locate the Indians. This was about five o'clock in the evening. It soon got dark on us and the trail was [so] obstructed with lodge pole pine that in places it was almost impossible to lead our horses through and owing to [that] delay we did not get down until daylight.

We located the Indians all right and after we had found them the only thing for us to do was not to let them find us until we could join forces with General Gibbons, who finally reached us at night, after we had remained hidden the entire day.[35]

Since there was no possibility of driving off the horse herd in daylight, Bradley sent a courier to Gibbon with word that they had found the Indians, then, with his men left in charge of Captain Catlin and Sergeant Wilson in a cove three or four miles up Trail Creek from its junction with Ruby Creek,[36] he and Lieutenant Jacobs set out to scout the Indian camp. There are a number of con-

---

[33]Constant Williams is another of those officers who came out of the ranks during the Civil War.

[34]Will Cave, "Most Bitter Indian Battle Near Missoula," in *The Sunday Missoulian,* August 7, 1921; Special Features, p. 7.

[35]"The Battle of the Big Hole," (MS) pp. 2-3; cited in Note 29. In addition to Catlin's men, the volunteers with Bradley's command included Lt. J. W. Jacobs, regimental quartermaster, his nephew (Mr. S. J. Herron, of Kentucky), Sgt. Mildon Wilson of Co. I, and the Fort Shaw guide, Henry S. Bostwick.

[36]There are two possibilities for this site, which is also the place where Gibbon's wagon train was parked: Placer Creek, 2.8 up Trail Creek from its junction with Ruby Creek, and Cascade Creek at 4.3 miles. Paul Hedron, a former historian at Big Hole National Battlefield, who had the help of Forest Service personnel in an inconclusive attempt to determine the location, believes Cascade Creek to be most likely. However, A. J. Noyes indicates that Tom Sherrill identified the creek the wagons were parked on as *"Fool Hen Creek"* (see, T. C. Sherrill, as told to Noyes, in "The Battle of the Big Hole As I Saw It," typescript in the collection of the Montana Historical Society, n.d., p. 3). That is confirmed by Will Cave, who places the cove on *"a small tributary [of Trail Creek] then called Fool Hen creek (now Placer) about three and one-half miles from the battleground."* (See, article cited in Note 33). I am inclined to trust Cave's identification of the site because he visited the battlefield in 1916 with his uncle, Captain John Catlin, and had the advantage of the captain's first-hand knowledge of the fight. His estimate of the distance from Placer Creek to the *"battleground"* is reasonable; 3.5 miles *is* the distance to the Indian encampment, and the siege area is 3.0 miles by the old Model-T road, which is essentially the line of the *"dry trail"* used by the soldiers.

flicting accounts of this scouting activity, all but one of them rather unlikely (unfortunately Bradley died the next day and Jacobs never wrote about their scouting).

Colonel Gibbon's adjutant, Lieutenant Charles A. Woodruff, fortunately included this in his account of the battle:

> . . . Bradley and Jacobs, keeping under cover as much as possible, went forward until they could hear the sound of axes in the woods where they were. Then crawling along until they could distinguish the voices of squaws, who were cutting lodge poles, they climbed a tall tree and a few hundred yards from them they saw the Indian camp.[37]

While Bradley's command waited out the 8th dangerously near the Nez Perce encampment, Gibbon's main force was toiling toward them. Leaving Ross Hole at five in the morning, the two miles to the summit of the Continental Divide required six hours of double-teaming to get the lightly loaded wagons up, with the sweating mules assisted by men hauling on drag ropes. What trace there was of a road — made mainly by descending emigrant wagons — was also badly obstructed by fallen timber which had to be removed or laboriously by-passed. Before the summit was reached, Bradley's courier arrived,

> . . . informing me that the distance he had to pass over was greater than supposed and daylight had overtaken him before he had succeeded in reaching the camp of the Indians. We pushed ahead without waiting to rest or feed the animals, and later in the day I received another message from him [by Bostwick] informing me that he had discovered the location of the Indian camp, and had concealed his command in the hills and was awaiting my arrival. Fearing the Indians would discover him, I left the train under cover of one company — Logan's — to come forward as fast as possible, and started forward with the rest of the command and the mountain howitzer . . .[38]

---

[37]Gen. C. A. Woodruff, "The Battle of the Big Hole," in *Contributions To The Historical Society Of Montana*, Vol. 7 (1910), p. 104. M.A. Leeson, ed., in his *History Of Montana* (1885), p. 142, agrees *"that on the 8th Lt. Bradley managed to get close enough to observe the actions of the savages. At this time there were 89 lodges."* On the other hand, G.O. Shields in his hearsay account of the battle, has Bradley sending out *"scouts in different directions with instructions to proceed cautiously and stealthily about the valley,"* and he dresses up the tree-climbing incident with an impossible amount of detail. See, *The Battle Of The Big Hole* (Chicago and New York: Rand, McNally & Company, Publishers, 1889), pp. 39-40; or, "The Battle of the Big Hole," reprinted in Cyrus Brady's *Northwestern Fights And Fighters* (1909), pp. 168-69. The least believable version is the one A. J. Noyes got from *"Bunch"* Sherrill: *"Otto Leifer and John Sheehan had climbed to the top of the mountain, and Leifer climbed a tree and looking over the tops of the lower trees discovered the Indian village. Sheehan said when Leifer was climbing the tree, he took it slow but when he saw the Indian village, so close, he broke off some of the limbs in his haste to get down. An Indian had just left the spot where Leifer climbed the tree, as they found the entrails of a deer that had just been killed."* See, Montana Historical Society — manuscript SC-739.

[38]Gibbon's Report, pp. 522-23; cited in Note 31. Gibbon was still seven miles from Bradley when he received the second message.

From the summit, the *"road"* followed down Trail Creek for about 20 miles on a good grade, but much obstructed with fallen timber and with many stream crossings where the banks were abrupt. Thus, it was sunset before Gibbon reached the cove where Bradley was waiting, and later still before the wagon train was brought in and parked.

The men ate their rations cold, and without coffee, for they could have no fires with the Indian encampment so close. Pickets drawn from the volunteers were placed on the trail, probably for the very good reason that they had been able to rest all day, but that did not set well with Captain Catlin — *"The General did not have any use for civilians, but for all that he sent his adjutant to see if I would take two men and picket a trail."* — and, with the camp secure,

> . . . all laid down to rest until eleven o'clock. At that hour the command, now consisting of 17 officers, 132 men and 34 citizens,[39] started down the trail on foot, each man being provided with 90 rounds of ammunition . The howitzer could not accompany the column in consequence of the quantity of fallen timber obstructing the trail and the noise which would have to be made in removing it. Orders were therefore given that at early daylight it should start after us with a pack mule loaded with 2,000 rounds of extra [rifle] ammunition. The 34 citizens who volunteered to accompany us being joined to Lt. Bradley's command, the advance was given to him and the column moved in silence down the trail, the night being clear and starlight.[40]

That fragile, tongue-in-cheek *"treaty"* in which the Nez Perces had put their trust; that presumption of peace in Montana, was about about to be shattered violently — by a dawn attack upon their sleeping village.

---

[39]The last figure does not include four volunteers who remained with the wagons — Anthony Chaffin, age 54, Joseph G. Hull, age 42, Barnett Wilkerson, age 18 and Eugene Lent; however, adding Henry S. Bostwick, the Fort Shaw post guide, who went in with the attack force, the number of citizens was 35, which includes Captain Catlin (though a major in the Civil War, his present status as an officer of militia seems to have been recognized only obliquely). The number of enlisted men is shown as 132 because twelve remained with the wagon train.

[40]Gibbon's Report, P. 523; cited in Note 31. Several writers have put the amount of ammunition issued at 100 rounds per man, but Gibbon is likely correct because a soldier's belt held 50 rounds and two cardboard boxes of 20 rounds each carried in the haversack would have made the 90 rounds (weight, nearly 9 pounds).

Chapter 4

HOLOCAUST IN A MEADOW

The men of the force which was to attack the Nez Perce encampment were aroused an hour before midnight to begin the approach march which would put them in place to charge the camp at dawn on August 9. Stripped of all items not essential to combat — blanket rolls, overcoats and even blouses — they formed up and moved out with Lieutenant Bradley in the lead. As they groped their way down Trail Creek, an incident occurred of no very great importance at the time; however, it explained an earlier event, and was ultimately of some help to the troops.

Somewhere near the Indian encampment the scouts captured a halfbreed; that same Pete Matt who, with Billy Silverthorne, had given the first notice of the arrival of the Nez Perces at Lolo Hot Springs. He and August K. Gird (the volunteer who fired at the Nez Perces as they bypassed the barricade at Fort Fizzle) were convinced Colonel Gibbon intended to fight the Nez Perces, and they decided to put themselves in position to steal some Indian horses during the confusion of battle. They had managed to get ahead of Gibbon's column and were hiding in the brush beside Trail Creek when Lt. Bradley's detachment came along on their night march. Hearing a noise, Bradley investigated, but Matt and Gird escaped. The two would-be horse thieves went up on a mountain after daylight on the 8th, saw the Indian encampment, and, after dark, went down close to it in order *"to be in readiness to get the horses when the fight began."*[1]

Both Corporal Loynes and Private Coon indicate that Matt was viewed with suspicion, both mentioning that orders were given to shoot him if he tried to alert the Nez Perces, and the latter adds: *"For fear that the half-breed would give an alarm he was bound to a tree and gagged."*[2] The failure of either to mention Gird at this point hints that he was not caught or was somewhere else, and Indian accounts throw some light on where he might have been.

The evening of the second day that the Nez Perces were camped in the meadow they called *Iskumtselalik Pah* (place of ground squirrels), beside the North Fork of Big Hole River, the people were relaxed; there was feasting, parading, dancing and singing — even the few warriors who had wanted to scout their back

---

[1] T. C. Sherrill, as told to A. J. Noyes, in "The Battle of the Big Hole As I Saw It;" typescript in the collection of the Montana Historical Society, n.d., p. 3. Sherrill confuses Pete Matt with his brother, Alexander (a rancher), who was one of the volunteers at Fort Fizzle; and he calls Gird *"Joe,"* though he is identified from several sources as August K. Gird, a long-time resident of the Bitterroot Valley. Mark Brown tends to be skeptical of this episode as coming from a *"source of questionable reliability."* (*Flight Of The Nez Perce*, p. 249). However, in this instance there is enough confirmation in other accounts to indicate it is essentially correct.

[2] Homer Coon, "The Outbreak of Chief Joseph;" typescript in the collection of Yale University Library, n.d., p. 2. See also, Charles N. Loynes, "Battle of the 'Big Hole'," in *Winners Of The West*, March, 1925, p. 7.

trail for possible pursuers had accepted the word of Chief Looking Glass that it was unnecessary. A ten-year-old boy by the name of Red Elk remembers:

> Sun was going down.   I heard someone say he had seen a *shoyahpee* [white man] cross the canyon, riding down on horseback. A second time they saw him, this time going back. Some thought he must have been a spy. It was now nearly dark. I heard some of the older people talking that the white man must be working a mine somewhere . . . After dark we small boys had a bone game near the end of the camp. After playing awhile, I was ready to go home and sleep. I heard someone say that a *shoyahpee* was approaching. I saw a man standing wrapped in a blanket.   Standing in the firelight, I saw white on his forehead under his hat. I went home and all were sleeping. I did not wake them but went to bed and fell asleep.[3]

The column of soldiers, afoot except for Colonel Gibbon and Adjutant Charles A. Woodruff, followed the north side *"dry trail,"* down Trail Creek nearly to the mouth of its shallow canyon, then,

> . . . We turned to the left and following along the low foothills soon came within sight of the fires [in Indian lodges]. After proceeding about a mile from where we emerged from the mountains, we passed through a point of timber projecting into the valley and just beyond encountered a large herd of ponies grazing upon the hillside.[4]

The old Indian trail they were following forked in that *"point of timber,"* with the right hand branch crossing the swamp on a strip of dry ground to the meadow where the Nez Perces were camped, just as the road built to bring in the soldier monument in 1883 did later; the left hand branch, which the troops were on (later known as the Tie Creek Trail), skirted the base of Battle Mountain about thirty feet above the swamp bordering the North Fork of Big Hole River, and, as the column pushed past the lower edge of the herd, the Indian ponies began to neigh and whinny, starting dogs to barking in the camp across the river. But the herd moved up the hillside to resume its quiet grazing and the dogs ceased their alarm, leaving the night *"painfully still,"* as Captain Comba put it. They had not been discovered.

Colonel Gibbon called a halt at one o'clock on the morning of August 9, with his line of battle on the trail directly opposite the sleeping village. The men sat down in the grass and sage, to shiver in the cold night air (most were stripped to their shirt sleeves), and gaze at the shadowy tipis in the meadow three hundred yards to the east. Between them and the camp, though not distinguishable in the

---

[3]L. V. McWhorter, *Yellow Wolf: His Own Story* (Caldwell, Idaho: The Caxton Printers, Ltd., 1986), p. 141. The Nez Perce term for white man should be rendered as *"soyapo."*

[4]"Report of John Gibbon, Col. Seventh Infantry, Commanding, to Assistant Adjutant-General, Department of Dakota . . . Oct. 18, 1877," in *Report Of The Secretary Of War* (Washington: Government Printing Office, 1877), Vol. I, p. 503.

poor light, was a swamp through which the North Fork of Big Hole River serpentined; a place of willow thickets alternating with small, grassy opens and cut by deep sloughs which were the remnants of old meanders of the river. While they waited for dawn, here and there a tipi would be dimly illuminated as fuel was put on a fire, *"and every now and then the sleepy cry of a baby could be heard, or the chatter of a few wakeful squaws . . ."* Gibbon continues:

> . . . in the midst of this intense strain, I was startled by seeing, right in my lines, a bright light suddenly appear. An impatient soldier [Pvt. Patrick Fallon, Co. I], unmindful of his surroundings, and burning for the soothing effects of tobacco, had struck a match with which to light his pipe. Under other circumstances the man might well have been shot on the spot, or knocked over with the butt of a musket. But this would have been worse than the match, and he was quietly told by the nearest officer to put out his pipe, and give no further cause for alarm.[5]

Colonel Gibbon was aware that he had his men in exactly the position he had hoped Lt. Bradley's detachment would be in 24 hours earlier — between the Indians and most of their horses — and he wanted to take advantage of that. He told Henry Bostwick, his civilian guide from Fort Shaw, to *"get three or four of the citizens and drive this herd quietly back on our trail."* Amos Buck reports Bostwick as saying: *"General, you had better keep your command together, you are not fighting the Sioux now."*[6] In what was evidently a compromise based on Bostwick's long experience among Indians, the attempt to put the Nez Perces afoot was delayed until the signal to attack was given. Then, four of the Bitterroot volunteers, with several soldiers and Pete Matt made an unsuccessful attempt to drive off the pony herd (the inclusion of Matt in this party would indicate Gibbon had no objection to taking advantage of Pete's natural talents; and it throws some doubt on Pvt. Coon's statement that Matt was tied to a tree and gagged).[7]

There is a hint that Bostwick himself made an audacious reconnaissance of the Indian encampment while the troops waited. L. V. McWhorter notes that

[5]Brigadier-General John Gibbon, "The Battle of the Big Hole," in *Harper's Weekly*, Dec. 28, 1895, p. 1235. The soldier was identified by Cpl. Loynes, cited in Note 2; he was not a recruit, but a veteran of the Civil War and two previous enlistments in the Seventh Infantry. The severe wound received by Fallon in the subsequent battle led to a medical discharge within a year, and to an early death.

[6]Amos Buck, "Review of the Battle of the Big Hole," a speech delivered by the Hon. Amos Buck, at Hamilton, Montana, August 9th, 1908, on the 31st anniversary of the battle. Published in *Contributions To The Historical Society Of Montana*, Vol. 7 (1910), pp. 117-130. The Bostwick quotation, on p. 124, is the same as one in an account which appears, from internal evidence, to have been written by Captain John B. Catlin in the 1880's (catalogued as the Montana Historical Society's SC-52, and published under Catlin's name in the *Historian's Annual Report, Society Of Montana Pioneers*, 1927 — ten years after his death).

[7]Oral History Notes — Interview with *"Quiller"* Wilkerson, recorded by Yellowstone Assistant Chief Ranger Hugh Peyton in 1939. Typescript forwarded to the Superintendent, Big Hole National Battlefield, by the Superintendent, Coulee Dam National Recreation Area, May 8, 1985, from the effects of Hugh Peyton following his death. The Bitterroot men listed, in addition to Pete Matt, are John Shean, Bunch and Tom Sherrill and *"old"* John Armstrong. See p. 2.

Yellow Wolf told him, *"Before the soldiers charged from the hillside, I heard a horse cross the river slowly. Heard it pass down the camp, out of hearing,"* and a letter from Andrew Garcia provides this explanation:

> I well knew H. L. Bostwick, scout and post guide at Fort Shaw, where Colonel Gibbon held command. A half-blood Scotchman of determined mind, he ill-brooked military restraint. He is reputed as having rebelled against going afoot in a night reconnoitering of the Nez Perce camp, but rode his iron-grey saddler through the willow thickets with no particular attempt at concealment of movement. Doubtless he reasoned that the tramp of a horse would be less likely to attract the unfavorable attention of the enemy than would the sly movements of a footman. The animal could well be a rambler from their own herds, while the idea of a mounted spy passing noisily through the brush would be too rash to be entertained.[8]

After two hours of waiting, and a little before daylight, Adjutant C. A. Woodruff delivered orders to Captain Richard Comba to take his Company D

> . . . down to the river bottom and form line in the willows, connecting with Company K, Captain Sanno's on the left. About 20 minutes afterward, as day was clearing, I received an order from Lt. Woodruff to the effect that the General desired my company to move forward to the attack at once, and to approach as near the hostile camp as possible before commencing to fire . . .[9]

Lieutenant Bradley, who held the extreme left of the line with his mounted detachment (now on foot) and most of Catlin's volunteers, received a similar order — executed by Catlin in his peculiar way. That old soldier later wrote:

> I was asked to detail ten men for picket duty. I refused to make a detail but told the Adjutant I would furnish the required number. I then called for volunteers and the entire command volunteered. I then counted off the required number of men and by that time the Adjutant was back to know if I would take charge of the picket line . . . I told the Adjutant I would go with them as I would not ask men to go where I would not go myself.[10]

---

[8]Yellow Wolf, pp. 114-15; cited in Note 3. This hearsay statement is unconfirmed as Garcia was not a battle participant, nor could he have obtained his information from Bostwick, who died in the battle. On the other hand, Adjutant Woodruff was positive in stating: *"The Genl. and I were the only ones mounted, both our horses were shot."* See, Edgar Stewart, "Letters from the Big Hole," in *The Montana Magazine Of History*, 2/4 (October, 1952), p. 55.

[9]Official report of Captain Comba, Commanding Company D, 7th Infantry, dated Camp Baker, M.T., September 11th, 1877, of the operations of his Company during the Nez Perce Campaign of 1877, to Assistant Adjutant General, District of Montana, Fort Shaw, M. T., pp. 1-2. Typescript in the Big Hole National Battlefield library.

[10]"The Battle of the Big Hole;" cited in Note 6. See also, "Communication from Gen. Woodruff," in *Contributions To The Historical Society Of Montana*, Vol. 7 (1910), pp. 132-34.

Upon receiving the order to advance on the camp, at *"exactly 4 o'clock"* (as noted by Adjutant Woodruff), the skirmish line moved forward through the swamp. Then, as now, the brownish waters of the slough which roughly paralleled the base of the hill were waist deep in places. Beyond that thirty-foot barrier, impenetrable clumps of willow brush fractured the skirmish line, so that the advance became somewhat disjointed. Before Captain Catlin's men reached the serpentining river, they met a solitary Indian riding directly toward them on his way to the pony herd on the hillside. This *"large, well built fellow . . . did not notice our men until he was within a few yards of us. He then put spurs to his horse and attempted to ride through our lines. Four shots were fired almost simultaneously and the great Nez Perce medicine man was no more."*[11]

Chief White Bird, who was also going to look after his horses, but afoot, was about forty steps behind Wetistokaith when he saw the gun flashes and heard the reports, and he was able to turn back and give the alarm. Young Red Elk, drowsing in his father's tipi, remembered that warning cry:

About early morning I was awakened. My father and Chief Yellow Bull were standing, talking low. They thought they saw soldiers across the creek. Next instant we heard shots from above the creek across the canyon, maybe a quarter mile away. I heard the loud call, 'We are attacked!' . . . After these two or three shots there broke a heavy fighting. Soldiers soon came rushing among the tepees. Bullets flying everywhere.[12]

Upon hearing those first shots, the men of D Company made a rapid advance, pausing about 75 feet short of the river bank to fire a volley low into the tipis. At that point, according to Captain Comba, *"Seeing that the stream was fordable, I gave the order to charge. The men obeyed promptly and with a loud cheer we were in an instant fighting in the enemies camp."* At the same time, K Company,

---

[11]"Review of the Battle of the Big Hole," pp. 124-25; cited in Note 6. The Indian was not *"Cul-Cul-Se-Ne-Na, their great medicine man,"* as Buck, or Catlin, thought, but only an old man of Chief Joseph's band — Wetistokaith, sometimes called Natalekin — of whom Yellow Wolf said: *"He could not see very well."* Yellow Wolf, p. 127; cited in Note 3. The first shot, which had the effect of opening the battle, has been credited to several individuals, particularly to Captain Catlin and to Campbell Mitchell; however, *"Bunch"* Sherrill says, *"several claim the honor of killing the first Indian, but my idea is that no one knows who did kill him."* Catlin's statement, *"Some four or five of the boys helped him on his way,"* should be a sufficient notice that it was not an individual act, but more like the work of a firing squad. With regard to Buck's personification of this Indian, Editor Barbour used an almost identical name — Col-Col-See-Nee-Nah — when speaking of Chief Red Owl's presumed death in the attack on the village of Looking Glass (see Chapt. 1), and that may be where that name came from. The Indian's horse has been called both *"a large iron-gray"* and *"an ordinary 'buckskin' pony with a stripe along its back;"* so much for battlefield observations. Chief Joseph's comment on this killing was: *". . . about daybreak one of my men went out to look after his horses. The soldiers saw him and shot him down like a coyote."*

[12]Yellow Wolf, pp. 139 and 141; cited in Note 3.

"on the left took up the charge, both companies entering the camp almost at the same time. "[13]

Momentarily, there was little resistance, but, as Indians got into the brush and found shelter behind the creek bank, the soldiers came under fire. They received immediate support from Captain Logan's Company A, which was *"sent in on the run on the extreme right. "* These men came in directly at the back of some of the Indians sheltering by the stream, *"and here the greatest slaughter took place. In less than 20 minutes we had possession of the whole camp [actually, only the upper or southern half of it was entirely overrun] and orders were given to commence destroying it. "*[14]

Captain Sanno's men, who were already across the river before they broke out of the willows opposite the center of the village, paused 180 feet from the nearest tipi — a maternity lodge, at the apex of that very flat "v" which Gibbon assumed to be the shape of the village — and fired two volleys from a ragged company front 300 feet in length. Don Rickey, Jr., who discovered this firing line in the course of an official metal-locator reconnaissance in July of 1958, noted:

> I found a line of 22 45/70 Government cartridges (19 empty and 3 loaded). These shells were usually found in groups of 2 with an interval of about 3 or 4 yards between groups. It appears that a line of soldiers had burst through the concealment of the willows at this point and fired two volleys before charging the Nez Perce camp. Two of the loaded cartridges were found together, with no empty cases nearby, perhaps revealing that an excited soldier had run two loads through the action of his rifle, forgetting to pull the hammer back to full cock for firing.[15]

The occupants of the maternity tipi — Weyatanatoo Latpat's wife, who had just delivered a baby, and Tissaikpee, an older woman acting as nurse — were probably killed by the volley firing.

Yellow Wolf said that when the soldiers were driven out of the village, *"This tepee here [stake M-5] was standing and silent. Inside we found the two women lying in their blankets dead. Both had been shot. The mother had her newborn*

---

[13] Official Report of Captain Comba, p. 2; cited in Note 9. Artifact recovery has established the firing line from which the volley was fired. The distance to the nearest tipis was fifty yards.

[14]"Report of John Gibbon," p. 503; cited in Note 4. The account of Pvt. Homer Coon has the Looking Glass band at the upstream end of the camp, White Bird's band in the center and Joseph's band at the downstream end; but Jack Williams informs me that, unlike the Plains Indians, the Nez Perces did not have specially delineated locations in the camp for the different bands. Instead, they tended to camp either in family or friendship clusters. That is confirmed by the tipi locations shown on L. V. McWhorter's map of those sites pointed out by Yellow Wolf in 1937 (the tipis of Looking Glass, White Bird, Joseph and several subchiefs being close together, somewhat south of the apex of the camp).

[15]Don Rickey, Jr., "Field Research, Big Hole Battlefield National Monument, July 16-22, 1959," typescript. See Attachment B.

baby in her arms. Its head was smashed, as by a gun breech or bootheel. "[16] In Yellow Wolf's opinion, *"Some soldiers acted with crazy minds. "*

It would appear that the men of Company K met an immediate and determined resistance when they attempted to move forward through the thin screen of willows which separated their initial firing line from the open meadow where the tipis had been set up. Subsequent investigation has established that only the right hand third, and a few men on the extreme left, advanced; and then only for fifty feet, to new positions from which they continued firing.

This evident failure of Company K to break into the village at once, can be explained by the fact that, as they came out of the willows, they were under the fire of two warriors — Wahlitits and Rainbow — who had taken positions about 200 feet ahead of the right end of the line from which the volleys were fired. Wahlitits, and his wife, sheltered in a slight hollow, with Rainbow about four steps to the left of them. Yellow Wolf has described this incident:

> Here [stake M-10] Wahlitits was killed early in the fight. It happened immediately after I passed on my way to where the soldiers were mixing the Indians up [Captain Comba's charge]. His tepee stood just south of here, in the main village line [stake M-21]. Like all the warriors, he was bothered to get moccasins and rifle. He sprang out and ran to this place. He dropped flat in the sink behind a log thick as a man's leg. Across this log, his rifle pointed at the willows over there where the soldiers would be first seen. He killed a soldier who stepped from the willows [stake M-9A]. I do not know how, but Wahlitits was then killed by another soldier. When hit, he must have raised up, for he was found lying on his back.
>
> Wahlitits' wife, a brave woman, was with him. When he fell, she grabbed his gun and fired at a near soldier. I do not know if more shots than one. Some said she killed the soldier who had killed Wahlitits [stake M-11], and then was quickly killed herself.
>
> We found her lying across her husband's body as if protecting him. I heard she had been wounded before Wahlitits was killed. She was the only woman who did fighting in that battle that I knew about.[17]

It must be added that Company K was undermanned, with only 21 men, of whom two-thirds were recruits, for its 300-foot front, and loss of two men to the resolute stand of Wahlitits and his wife appears to have robbed the line of its momentum. That there was a soldier killed where the line broke out of the willows is indicated in the finding of the remnant of a soldier's boot, Model 1872, which

---

[16]Yellow Wolf, pp. 131-32; cited in Note 3. The soldiers awaiting the hour of attack had noticed the activity at that tipi but attributed it to gamblers continuing their game into the morning hours. Sites with an "M" prefix are on the map of the Nez Perce camp.

[17]Yellow Wolf, p. 133; cited in Note 3. See the statement of John Pinkham (p. 135), who adds that Rainbow, from his prone position, also fired on the soldiers, but left when Wahlitits was killed.

had lain 87 years in the mud of an overflow channel,[18] and, nearby, a man-made depression of the right dimensions to have served as a temporary grave. More will be said about this later.

While Colonel Gibbon's report does not specify when and where the other companies (F, Captain Constant Williams; G, Captain George L. Browning, and I, Captain Charles C. Rawn) were committed, they must have been sent in soon and at the center and right, where they not only assisted K Company to get into the village but also countered Indian fire from the brush, the bluff on the east, and soon, the hillside on the west. The statement of G. O. Shields that *"Logan, Williams and Rawn, with their companies, were sent to the extreme right,"*[19] would indicate that the center got only Browning's Company G as its reinforcement. Colonel Gibbon comments that Captain Browning started for the bluff on the east, with the intention of driving off the Indian marksmen that had taken up positions there (from whence they were doing considerable damage with their long-range shooting); but such a division of his small force was too risky, and Browning and his men were called back.

The left wing of the attack was a mixed force of dismounted regulars and volunteers under 1st Lt. James Bradley. In addition to his 11-man mounted detachment (7th Infantry) from Fort Shaw, there were 8 cavalrymen from Fort Ellis (2nd Cavalry), and 27 of Catlin's Bitterroot Valley boys. After opening the battle by killing Wetistokaith, they had to cross the river and make their way through thick willow brush for 300 feet parallel to the stream. Just before breaking out of the brush, but with the village evidently visible, a short firing line was established and several volleys were fired, and it may have been in forcing his way through the remaining screen of brush that Bradley was killed, *"at my side early in the engagement,"* according to Captain Catlin.[20] David Morrow, one of the volunteers, was killed soon after, but whether there in the willow brush or on the firing line established beyond it, is not recorded. A visitor to the battleground immediately after the fight noted: *"In our stroll we came to the grave of our dear*

---

[18]Kermit M. Edmonds, "Historian's Report - Nez Perce Encampment Area Relic," Big Hole National Battlefield, September 8, 1964. 2 pp. & sketch. Company K did lose two men killed, in addition to its 1st sergeant (killed fighting among the tipis).

[19]G. O. Shields, *The Battle Of The Big Hole* (Chicago and New York: Rand McNally & Company, Publishers, 1889), p. 47. See also, "The Battle of the Big Hole," Ch. 10 in Cyrus T. Brady's *Northwestern Fights And Fighters* (New York: Doubleday, Page & Company, 1909), p. 173.

[20]"The Battle of the Big Hole," p. 11; cited in Note 6. In an unsubstantiated statement, Shields says, *"General Gibbon had cautioned him to exercise great care going into the brush at that point, and told him to keep under cover of the brush and riverbank as much as possible, but the brave young man knew no fear and bade his men follow him. One of them called to him just as he was entering a thicket where a party of Indians were believed to be lurking, and said: 'Hold on, Lieutenant; don't go in there; it's sure death.'"* (See p.58 in the account cited in Note 19). In a letter Lieutenant Woodruff wrote to his wife on the 11th, he states that Private Hurlburt, of K Company, killed the Indian who shot Bradley ("Letters from the Big Hole," as cited in Note 8). McWhorter's suggestion that this incident occurred at stake M-1A is not in agreement with the evidence of the Bradley firing lines.

*friend Dave Morrow. His hat was lying on the ground having a bullet hole through the crown, plainly telling the cause of death. " * [21]

Just clear of the screening brush, a longer firing line was established behind a protecting break in the surface of the meadow. The many fired shell cases — .45-55, .45-70 and .50-70 Government — found along that 180-foot line were closely-spaced, as if ejected during prone firing. Also, several slugs, including a musket ball, recovered from the ground there, testify to return fire by Indians. Unable or unwilling to advance farther down stream, the leaderless men of the left wing remained where they were for a time and then merged with the center in its not-so-successful attempt to burn hide tipis damp with the morning dew.

The successful defense of the lower end of the village was accomplished by a few *"real men"* — buffalo hunters who had become skilled fighters in their conflicts with Blackfoot and Sioux enemies in eastern Montana, and with the Shoshonis of central Idaho. Black Eagle, a sixteen-year-old youth sleeping in one of the last tipis has stated: *"Only a very few warriors with guns, maybe three, held them . . . "* But it *was* dangerous there. After initially bolting to the river, Black Eagle remembered his horsehair rope and ran back to the tipi to get it. *"While doing this bullets passed through the tepee . . . "*[22]

The rallying of those startled warriors who had fled to the willows was largely the work of two chiefs, White Bird and Looking Glass. White Bird, who had a strong voice,

> . . . was first to rally his warriors to a charge upon the soldiers. "Why are we retreating?" he shouted in Nez Perce. "Since the world was made brave men fight for their women and children. Are we going to run to the mountains and let the whites kill our women and children before our eyes? It is better we should be killed fighting. Now is our time to fight! These soldiers cannot fight harder than the ones we defeated in White Bird Canon. Fight! Shoot them down. We can shoot as well as any of these soldiers." At the words the warriors wheeled around and started back to fight the soldiers in their camp.
>
> Looking Glass was at the other end of the camp. His voice was heard calling out, "Wallitze! Tap-sic-ill-pilp! Um-til-lilp-Cown! This is a battle! These men are not asleep as those you murdered in Idaho! These soldiers mean battle! You tried to break my promise at Lo Lo, you wanted to fight at the fortified place. Now it is time to show your courage and fight. You can kill right and left. I would rather see you killed than the rest of the warriors, for you commenced the war. Now go ahead and fight." The warriors addressed were so angered and

---

[21]Henry Buck, "The Story of the Nez Perce Indian Campaign During the Summer of 1877," typescript [1925], Montana Historical Society, Helena, p. 27.

[22]Yellow Wolf, p. 145; cited in Note 3. The McWhorter map places the lower end of the camp at stake M-1, but artifactual evidence indicates it probably extended at least 250 feet farther — nearly to the present boundary fence.

aroused they did not care for their lives, and rallied to the charge with those led by White Bird.[23]

Going back to the pony herd on the open slope of Battle Mountain, and to the party detailed to secure the Indian horses, M. F. "Bunch" Sherrill has left an account of that fruitless endeavor. Bunch puts the horse-stealing detail at twenty men, where "Quiller" Wilkerson says five, but, whichever,

> We were all sent up the Bald Side of the Mountain north of the Indian Village. We went up as far as the timber and waited . . . John Sheehan and I went over to the break of the canyon that runs down and through what afterwards was our rifle pits. An Indian came up a horse-back and tried to stampede the horses. So John and I turned loose on him. It took three shots apiece before we succeeded in sunning his moccasin [sic]. I stayed where we were and John went back. Pretty soon, John Armstrong come my way, and about [that] time the horses stampeded for the timber. We cut off about half of them. About that time there was eight warriors come out of the canyon to where I was. They gave the war whoop and stampeded the horses. Well, about that time I stampeded too; as I run by John Armstrong, I hollered to him to run. The last thing I heard him say was, "I was sent up here to hold these horses, and by God, I am going to do it." The Indians cut him off and drove him to the timber, and about the middle of the afternoon he made a break to get to us. (We were in our rifle pits then). He succeeded in covering about two thirds of the way from the timber, when they killed him. Another party of Indians came up from the west to meet these that come up on my side. The soldiers run to meet us and the Indians aimed to cut us off from the main command. There was two Indians that got in the shelter of the big fir tree. My brother, Tom, stopped and took a shot at one of them, but did not hit him, and as I once more looked around one of the Indians was just lowering his gun and I saw one of the soldiers fall. Well, talk about foot racing! I know I made the best time on record for Five Hundred yards, the time was never beaten and never will be beat. Be a little excited, and have a down hill pull with bullets flying around you, I reckon you will go some.[24]

---

[23]Duncan McDonald, "The Nez Perces Indian War of 1877 — The Inside History from Indian Sources," in *The New North-West*, Deer Lodge, M. T., January 24, 1879.

[24]As told to A. J. Noyes, 1916. Typescript in the collection of the Montana Historical Society, Helena (SC-739), p.2. Nothing is known of John Armstrong's background. Tom Sherrill says, *"We found him after the battle about a half of a mile from the breast work, up on the side of a mountain. He was shot through under the right arm, the bullet passing through his body. He was stripped stark naked when found."* ("The Battle of the Big Hole As I Saw It," pp. 18-19; cited in Note 1). Cpl. Loynes dismissed this venture with the remark, *"Those detailed to run off the Indian ponies had failed in their mission."* *Winners Of The West*, p. 7; cited in Note 2.

Yellow Wolf has a different, and much simpler, version of the saving of the pony herd.

> [He] . . . saw Chief Joseph and No Heart, a young man, up the hillside going afoot after the horses. Both were barefooted, and Joseph had no leggings. Only shirt and blanket. Reaching their own horses, they mounted and drove the herd farther up the hill. Out of sight of soldiers and the fighting.
> Up there No Heart was killed. Shot through mistake by a friend. Word had gone out that Flathead Indians were driving the horses away. This was not true, and cost the life of a good young man. Afterward the Indian who shot No Heart went back to bury his body, but it could not be found. Nor could No Heart's horse be seen anywhere. Maybe No Heart came back to life soon after he was shot, and went away and died.[25]

Returning to the fighting in the encampment, the south end of the village — that part which the soldiers broke into in their initial charge — quickly became the focus of scattered, individual conflicts, and it was there that many of the casualties occurred. The last tipi at that end belonged to Pahka Pahtahank (Five Fogs), a man of *"about thirty snows."* According to Yellow Wolf, *"he was of an old-time mind. He did not understand the gun."* And so, he undertook to defend his home with a hunting bow.

> He was just in front of his own tepee [stake M-50]. Soldiers were this side [in the willows across the river], not far from him. He stood there shooting arrows at his enemies. The soldiers saw, and fired at him. That Indian stepped about a little, but continued sending his arrows. Three times those soldiers fired and missed him. The fourth round killed him.
> Looks wonderful to me, three volleys — not exactly volleys together — should miss him not more than ten steps away. I do not know if he hit any soldiers.[26]

But soldiers did die in the twenty-minute melee among the tipis. Captain William Logan was shot in the head and killed [stake M-13] beside the tipi Wahlitits and his wife ran from [stake M-21]. G. O. Shields claimed to have the story of Logan's death from a surviving Nez Perce Indian, but he actually took his details from the story published by Duncan McDonald:

> In a fight between an officer and a warrior the warrior was shot down dead. The warriors sister was standing by him when he fell, and as he lay there his six-shooter lay by his side. The woman seeing her

---

[25]Yellow Wolf, p. 145; cited in Note 3.
[26]Yellow Wolf, p. 119; cited in Note 3. After the battle, Scout S. G. Fisher recovered the bow and quiver, which is now in the battlefield museum collection. The quiver contained ten arrows when found.

brother dying and the blood running from his mouth, seized the six-shooter, leveled it at the officer, fired, and shot him through the head and killed him. From all the information I can obtain, I believe the officer was Captain Logan.[27]

Corporal Loynes did not mention Captain Logan's death, but he did remember Pvt. Herman Broetz, a 23-year-old immigrant boy who had been a baker in his home town of Nassau, Germany, *"whose knee had been shattered by a ball,"* and how he *"reached up and grasped Sergeant Murphy's rifle and would not let go."* Even how *"the sergeant quickly found another."*[28] The trouble with his story is that there were four Murphys in the battle, and not one was a sergeant (Company I did have a Pvt. Nicholas Murphy). But there is no doubt that Broetz died there in the village, amidst the wreckage of overturned and half-burned tipis [stake M-33].

Other soldiers lost their lives in that desperate attempt to destroy the part of the village they had taken; G Company's Pvt. Gottlieb Mantz, another young German immigrant who would never see his native Wurttemburg again, nor cut any more stone [stake M-34], and Cpl. Dominick O'Conner, a 29-year-old Irishman who had given up bookbinding for the military life and was well into his second enlistment when struck down [stake M-32]. In addition to Pvt. Broetz, Company I lost Sgt. Michael Hogan, a 25-year-old immigrant from County Clare, Ireland [stake M-31], and Cpl. Daniel McCafferey of Canada, a butcher by trade [stake M-30]. A year younger than Hogan, whom he died beside, McCafferey, too, was in his first enlistment.

Company K lost 1st Sergeant Frederick Stortz in that bloody melee; the man Yellow Wolf saw standing in a clump of willows — rigid in death. *"Some kind of marks or stripes were on his upper arms or shoulders, as if an officer. I thought he was alive, and brought my gun to shoot. He could see me, but did not move [Stake M-29]. Then I understood, that soldier was dead!"*[29].

The Nez Perce loss was great there also. Wetyetmas Likleinen (Circling Swan) died with his wife at their tipi [stake M-22], and, nearby, Tewit Toitoi also [stake M-23]. Yellow Wolf recalled one wounding that appears to defy ordinary mortality:

> Here by his tepee [stake M-24] sat smoking, Wahnistas Aswetesk, a very old man. He was shot many times! As he sat on his buffalo robe, one soldier shot him. Still he sat there. Others shot him. He did not move, just sat there smoking as if only raindrops struck him! Must have been twenty bullets entered his body. He did not feel the shots!

---

[27]Text from *The New North-West* article cited in Note 23. Cf. Shields (*The Battle Of The Big Hole*, p. 53; cited in Note 19, or in Brady's *Northwestern Fights And Fighters*, pp. 176-77).

[28]*Winners Of The West*, p. 7; cited in Note 2.

[29]Yellow Wolf, p. 122; cited in Note 3. Stortz was not an immigrant, but hailed from Rochester, New York, where he had been a clerk before beginning an Army career (he was in his second enlistment). Here, Loynes has romanced the facts. He spoke of *"the glaze of death coming in his light blue eyes,"* but the company muster roll indicates Stortz had *hazel* eyes!

After the battle, he rode horseback out from there. He grew well, but died of sickness in the Eeikish Pah where he was sent after the surrender.[30]

The tactics used in this fight — short-range volley firing aimed low into the tipis of unsuspecting Indians — combined with the difficulty of telling the warriors from the women, children and old people, under the conditions of poor light, masking gun smoke and noise existing in the village, contributed to the high proportion of noncombatant casualties. Those who escaped from their beds sought shelter in shallow depressions, under cut banks, in the river and among the willows across the stream; often to die from rifle fire intended for the Indian marksmen who had also taken their positions in just such sheltered places.

Among those who remembered how easily death overtook noncombatants on that terrible day was Josiah Red Wolf, who, though only a five-year-old at the time of the battle, lived long enough to turn the first shovel of earth at the ground-breaking for the present visitor center in 1967. His death, March 23, 1971, broke the last direct link with that holocaust.[31] As he described it:

> . . . we were awakened by shots and the neighing of our horses. My two brothers ran from our tepee to take cover in the willows. My mother gathered up little sister and, taking me by the right hand, she started to run after them. A single shot passed through the baby and her. She dropped down without saying a word . . . My father bent over her and, although I did not realize it, she was dead . . . He tried to take my hand and pull me with him, but I would not leave my mother . . . seeing I was determined to stay there, he covered me with our big buffalo robe and cautioned me to stay perfectly still . . . I was very frightened as sound of guns and screams of wounded increased . . . but I never moved. I tried not to cry, I must be brave.[32]

Sahm Keen (Shirt On), a ten-year-old whose later white name was Samuel Tilden, herded the family horses during the retreat. When the village was attacked at Big Hole, he was sleeping beside his grandmother, Chee-Nah (Martha Joseph). When they were awakened by the shooting, *"Chee-Nah rose to peer out and a bullet pierced her shoulder . . . blood streamed from the wound as she pushed me from the tepee crying, 'Suhm-Keen run to the trees and hide'."* He ran to the ridge above the mouth of Battle Gulch, while *"bullets kept whizzing past clipping off*

[30]*Ibid.*, p. 123. The *"Eeikish Pah,"* or Hot Place, was the Nez Perce name for the Indian Territory (present Oklahoma).

[31]"Last Survivor of Indian War Dies," in *The Morning Tribune*, Lewiston, Idaho, March 24, 1971; also, "What is an Old Indian Thinking," March 25, 1971, and "War's Last Survivor Is Buried," March 28, 1971.

[32]Rowena L. and Gordon D. Alcorn, "Aged Tribesman Was a Frightened Five-Year-Old in 1877 As His People Struggled Towards Sanctuary In Canada," in *Montana*, Vol.15, No.4 (Oct., 1965), p. 63.

leaves and branches all around me. I was very afraid . . . soon some other boys joined me there and we watched trembling at the awful sight below. "[33]

Some children were deliberately left in tipis because their parents thought they would be safer there. Pahit Palikt, was one of those.

> I remember only one time in that war. I was so small. It was early morning the soldiers came . . . My father and mother ran from the tepee, leaving me, my brother twelve years old, and a cousin thirteen, sleeping under blankets. We would be safer there. Bullets would go over us.
>
> Soldiers came and shot my dog in the tepee. I did not hear. They must not have seen us, all covered feet and head. When the soldiers left, my brother shook me and said, 'Wake up! Bring that blanket and come!'
>
> I grabbed my blanket and we all three ran from the tepee. Guns were going fast, popping loud! We ran maybe thirty steps, when my brother leaped over the creek bank and called to me,'Jump down here!'
>
> I jumped to where he was. We stayed there maybe half hour, maybe one hour; I do not know . . . Soldiers seemed shooting at me. I heard the bullets going past my head. My brother was killed there under the bank. I missed my blanket. I thought, 'Where is my blanket?'
>
> I had dropped it while running for the bank. I ran back and got my blanket.[34]

Of course, the parents who left children in the tipis did not know the soldiers would try to burn the village (in order to prevent further flight by leaving the Indians destitute). Owyeen, an old woman when she told McWhorter this, said: *"They set fire to a few tepees. Little children were in some of those tepees. Sleeping in blankets, they were burned to death [stake M-73]. We heard them screaming. We found the bodies all burned and naked. Lying where they had slept or fallen before reaching the doorway."* On the other hand, Black Eagle recalled that two little boys survived such a fire; covered with blankets and a buffalo robe, they escaped unhurt [stake M-74].[35]

On seeing some of the tipis burning, a warrior by the name of Kowtoliks rallied other fighters by calling in a loud voice: *"My brothers! Our tepees are on fire! Get ready your arms! Make resistance! You are here for that purpose!"*[36]

There was one casualty, remarked by both Indians and whites, which can stand as a symbol of the terrible, needless killing and maiming of that dawn attack. *"A squaw was found lying on her back, dead, with wide open eyes staring*

---

[33]Rowena L. and Gordon D. Alcorn, "Old Nez Perce Recalls Tragic Retreat of 1877," in *Montana: The Magazine Of Western History*, Winter 1963, p. 66. See also, Yellow Wolf, p. 146; cited in Note 3.

[34]*Ibid.*, p. 143.

[35]*Ibid.*, pp. 137 and 145.

[36]*Ibid.*, p. 118.

heavenward, an infant upon her bare breast, alive, and crying as it painfully waved its little arm, which had been shattered by a bullet. " [stake M-35] After Forty-eight years, that shocking image Corporal Loynes carried away had not dimmed, and an aged Indian also recalled that *"lifeless hand flapping at the wrist. "*[37]

In general, the Indian wounded have been lost sight of — though there were a great many of them. But one case, that of a young woman by the name of White Feather, stands out. During Captain Comba's initial attack on the south end of the village, White Feather was shot in the shoulder and her sister, Lucy, was killed. Lying on the ground in a delirious state during the subsequent melee among the tipis, she grabbed the leg of a soldier in a frantic attempt to pull herself up — and was smashed in the face with the butt of his rifle [stake M-37]. The blow broke off a tooth, giving her a new name, In-who-lise, or *"Broken Tooth. "*[38]

An analysis of the information provided L. V. McWhorter by Yellow Wolf in 1937 indicates that the casualties suffered by noncombatants — women, children and old people — were nearly double those of adult Indian men (who might, more reasonably, have been considered as adversaries by the soldiers). The number of *"warrior"* dead tabulated was 23, some of whom were unarmed through inability to get to their rifles and cartridge belts; but the number of noncombatant dead was 38, of which 7 were old men, 16 were women and 15 were children or youths. These figures do not represent the whole loss, just the deaths remembered by Yellow Wolf.

The disparity apparent in the foregoing figures was noticed almost at once. In the article written for the Deer Lodge *New North-West* a year later, Indian trader Duncan McDonald, who got much of his information through his Nez Perce relations, was blunt in his condemnation of the killing of women and children during the fight in the village, and it may have been a fact that some of the savagery displayed that day was predisposed. Mark Brown claims that Colonel Gibbon *"had let it be known that he did not want any prisoners taken during the attack, "* but the only support for that comes from Tom Sherrill, who is quoted thus about a conversation that *may* have taken place at the wagon train prior to the battle: *". . . we got to talking about what we would do with prisoners we were about to take, and Major Catlin went over and spoke to Gibbon concerning it. Gibbon said that we did not want any prisoners. He came back to us, made his report and said, 'Boys, you know what to do now. '"*[39]

Of course, that does not mean that Gibbon was willing to countenance an indiscriminate slaughter regardless of sex or age; such a statement — that no prisoners were wanted — could have been intended for *"warriors, "* which was assumed to be the status of every male Indian who was big enough. In fact, Private Coon has stated: *". . . we were told not to shoot the squaws and I honestly*

---

[37]*Winners Of The West*, p. 7, cited in Note 2; and, Yellow Wolf, p. 137, cited in Note 3.
[38]Andrew Garcia, "Graves and Grizzlies," in *American Heritage*, June, 1967, p. 36.
[39]"The Battle of the Big Hole As I Saw It," p. 4; cited in Note 1.

can say it was not done on purpose. "[40] On the other hand, quite apart from any pre-battle instruction, there were other factors that led to wanton killing. The very tactic employed — the dawn attack, with volley firing low into the tipis — was bound to take a toll of noncombatants. In Gibbon's defense, it must be said that he was *expected* to conduct the attack in that manner; it was the proven recipe for success in combating the mobile tribes of the Plains during the post Civil War period.[41]

Another factor emerges in the letter Dr. John FitzGerald, one of General Howard's medical officers, wrote to his wife after helping dress the wounds of the men injured in the battle: *"I was told by one of General Gibbon's officers that the squaws were not shot at until two officers were wounded by them, and a soldier or two killed. Then the men shot every Indian they caught sight of — men, women and children.* "[42] The grounds for such an attitude, insofar as the record is concerned, do not seem sufficient to warrant a general slaughter.

Mark Brown also states that Pvt. George Lehr was dragged into a tipi by a woman, presumably bent on finishing the job a grazing shot had failed to do, but he regained consciousness and escaped, and Pvt. Charles Alberts was almost cornered by knife and hatchet wielding women and boys in a tipi he entered. The finding of a dead soldier under the ruin of a tipi [stake M-97] hints that entering a tipi during the fight could have fatal consequences. Yet the only instances of women taking part in the fighting which can be documented are Wahlitits' wife, the girl said to have killed Captain Logan after he killed her brother, and this reminiscence concerning Lieut. Woodruff:

> The story is still very clear to me, from Grandfather's accounts. I remember among other things his [telling of] wading into the stream to wash his wounds [upper thighs or buttocks], lowering his trousers to get a better look, and being shot at by a squaw on the bank while he was thus embarrassingly situated. Fortunately, she was a poor shot.[43]

On the other hand, some accounts have made sweeping but unspecific charges that the women were as dangerous as the men, using that as an excuse for some acts of outright barbarity. G. O. Shields wrote:

> During the progress of the fight among the tepees, the squaws and young boys seized the weapons of slain warriors, and from their hiding places in the brush fought with the desperation of fiends. Several instances are related by survivors of the fight, in which the she devils met soldiers or scouts face to face, and, thrusting their rifles almost into the faces of the white men, fired point blank at them. Several of our

---

[40]"The Outbreak of Chief Joseph," p. 5; cited in Note 2.

[41]Jerome A. Greene, *Slim Buttes, 1876* (Norman: University of Oklahoma Press, (1982), pp. 57-8. Greene says, among other things: *"The tactic was immoral, but for an army charged with subjugating the Sioux and other dissident Plains tribes, it was justified for the simple reason that it worked."*

[42]Mark Brown, *The Flight Of The Nez Perce*, pp. 253-54.

men are known to have been killed by the squaws, and several of the latter were shot down in retaliation by the enraged soldiers or citizens.[44]

Amos Buck (Note 6, pp. 7-8) mentions *"the squaws with their Winchesters doing as much execution as the bucks,"* and Cpl. Charles Loynes (Note 2, p. 4) similarly writes of *"the screeching of the squaws, who with Winchesters in their hands, were as much to be feared as the bucks."* Even Captain Catlin, he who had said to his men, *"Boys, you know what to do now,"* later felt the need to offer an apology. He wrote:

> You may ask why did we kill the women and children? We answer that when we came up on the second charge, we found that the women were using the Winchesters with as much skill, and as bravely, as did the Bucks. As to the children, though many were killed, we do not think that a citizen or soldier, killed a child on purpose.[45]

Yellow Wolf's answer, when McWhorter informed him of the foregoing statements, was: *"There was no fighting in the brush by women as you tell me. No women had guns. Only few men got hold of their rifles in the camp fighting."*[46]

Some terrible things happened in the willows and along the stream where the women, children and old people who had escaped from the tipis sought shelter. Regardless of Gibbon's statement that *"the poor terrified and inoffensive women and children crouching in the brush were in no way disturbed,"* some were killed deliberately by enraged soldiers or volunteers. Tom Sherrill's account of such an incident, which sounds so very similar to one recounted by G. O. Shields that they must refer to the same happening, is an example of this particular type of brutality. After coming back from the failed attempt to run off the Indian horses, an officer put Tom to work burning tipis, but he found them too damp,

> . . . so I left and went down the creek for a short distance where I saw two squaws, one of them holding a papoose, near a bunch of willows that had become uprooted and had fallen into the water. I pulled my pistol and took aim at the old squaw who was holding the child. I was a good shot and aimed right at her head, but she did not waver a particle. She looked me in the eye, and say, I began to think. Why should I shoot an Indian woman, one who had never injured me a bit in the world.
>
> I put up my gun and left. A little later in the day I heard a fellow bragging that he had killed those two women. I could never have forgiven myself if I had been that man.[47]

---

[43]Malin Craig, Jr., letter to Don Rickey, Feb. 9, 1956 (copy furnished the author).

[44]*The Battle Of The Big Hole*, p. 60; cited in Note 19 (or *Northwestern Fights And Fighters*, p. 181).

[45]"The Battle of the Big Hole," p. 7; cited in Note 6.

[46]*Yellow Wolf*, p. 136; cited in Note 3.

Fortunately, there were instances where mercy prevailed. Nine-year-old White Bird — the nephew of Chief White Bird — remembered being in the water, sheltering behind a thin screen of willows with his mother and five other women and little children, when *"Some soldiers leveled their guns at us. My mother threw up her hand and called, 'Only women! Only women!' as she jerked me entirely under water. An officer spoke to the soldiers, who let down their guns and went away."*[48]

An act of mercy on the part of an officer is recorded by Will Cave. He states that during the fight two Indian women came directly toward Captain Browning, *"one holding an infant in her hands. He motioned them to pass through the lines, which they did . . ."* This occurrence was told to Duncan McDonald, who was certainly no admirer of the Seventh Infantry, and when he visited White Bird's band in Canada in 1878, Duncan asked the chief *"if he ever heard of such an incident. White Bird answered: 'Yes, the woman with the infant was my wife.' Afterward, when the Indians began getting the better of the scrap, White Bird's wife started back into the camp and was shot through the body, a wide leather belt she was wearing being pierced by the bullet. However, she survived . . ."*[49]

One more story concerning the many incidents along the river bank and in the willows must suffice. Owyeen (Wounded), described as *"a woman of venerable age"* in 1926, when McWhorter interviewed her, crossed the river into the brush.

> Some women and the old medicine man, Kapots, were there. One of the women requested of him, 'Why not do something against soldiers' killing? You must have some strong Power?'
>
> Kapots replied, 'I can do nothing. I have tried, but my Power is not effective. I feel helpless. So, my niece, you better look out for yourself, how you can save your life. Go farther down the creek!'
>
> The woman did as directed and was saved . . .[50]

Soon after the upper end of the village was secured, Colonel Gibbon left his command position on the old Indian trail at the base of Battle Mountain and rode over to where the soldiers were pulling down and attempting to burn tipis. But he found that a man on horseback made an attractive target for Indian marksmen firing from the bluff on the east and the mountain on the west.

> Hastily dismounting and holding my horse's rein, I stood looking at the scene around me, when an officer close by called my attention to the fact that my horse was wounded, and glancing around, I discovered

---

[47]"The Battle of the Big Hole As I Saw It," p. 7; cited in Note 1. Cf. *The Battle Of The Big Hole*, p. 61; cited in Note 19. There Shields manages to make the killing justifiable.

[48]Yellow Wolf, p. 140; cited in Note 3.

[49]Will Cave, "Most Bitter Indian Battle Near Missoula," in *The Sunday Missoulian*, Aug. 7, 1921, pp. 1, 5, 7 & 10. See p. 7.

that the poor beast had his foreleg broken near the knee. I had, in a dim way, realized the fact that I had received a shock of some kind, but it took me a second or two to discover that the same bullet which broke my horse's leg had passed through mine; but I was more fortunate in the fact that it had not broken the bone. It is said that frequently the first impulse of a man when shot is to run away. I am not very clear as to whether this was true of me or not. I can only say that what I did was to run or hobble back a few steps and plunge into the cold water of the stream over my boottops. If I had any intention of running away farther, the cold water must have recalled me to my senses, and made me realize the fact that my little force was in what is said to have been "the ideal position" — surrounded. [A Civil War joke].[51]

The battle for the village proper was over and the tables were turned. The attackers must now fight for *their* lives.

[50]*Ibid.*, p. 137. The old medicine man, Kapots, was so sick and weak that he had to be left by the trail several days later (probably at his own request), where he was found and killed by General Howard's Bannock scouts.

[51]"The Battle of the Big Hole," p. 1235; cited in Note 5. Of the two horses taken into the battle, Gibbon's was the first one lost to rifle fire. This gray horse was left standing in the village. Later, Young White Bird, son of the Chief, recalled seeing an Indian run up and jump on Gibbon's horse, but he couldn't make him go. The animal had been paralyzed by that or another wound. See also, L. V. McWhorter, *Hear Me, My Chiefs!* (Caldwell, Idaho: Caxton Printers, 1952), p. 378.

Bone-handled table knife found in the north end of the Nez Perce encampment in 1971. Probably lost in the wreckage of a tipi (cat. 810).

Army shoe (Model 1872) found west of the Nez Perce encampment in 1964. It was on the Co. K firing line and may have been worn by a soldier killed in that area (Cat. 60).

Iron picket pin (cavalry issue) found adjacent to a rifle pit on the northeast side of the Siege area. Probably used to secure Lt. Woodruff's horse before it was killed (Cat. 51).

Photos by ALH, 1989

Chapter 5

SOLDIERS BURIED THEMSELVES

Within an hour of the time his men had overrun the upper two-thirds of the village, Colonel John Gibbon had good reason to recall that poet Bobby Burns had something to say about *"The best laid schemes o' mice an' men . . ."*

With Indian marksmen in the willows along the river, and on the high ground on each side of the valley,

One thing had now become very apparent. We were occupying an untenable position, and longer continuance in it could result only in increased losses and inability on our part to retaliate. The men were therefore collected, and orders given to move back towards the bluff we had left in the morning, and in the direction of the point of timber jutting down into the valley, and heretofore mentioned. Every one knows the demoralizing effect of a retreat in the face of an enemy. We had to pass an open glade in the valley, where the Indian sharp-shooters posted on the high ground had us in plain view, and here several of the party were shot down. As we reached the foot of the bluff and commenced to rise toward the timber, a young corporal cried out, in a loud voice, "To the top of the hill — to the top of the hill, or we're lost!" I have never witnessed a more striking instance of the value of discipline than was now presented. To the top of the hill was the last place I wanted to go, or could go, and I called out to the corporal to remind him that he was not in command of the party. The men about him burst into laughter. Amongst regular soldiers the height of absurdity is reached when a corporal attempts to take command of his colonel, and the incident really had a good effect by calling attention to the fact that the commanding officer was still alive.[1]

Actually, that retrograde movement got off to a halting start, and there was evidence of disorder before the men were out of the willow swamp. Tom Sherrill says, *"We seemed to be waiting for orders, and as we were bunched together that Indian behind the big tree was simply giving us hell. The fact is we were so close together that he couldn't miss us and several were killed right there."*[2] An article which appeared in *The Dillon Examiner* in 1902 has much to say about the Indian

---

[1]Brigadier-General John Gibbon, "The Battle of the Big Hole," in *Harper's Weekly*, December 28, 1895, p. 1235.

[2]"The Battle of the Big Hole As I Saw It," as told to A. J. Noyes, n.d. Typescript in the collection of the Montana Historical Society, Helena, p. 8.

marksman whose long-range (300 to 500-yard) shooting was so deadly. However, since Amede Bessette was not a battle participant, but only a visitor to the scene some time afterward, his statement may not be entirely factual, and at best, it is exaggerated. He wrote that the Indian

> . . . took a position behind the east tree and killed nine soldiers during the bad retreat of the soldiers to the wooded point. Every time the Indian's gun would crack, a soldier would fall. For a long time no one could tell from where the shooting came. At last Gibbons detected him behind the tree. He ordered two of his best shots to go and dislodge him. They started at once, following the base of the hill. Soon they came to a tree made like a chair, with two crooks in it. The two leaned their guns upon it and at first fire the Indian leaped six feet in the air, and never stopped rolling until permitted by the laws of gravitation, within a few feet from the tree from which he was shot. The Indians did not bury this one, they wrapped him up in two old grey blankets, and cast about one-half of an old buffalo robe over his face. A beast had taken a meal from his flesh above the right knee. His face had not been touched. We measured him. He was seven feet, strong, in height. In the place where the Indian stood behind the tree, we found 11 empty shells. I was quite interested in these shells, well knowing that nine of them had done effective work, and killed nine soldiers.[3]

There were some reasons for the delay which vexed Tom Sherrill. There was the difficulty of getting word of the retrograde movement to all units; the guns of fallen comrades had to be broken or thrown into the river, along with those captured from the Indians; there were wounded to find and assist,[4] and there were stragglers to account for (Bunch Sherrill missed his brother, Tom, and went back into the abandoned village looking for him). Captain Rawn's company covered the

---

[3]"A Good Story of '77," in the issue of Sept. 27, 1902. The caption hints that the editor was skeptical; however, in 1972 Historian Kermit Edmonds found a .50-450 bullet (the type fired in the obsolete pattern rifles issued to the volunteers) nearly ten feet north of the northerly tree. If fired from the direction of the willow swamp through which the soldiers retreated, it would have barely missed the trunk of that tree, which is the *"east tree,"* as seen from the retreat route. By following the base of the hill, the two marksmen could have got as close as 200 yards from the Indian; thus, Bessette's story about how the sniper was dislodged may be a *"tall story"* mainly in the height of the Indian! The tallest of those Nez Perces was Chief Toohoolhoolzote at six and one-half feet, and he did not die there. Forest Supervisor C. K. Wyman stated in 1908 that *"This Indian was buried where he fell at the foot of the tree,"* but he did not give the source of his information. (See, Letter to F. A. Silcox, Forester, May 2, 1908, Big Hole National Battlefield files).

[4]Colonel Gibbon, in his epic poem written five years later, *A Vision Of The 'Big Hole'* (privately printed, Ft. Snelling, Minn, Aug. 9th, 1882), p. 11:

> *"We take along such wounded as we find,*
> *And seek the shelter of the friendly bluff,*
> *Leaving our badly wounded and our dead behind,*
> *And run a gauntlet which to us is rough."*

retreat, but, as in all chaotic situations, there were vicious little confrontations where the outcome depended solely on the participants.

Yellow Wolf mentions coming upon a soldier who was standing, looking the other way through the willows. Intending to get close enough to touch him and thus *"count coup,"* he was within four steps of him when the soldier sensed his presence and whirled around; but Yellow Wolf was ready and killed him [stake M-101].

A similar duel in those willows had a different outcome, resulting in the loss of one of the *"great warriors"* of the Nez Perce. Wahchumyus, whose name translates as *"Rainbow,"* confronted a tall soldier at *"about four steps"* and, *"both raised guns at the same time. The Indian was the quickest, but his gun snapped. The tall soldier shot him through the heart. He fell backwards, dead."*[5] Wahchumyus was known to enjoy the special protection of his *wyakin*, or guardian spirit. In any battle he engaged in after sunrise, he had a guarantee that he would not be killed; but, the sun was not up when he met his adversary, and he died.[6]

After killing Wahchumyus, the tall man ran south about fifty feet to a clump of willows, but

> Hohots Elotoht [Bad Boy Grizzly Bear] was back of those willows. Both their guns were empty. They clubbed with their guns, then grabbed each other. They wrestled. The big soldier was too much for the short Indian and threw him. Both struggled for their lives. The big soldier was on top. The Indian called twice to his **wyakin** for help. He was heard and was given strength to break from his enemy.
>
> The two stood up. Not equally matched, again Elotoht was thrown. His arm was doubled under the tall soldier who was now choking him. Elotoht could no longer free himself.
>
> A brave warrior, Lakochets Kunnin, came running. He shot the tall soldier and killed him. The bullet broke one bone in Elotoht's arm above his wrist.[7]

Lakochets Kunnin (Rattle on Blanket) was involved in another furious, hand-to-hand struggle below the bench the soldiers took refuge on. Yellow Wolf remembered:

---

[5]L. V. McWhorter, *Yellow Wolf: His Own Story* (Caldwell, Idaho: The Caxton Printers, Ltd., 1986), p. 124. This *"tall soldier,"* described by Yellow Wolf as *"near seven feet,"* does not appear in the muster rolls of the six companies of the 7th Infantry involved in the battle. All the regulars present were under six feet; ranging down to four feet eleven inches in the case of John McLennon, a musician in Company A. If Yellow wolf was correct in estimating the man's height at well over six feet, he would have had to be one of the citizen volunteers — possibly Alvin Lockwood (see Note 7).

[6]L.V. McWhorter, *Hear Me, My Chiefs!* (Caldwell, Idaho: The Caxton Printers, Ltd., 1983), p. 386.

[7]Ibid., p. 125. The man killed in this encounter — if he was one of the citizen volunteers — would be Alvin Lockwood because all the others who died are accounted for: John Armstrong on Battle Mountain; Dave Morrow in the willows, immediately after Lt. Bradley was killed; Campbell Mitchell in the village, after he was found wounded, and Lynde Elliott in a rifle pit at the siege area.

Lakochets, there, where I showed you [stake M-107], mixed a soldier in hand to hand fight. The soldier had a gun and was getting the best of Lakochets. Peopeo Tholekt rushed in and wrenched the gun away from the soldier, and Lakochets then killed him. It was hard struggling and the soldier would have come out best had Peo not been quick.[8]

There were only a few Indians in the point of timber toward which Colonel Gibbon directed his men, and a determined charge forced them back up the gulch and onto the hillside where several found firing positions behind trees and logs. Upon gaining the bench — really an old alluvial fan of debris washed out of *"Battle Gulch"* — the soldiers began to fortify a vase-shaped area with maximum dimensions roughly 100 feet each way. The smaller base of fifty feet faced northwest, that is, up the gulch, while the broad lip was parallel to the outer edge of the bench and 50 to 75 feet back from it. Several isolated rifle pits on the rim of the dry draw south of the trenches served to keep it clear of Indians and prevent a close approach on that side.

It was a reasonably good defensive position except that the hillside to the north provided the Indians with a plunging fire into the works. That defect was not lost on Captain Catlin — though his former service as a major in the Union Army should have told him there was no better position in the vicinity. Arriving among the last to reach the siege area Catlin vented his displeasure with, *"Who the hell called a halt here?"* Learning that Gibbon had picked that place, he added, *"I don't give a damn, it is a hell of a place to camp."*[9]

While some of the soldiers fired at the Indians who were harassing them from positions on the hillside and in the swamp, others pulled logs and stumps into place around the perimeter and piled up rocks, and, behind those flimsy barricades, the men began excavating rifle pits. Since only two companies had been issued that all-purpose digging, cutting, fighting implement — the Rice trowel bayonet — other men used whatever they had, particularly knives and mess gear. M. F. *"Bunch"* Sherrill, one of the Bitterroot boys, later said:

Several of us young fellows had taken from home, a butcher knife. We had ground them sharp and on the road over to the Big Hole, we would take our knives out of the scabbard and run a thumb over the edge to see if they were in good shape to raise a scalp with. Well the first work I had for my scalping-knife, was to dig a hole to get into. It looked like a saw blade next morning.[10]

---

[8]*Ibid.*, p. 126.

[9]Amos Buck, "Review of the Battle of the Big Hole," from a speech delivered at Hamilton, Montana, August 9, 1908, on the 31st Anniversary of the battle (published under the same title in *Contributions To The Historical Society Of Montana*, Vol. 7, 1910, p. 126).

[10]As told to A. J. Noyes, [1916], p. 4. Montana Historical Society manuscript SC-739. While several of the volunteers carried scalping knives, there is no evidence hair was *"lifted"* by any but General Howard's Bannock scouts. The Nez Perces did not scalp or mutilate their enemies.

Metal locator research in 1965 in the dry draw southwest of the perimeter discovered a firing position intended to command the mouth of the draw. There, on a small platform behind the stump of a tree, two unfired .45-70 Government cartridges and an Army mess kit spoon were found [See the siege area map]. The "F" stamped on the handle of the spoon identified it as having been issued to a soldier of Captain Constant Williams' company from Fort Benton. It seems likely the soldier had laid out two rounds to facilitate rapid loading of his Model 1873, single shot Springfield rifle, and was digging with the spoon to improve his position when somehow interrupted.

There were several casualties among the troops while occupying the siege area. When Colonel Gibbon was wounded in the Indian encampment, losing his gray horse at the same time, Adjutant Woodruff offered him his large sorrel, which was still serviceable; but Gibbon refused and one of the wounded men was put on the horse for the retreat through the willows. Upon arrival at the defense perimeter an Indian marksman killed the wounded soldier before he could be taken off the horse, which also was soon so badly wounded he had to be killed within the lines. The regulation picket pin recovered in 1959 just inside the trench line, on the north side, probably marked the place where the horse was tethered before his kicking and plunging made him a danger to the nearby men [siege area map].[11]

At this time Colonel Gibbon and several officers were standing outside the perimeter, on the east side [site 22], watching the men prepare the defenses, *"when suddenly a shot was heard, and Lieutenant English, standing by my side, fell backward with a cry. A bullet had gone through his body."*[12] Private Philo O. Hurlburt — the soldier credited with killing the Indian who shot Lieutenant Bradley early in the attack on the village — got him within the barricade. He said: *"We were building breast works. My Lieutenant was shot and I carried him inside the works. I had just laid him down when a ball struck me and I fell."* [13] Hurlburt had been hit in the left shoulder and lay beside Lieutenant English, suffering terribly for the next 24 hours.

Nearly coincident with the taking of the timbered bench — a success Corporal Loynes thought was managed because *"many Indians had gone in the direction of our field piece, which was hurrying to our relief,"* the boom of the howitzer was heard on the ridge above them, and that shot was followed by another; then, silence. Sergeant Wilson told the editor of the Deer Lodge *New North-West* that when the gun was silenced, *"a portion of the men thought there was an order to go back and capture it. And quite a number started back on that mission . . ."* but there was no such order and they were recalled.[14]

The gun — a 12-pounder mountain howitzer — started from the wagon train at daylight with a six-man gun crew consisting of four G Company men — Sgt.

---

[11]The picket pin is in the museum study collection (Master list, No.51).

[12]"The Battle of the Big Hole," p. 6; cited in Note 1.

[13]Statement from the pension file of Philo O. Hurlburt (copy in the Big Hole National Battlefield library).

[14]"The Battle of the Big Hole," in the *New North-West* of August 17, 1877.

John W. H. Frederick, a 30-year-old veteran of the Civil War with a previous enlistment in the 7th Infantry, and, a record marked *most exceptional*; Cpl. Robert E. Sale, a 29-year-old recruit, whose record was exceptional only in the wildness of his lifestyle *and* his devotion to duty; Pvt. Malcolm McGregor, a 31-year-old Scot from Glasgow, with one prior enlistment, and Pvt. John H. Goale, a 26-year-old recruit from Cincinnati. The other two men were Sgt. Patrick C. Daly, of D Company, a 44-year-old Irishman from Limerick, with three prior enlistments in the 7th Infantry and an excellent record, and Pvt. John O. Bennett, of B Company, a 56-year-old who personified the *"old army"* soldier. With seven prior enlistments, he had fought in the Mexican War and the Civil War; *"brave old John Bennett"* Colonel Gibbon called him!

The howitzer party was accompanied by two civilians: William Woodcock, the black man-servant of Lieut. Jacobs, who led a packhorse loaded with 2,000 rounds of rifle ammunition, and Joseph F. Blodgett, who was to guide the party to the battlefield. Blodgett came to Montana before it *was* Montana (in fact, the Bitterroot Valley had only 29 white residents when he arrived in 1859). In 1862, he brought wagons in from Bannack by way of the Big Hole and Trail Creek, opening a wagon route used by the 1864 Chaffin-Mitchell party of immigrants, and by the Mitchell-Reed party in 1869. It was by that abandoned track, which was on the south side of Trail Creek in that vicinity, that he brought the gun forward. Near the mouth of the canyon, they took the gun

> . . . across Trail Creek and up on the bluff, where they were in the act of putting it in position to open fire, when a body of about thirty mounted Indians saw it, and ascertaining that only a few men were with it charged with the intention of capturing it.[15]

Colonel Gibbon's official report briefly outlined the sequence of events on the ridge:

> The non-commissioned officers in charge, Sergeants Daly and Fredrics and Corporal Sales, made the best resistance they could, whilst the two privates cowardly fled at the first appearance of danger and never stopped till they had put a hundred miles between themselves and the battlefield, spreading, of course, as such cowards always do, the most exaggerated reports of the dire calamity which had overtaken the entire command. The piece was fired twice, and as the Indians closed

---

[15]G. O. Shields, *The Battle Of The Big Hole* (Chicago and New York: Rand, McNally & Company, Publishers, 1889), p. 68 (also, "The Battle of the Big Hole," in Brady's *Northwestern Fights And Fighters* (New York: Doubleday, Page & Company, 1909), p. 185. I believe that Shields is right in his explanation of why the gun was on the ridge when attacked. Blodgett undoubtedly had told them it could not be taken across the swamp (the gun, on its prairie carriage, with caisson, ammunition and accessories, weighed 1,500 pounds), so it was decided to emplace it on the ridge, from where the gun could command the entire Indian encampment. At one time I thought the howitzer party had gone up the ridge to avoid the sidehill which the Indian trail traversed, approximately on the alignment of the now abandoned Model-T road, but a computation to determine the center of gravity for such a gun, established that it could be safely drawn over side slopes even steeper.

around it the men used their rifles. Corporal Sales was killed, the two sergeants wounded, the animal was shot down, and Private John O. Bennett, the driver, entangled in the fall, cutting himself loose, succeeded in reaching the brush and escaped to the train, which the two sergeants, Blodgett, the guide, and William [Woodcock], a colored servant of Lieutenant Jacobs, also reached.[16]

It has been generally assumed that the howitzer was fired defensively when the crew was *"on the road to us, intercepted by the Indians. "* However, the chance finding of a cannon ball fired from the howitzer, in the meadow, at the south end of the village,[17] raises the possibility that the target was Indian activity there, not attackers approaching the gun *up* a slope of 30 to 40 degrees. The firing tables indicate that an elevation of eight degrees would have been required to lob a spherical case shot that far — 3,200 feet, which is slightly beyond the gun's maximum range of 1,005 yards. The gunner may have decided to use a shell — lighter by two pounds — to increase the *"reach"* (particularly if he had estimated the range correctly).

Captain Ware, while describing his experience with the mountain howitzers he used against the Sioux, noted that a downward angle of fifteen degrees was *"the utmost angle of safety in firing the howitzer;"* and even then, *"unless the trail was fixed properly, the piece was liable to turn a summerset. "*[18] It is extremely unlikely that the gun was hastily put *"in battery"* merely to defend against horsemen charging up a 30 to 40 degree slope; anyhow, canister, which was in the ammunition chests and required no fusing, would have been the choice for such a purpose because the shotgun effect of its 148 lead balls was particularly deadly — if it could be brought to bear. Each ammunition chest was packed with two shells, five

---

[16]John Gibbon, Colonel 7th Infantry, Commanding, to Assistant Adjutant General, Department of Dakota, Saint Paul, Minn., "Report of the battle of Big Hole, M.T., Aug. 9, 1877, with list of killed and wounded," September 20, 1877, p. 11.

[17]Arthur M. Woods, letter to Superintendent Jack R. Williams, July 20, 1961, concerning the cannonball he found on the battlefield August 16, 1936. In his letter, Mr. Woods stated:

". . . the camp of the Indians was on the large meadow. May be some 75 acres. And I found the cannon ball some 200 feet from the stream, in the grass where the cattle were feeding . . . It was a beautiful meadow in 1936. I was looking for arrow heads when I saw a round iron in the grass. It was four fifths buried but I pulled the grass away and found it had never exploded. I brought it home and we drilled into it and found it was no longer dangerous. "

What Mr. Woods had was a 4.5-inch diameter *"shell,"* containing 7 ounces of rifle powder (black) as a bursting charge. The fuse port was still capped, and failure to detonate was due to the fact that the shell had not been fused before firing. Drilling into the shell, which was done with Mr. Woods' brother-in-law pouring water on the drill bit, was an extremely dangerous experiment — as he was later told at Fort Missoula. Fortunately, the powder was deactivated, either by age or the water used in the drilling. The shell was donated to Big Hole National Battlefield and is now included in the study collection. See, Carl P. Russell, *Guns On The Early Frontier* (Berkeley, Cal.: University of California Press, 1957), pp. 276-77, for information on the ammunition used in this gun.

[18]Eugene Fitch Ware, *The Indian War Of 1864* (New York: St. Martin's Press, 1960), p. 62.

spherical cases and one canister, and there were two chests on the caisson, a total of sixteen rounds available.[19]

What remains to be accounted for is why the shell fired toward the Indian encampment was not fused. The gun crew consisted of men from three different companies, who were to serve as artillerists. Available records indicate that only Sergeant Frederick had prior experience with artillery (he served in the navy during the Civil War — aboard the gunboat *Louisville* on the Mississippi River), nor is there any evidence this pro tempore gun crew was drilled in the complicated routine of loading and firing a mountain howitzer,[20] prior to taking it forward as Colonel Gibbon had ordered. Ordinarily, a gun crew consisted of a Chief of Section, a gunner and five men, each with specific duties. In this case with only five men available (Pvt. Bennett, as driver, remained astride the left leader of the team he managed), the gunner commanded, as well as pointing the piece, determining the range and tending vent; No. 1 sponged and rammed; No. 2 loaded; No. 3 primed and fired and No. 4 attended at the ammunition chest and served to No. 2. It was a routine which could keep well-trained men busy, but these men were not endlessly trained in the service-of-the-piece, to which it must be added that two were recruits. No wonder someone forgot to fuse the shell for a burst at the proper range! So, at least one shell was fired unfused, to bury itself harmlessly in the meadow soil. The nature of the other shot and what its target was remains a mystery.

Additional information on the action around the howitzer comes from Indian accounts which are, unfortunately, contradictory. Even L. V. McWhorter was led to write: *"Perhaps no unalloyed version of the Indian disposal of the howitzer can ever be obtained,"* and he erroneously located the capture site a half mile from the Siege Area, on the old Model-T road [stake M-142].[21] But even at that time there was recognition of the existence of another site on the ridge directly above [stake M-141], which was described as *"Pit reputed to be position of Howitzer before it was captured by the Nez Perce."*

The *"howitzer pit,"* as it was called for years, marked the place where a Forest Service employee engaged in surveying pine beetle damage found cannon balls in 1928. An attempt to trace those cannon balls brought an interesting letter from Neil Fullerton, of Thompson Falls, Montana. He wrote:

Replying to your letter of September 14, I must say that I was agreeably surprised that someone has taken up the problem of trying to

---

[19]Sergeant O. Sutherland's letter to General Howard, written at the wagon train between 11:00 A.M. and noon on the 9th, states: *"Howitzer lost with fifteen rounds of ammunition."* See, O. O. Howard, *Nez Perce Joseph* (Boston: Lee and Shepard Publishers, 1881), p. 200. Actually, since two rounds were fired, the ammunition destroyed by the Indians would have been 14 rounds.

[20]See, Stephen R. Pinckney, "Mountain Howitzer: Service of the Piece," in *National Guard Manual* (95th New York National Guard, 1864), 5 pp. Big Hole National Battlefield Library.

[21]L. V. McWhorter, "Stake Tabulation, Big Hole Battlefield," Sept., 1937, with a "Supplement, 8/31/38," and also, his letter to Floyd Henderson, October 10, 1936. For the location of this site, see Henderson's map of July 22, 1938. The sign which stood beside the road for many years stated, *"Here the Indians Captured the Cannon . . ."*

trace the present whereabouts of the two cannon balls found close to the vicinity of the Big Hole Battle.

About May 8th or 9th, 1928, a fellow forest officer named Kenneth Ford and I reported to Wisdom for work on the first large insect control job in Region One of the Forest Service. We were from the old Kaniksu Forest, the headquarters of which was at Newport, Washington.

Our initial assignment was to the old Battlefield Ranger Station. The first field operation on the control job was what we called 'spotting.' That is finding the exact location of groups of insect infested trees so that they could be treated by the treating crews.

Ford's spotting area was uphill back of the Ranger Station . . . One evening when Ford was coming back to the Ranger Station along the ridge he found two cannon balls and brought them in. They were both close together at the same place . . . were of course rusty, scaly and dirt encrusted . . . by their heft they did not seem to be solid cast iron . . .[22]

Those cannon balls were sent to the Forest Supervisor's office at Hamilton, Montana, but knowledge of the site persisted locally. Tom Sherrill is said to have dug there while caretaker, and George Minnick, a seasonal laborer at the Battlefield Ranger Station from 1921 to 1947, dug up two cannonballs which were displayed with the howitzer until stolen in 1940. Another cannon ball in the possession of Leslie Molls, of Darby, Montana, is one of two found by him and Louise Ramsey (daughter of Ranger Marshall Ramsey) in 1919 or 1920, "up the draw north of the ranger station."[23]

Unauthorized digging at the site, which was not officially a part of the battlefield until the nineteen-sixties, created the *"pit"* appearance and may have destroyed artifactual evidence. After the boundary readjustment which made the *"howitzer pit"* a part of the battlefield, a trail was built to the site in order to place an interpretive panel there, and a fortunate result of that work was discovery, by Historian Kermit Edmonds, of significant artifacts tending to confirm some aspects of the confusing Indian accounts of the capture of the gun.[24]

Since the recovered artifacts have particular relevance in the light of the Indian accounts, it is necessary to examine those accounts first. There are two: the first, obtained from Yellow Wolf, breaks the incident into two distinct parts which do not correlate well, and the other from Earth Blanket is limited in scope but fits better. Yellow Wolf's begins:

---

[22]Neil Fullerton, letter to the author, September 29, 1965.

[23]"Notes from Seasonal Ranger Olk's conversation with Leslie Molls, Darby resident, 8-11-85." Typescript in Big Hole National Battlefield files.

[24]Kermit M. Edmonds, "Field Research Project Report, Big Hole National Battlefield, June, July, August, 1964," September 7, 1964. Typescript, with 2 maps, Big Hole National Battlefield files.

I will tell you how we got this gun. Six of us were mounted and this side [southwest] of the entrenched soldiers. They were my uncle, Old Yellow Wolf . . . Tenahtahkah Weyun (Dropping from a Cliff), Weyatanatoo Latpat (Sun Tied), Pitpillooheen [Calf of Leg], Ketalkpoosmin [Stripes Turned Down], and I, Yellow Wolf.

We were scouts on the lookout. Scouts everywhere that enemies might be coming. From across the valley south of us, I heard a voice — a Nez Perce voice — call a warning, "Look this way!"

Looking we saw three scouts riding fast toward us. Drawing near, one of them yelled, "Two white men riding on trail towards you!"

We ran our horses in that direction. Soon we saw them! We chased those two white men back the way they came. We fired at them. Up there we found the cannon. We saw the big gun on a wagon with men. Four, maybe six, mules hitched to that gun wagon. While we charged this cannon, the men having it in keeping fired it twice. But some distance away, we scattered, and nobody hurt. I saw a warrior off his horse running afoot towards this cannon from the opposite side. This was Seeyakoon Ilppilp, a brave man, good fighter. He came running, dodging, getting closer to the main cannonman. That soldier did not see him. Then Seeyakoon, still at a good distance, shot him in the back, killing him. At the same time Tenahtahkah dropped the right-hand lead mule. The cannon was completely stopped. Some other soldiers with it skipped to the brush escaping with their lives.[25]

That much of Yellow Wolf's account is in reasonable agreement with the story of Wattes Kunnin (Earth Blanket), also known by the name of *"Big Joe."* He had no gun but arrived in time to see the capture completed. He told McWhorter:

Riding up the hill I came to a kind of small canyon forks. From there I saw the big gun and soldiers running away from it. Two Indians afoot came down the hill towards the cannon. I galloped up the hill a short way, and when I came again to where I could see, just one white man was there. Only one left. He was shooting back; sort of back of himself and not ahead.

The two Indians were getting closer. I saw the white man sinking down. I thought he was going to shoot at me. No! he was dying.

When I saw him go down, I galloped faster. When I reached the cannon there stood not far away a bay horse with packs on his back. Those packs were gun cartridges. Lots of them.[26]

It is in the matter of the packhorse with the reserve ammunition that a problem develops. In Yellow Wolf's account the capture of the packhorse is a sep-

---

[25]*Yellow Wolf*, pp. 149-50; cited in Note 5.
[26]*Ibid.*, p. 149n.

arate incident, unrelated to the capture of the howitzer. Continuing the story with
his narrative:

> This little fight over, we again heard one scout across the creek
> calling, "Coming down this way leading one pack horse, about ten
> soldiers!"
>
> We mounted in a hurry and went to meet these new enemies. As
> far to our camp [600 yards] one of the soldiers was leading the pack
> horse. My uncle, Espowyes [Light in the Mountain], was some
> distance ahead of us. I saw him head this soldier off and take the pack
> horse. That soldier put up no fight. He skipped for his life. We fired
> at him, but did not stop him. Espowyes was brother [relation] to Chief
> Joseph. Those ten or eleven soldiers ran their horses fast back up the
> trail. When we got to that pack horse, we cut the ropes holding the
> packs, dropping them to the ground. With rocks the boxes were broken
> open. It was ammunition, more than two thousand cartridges.
>
> I paid no attention, but about thirty Indians were there by this
> time. We all piled after that ammunition. Some got only few
> cartridges, some got more. Later it was evenly divided by the chiefs.
> Just one kind of rifles it fit — those we took from the soldiers.
>
> Most of the warriors now went back to fight the soldiers in their
> trenches, while several scouted the woods above us, the mountainside.
> Might be soldiers coming through that way.
>
> Only my uncle and I rode up the trail where the ten soldiers had
> fled. We went quite a way and decided those soldiers had left for
> Bitterroot Valley. We turned back.[27]

Artifact recovery in the vicinity of the howitzer pit provides confirmation for
both versions of the killing of the cannoneer. A string of four .45-70 Government
rifle cases were found approaching the gun position from the north; the farthest
174 feet away, the second 155 feet, the third 125 feet, and the last at 88 feet.
These ejected cases could be from Seeyakoon Ilppilp's shots, fired while *"running,
dodging"* — the intervals are about right. Of course, the ammunition used was
military, but that does not preclude its use by the Nez Perces since they had
captured both arms and ammunition in their previous encounters with the troops.

Two feet behind the second item mentioned above, and slightly to the right,
a .50-70 Government case was found, which is in agreement with Yellow Wolf's
mention of a second Nez Perce — Tenahtahka — shooting a lead-mule of the team
(the team would have pulled the caisson to the right, or west of the gun; in fact,
the separation was supposed to be 15 yards when the gun was in position to fire).
With the team facing west, the right-hand leader would have been the one most
likely hit.

Most of the remaining artifacts recovered comprised two groups, roughly
thirty feet apart. There were only small arms ammunition items in the eastern

---

[27]*Ibid.*, pp. 150-51.

group; nothing definitely associated with the howitzer, though the site would have been the proper one for emplacing the gun. The western group also yielded small arms ammunition items, but with them were pieces of sabot strapping (the metal bands which held a cannonball on its *"sabot,"* or wooden block intended to serve both as wadding and an attachment for the flannel bag holding the powder charge). All the items of the western group were on the lower side of the old howitzer pit and might have been displaced from it by the digging of persons hunting cannonballs. That the ammunition chests were thrown off the caisson — one to each side — while it stood just above or northwest of the pit, seems likely since more sabot strapping was found forty feet northwest of the pit.

The ammunition items in each group included some conspicuously of nonmilitary origin, as, a percussion cap of the proper size for a muzzleloading musket (perhaps the one to which the ramrod for a Model 1841 Mississippi rifle, found near the pit years ago, belonged); a .45-70 Government cartridge case ruptured from being fired in a rifle chambered for .50-70 — a very Indian adaptation; .50-70 commercial cartridge cases as well as Government, and two .44 Henry cartridge cases which had misfired. These latter are interesting as hinting at a shortage of ammunition for that type of weapon (Henry repeating rifle, or Model 1866 Winchester). The Henry cartridge was a rim fire ignited by a two-pronged firing pin, and two out of the seven cases bore more than one set of firing pin marks; one case had two sets of marks and the other five. Each new attempt requiring rotation of the cartridge in the chamber!

The fifteen .45-70 Government cartridge cases found in the two groups are even more speculative, since they could have been fired by gun crew or Nez Perces. One such case recovered 95 feet west of the howitzer pit raises the possibility that it represents a shot by one of the departing soldiers at the attackers near the gun; but the most that can be certainly concluded from the considerable recovery of ammunition items is that there was a hot little fire fight around the gun position.

The disposal of the howitzer after its capture is also shrouded in some uncertainty. Continuing with Yellow Wolf's account (p. 151):

> While we chased those soldiers and captured the ammunition, other Indians knocked out whatever was used in firing the cannon. Took off the wheels and rolled them down a steep place to the swamp or creek brush. We could have fought the soldiers with that gun had we known how to use it.[28] I understood Peopeo Tholekt shallow-buried it,

---

[28] According to Duncan McDonald, *"A few minutes later an Indian reached the gun and expressed great regret that it was rendered useless. He said: 'It is a great pity. I know how to use this kind of gun. I learned when I was with Col. Wright fighting Cayuses and Yakimas.'"* See, "The Nez Perce War of 1877 — The Inside History from Indian Sources," in *The New North-West,* Deer Lodge, M.T., January 24, 1879. Concerning this possibility, Col. Gibbon later wrote: *". . . as was afterwards learned, there were Indians in the party who knew something about artillery, and although it would have been a novelty, it would have been a disagreeable one to have been shelled in our wooded retreat with our own gun."* "The Battle of the Big Hole," p. 1236; cited in Note 1. It would

digging with his hunting knife. He came there as the fight ended. Poker Joe afterwards rolled it down the bluff to thick brush.

McWhorter adds that Peopeo's claim to having shallow-buried the howitzer — the barrel, presumably — was disputed by other Nez Perces, and certainly, the gun would have had to be intact if Lean Elk rolled it down into the swamp as some claimed. However, white statements are less ambiguous. Only *"Bunch"* Sherrill maintained that it was rolled into Trail Creek; the Deer Lodge *New North-West*, which had its information from Sergeant Mildon Wilson immediately after the battle, reported that, *". . . Indians destroyed all powder and gun ammunition, picked up the wheels between two horses and carried off and hid them and every possible portion of gun and carriage."* To that, Colonel Gibbon (who ought to know) added that the Indians, *"completely dismantled it, took off the wheels, concealed the howitzer in the brush, and carried off the sponge staff, handspike, and other implements to the top of a neighboring hill."*[29]

As for the gun crew, the two privates — Malcolm McGregor and John H. Goale — fled as the Indians charged, one yelling *"This is another Custer Massacre!"* They were listed on the Company G muster roll as deserters. Sergeant Frederick was wounded in the shoulder but able to escape with Sergeant Daly, who had a head wound. Driver Bennett, whose leg was caught under the fallen leader, freed himself by slashing the harness and prodding the dying animal with the knife until it moved a little (it is interesting that the only artifact recovered from the howitzer pit, proper, was a harness D-ring). The three soldiers, with scout Blodgett and Woodcock, made their way back to the wagon train, leaving behind the body of Corporal Sale, which was found two days later, stripped naked and wearing a horse collar.

With the howitzer disposed of, many of the warriors returned to the siege area to take up in earnest the investment of Gibbon's men by *"occupying the brush below and the timber above,"* and others established a picket post, or lookout, in the edge of the timber somewhat below the place where the gun had been captured — a good place to watch the Trail Creek route for the approach of any other soldiers. Yellow Wolf was with the latter group when word came that a noted warrior by the name of Sarpsis Ilppilp (Red Moccasin Tops), had been killed. This son of Chief Yellow Bull of the White Bird band was one of the three Nez Perces accused of starting the war; his partners in the killing of Salmon River settlers were Wahlitits, killed early in the fight for the encampment, and Wetyetmas Wahyaht (Swan Necklace).

The recovery of the body of Sarpsis, who had been fatally wounded in the throat while fighting near the west side of the trenches [site 38], became a major concern of the Nez Perces because, as his father said, *"We do not want to leave*

---

also have been something of a professional affront since John Gibbon began his military career as an artillery officer — in command of Light Battery B, Fourth United States Artillery.

[29]See, *The New North-West,* August 17, 1877; cited in Note 14. And also, "The Battle of the Big Hole," p. 1236; cited in Note 1.

him there. We do not want to leave him for crazy white people who might cut him in pieces to make fun of brave warrior." So, Yellow Bull, asked, *"Who will go bring his body away, bring him to this place?"*[30]

Yellow Wolf says that seven or eight of the warriors at the picket post started to the siege area under Tiphahlanah Kapskaps (Strong Eagle), a cousin of Sarpsis. When they reached the place where the old caretaker house used to stand, the timber thinned out and they had to move carefully to avoid rifle fire from the trenches. He adds:

> Weweetsa (Log), who had been wounded in the right side earlier in the fight, was the rear man. He became exposed and was killed [wounded at site 36] by a bullet from the trenches. It struck at the collarbone and came out at the left shoulder. Weweetsa soon regained life and remained with us two weeks. Then, with three other wounded men, he went to the Flathead Reservation. He got well of the shot but was killed soon afterwards by Flatheads in a quarrel.[31]

About three minutes after Weweetsa was wounded another man, Quiloishkish, was hit [site 35], shattering his right elbow. That ended the first attempt to recover the body of Sarpsis. But Yellow Wolf says:

> We thought to try again. Six or seven of us went this time. A shallow draw led down to where Sarpsis lay. Then Tipyahlanah sprang forward and caught up Sarpsis, who was still breathing. Only ran with him a few steps when he was shot through right side just below short rib. Wounded, he carried his brother [cousin] part way to safety, then fell [site 40]. Sarpsis there died. Tipyahlanah crawled back up to the benchland. We came back up here [to the picket post], our hearts feeling bad. After another council, we said we would try again.
>
> A third time we were ready to go. My uncle [old] Yellow Wolf told me he would go in my place . . .
>
> They went down. The dead man had a white wolfskin over his shoulders. His father, Yellow Bull, kept shouting from the wooded bench, "Who saves the body can have the wolfskin!" That wolfskin was strong medicine.
>
> I do not know only as they told when they came back. While the other warriors kept firing at the trenches from hiding places, Tahwis Tokaitat (Bighorn Bow), a strong man, crawled down to the body and pulled it away. As he brought the body behind a tree [site 41], Yellow Bull called to him, "You have done what you wanted! Come away!"

---

[30]*Yellow Wolf*, p. 153; cited in Note 5.

[31]*Ibid.*, p. 153. This interesting statement indicates that the Nez Perces managed to get some of their wounded to places where they could recover in safety.

They brought the body of Sarpsis Ilppilp up here [to the picket post] and buried it secretly. I saw the bullet mark. He was shot in the throat. The bullet cut one strand of his wampum beads.[32]

There is a sequel to this story. Tahwis Tokaitat did not get the wolfskin, as promised. Instead, Yellow Bull gave it to his wife, who was a magician. It was later taken away from her by a medicine man — Tahomchits Humkon — and he was wearing it at the Bear Paw fight when shot across the back of the neck. Yellow Wolf says he always shook after that.

Soon after the soldiers had retreated to the timbered bench, word filtered back to the village that Wahchumyus, the mighty Rainbow, lay dead among the willows. His war mate, Pahkatos Owyeen (Five Wounds), recalled their vow to die on the same day, in the same battle, as their fathers had. Yellow Wolf remembered him standing by the water, wrapped in a black blanket.

He seemed thinking to himself. Stepping one way, then another. Restless and not easy in mind. I knew his feelings. Thinking but not talking. After a few moments he said, "Any you brothers have two guns? Let me have one."

. . . One man a little way off, came stepping. Holding out a rifle, he spoke in quick words. "Take this gun. It has five shells in magazine and one in barrel."

Pahkatos took the rifle with the remark, "They are enough." He dropped his blanket.[33]

Pahkatos visited the body of his war mate, cried over him, drank a little whiskey from a canteen Otskai had taken from a dead soldier, and then joined an attack on the rifle pits. Two Moons, in telling of this, said that he (Two Moons) had reached a place from which he could fire, but,

Pahkatos kept going; Thomas Lindsay with him. Lindsay tried to stop him; tried to head him off from climbing the bluff to where the soldiers were entrenched, but could not do so. Reaching the brow of the bluff, Pahkatos was fired on by the soldiers and killed [site 8].

Another great warrior was gone. His mind no longer on the battle, his **wyakin** power had left him. There was nothing to protect him from enemy bullets.[34]

After the Nez Perces returned to the wrecked village, some warriors were searching the dead soldiers for guns and ammunition when they found a wounded volunteer — Campbell L. Mitchell — who was feigning death. There was, at first, an inclination to spare his life, but the situation soured and he was killed [stake M-92]. Though the two versions of this incident differ as to what led to his death,

[32]*Ibid.*, pp. 154-55.
[33]*Ibid.*, p. 116.
[34]*Hear Me, My Chiefs!*, pp. 387-88; cited in Note 6.

there was no torture, as Will Cave has hinted. Duncan McDonald got his information from the Nez Perce refugees he visited in Canada the following year, and this
is his version:

> Looking Glass ordered the warriors not to kill him, saying that he
> was a citizen, and that they might obtain information from him
> concerning Howard, etc. They then questioned him, and in reply he
> said that Howard would be there in a short time, and that plenty of
> volunteers were coming from Virginia [City] to head them off. While
> he was telling the news a woman who had lost her brother and some of
> her children in the fight came up. She was crying at the time, and on
> seeing the citizen slapped him in the face. On receiving the blow he
> instantly gave her a vigorous kick with his boot. He had no more than
> kicked her when some of the warriors killed him.[35]

Yellow Wolf's account of the incident is less ingenious, and more likely in
view of the anger generated by the dawn attack. As Lakochets Kunnin led the
prisoner passed a tipi, another warrior — Otskai — stepped from behind it and said:
"Do not waste time! Kill him!" Suiting action to words, he did just that with the
gun he had ready. His excuse to those gathered around was:

> No use! The difference is, had he been a woman, we would have
> saved him. Sent him home unhurt! Are not **warriors** to be fought?
> Look around! These babies, these children killed! Were **they** warriors?
> These young girls, these young women you see dead! Were **they**
> warriors? These young boys, these old men! Were **they** warriors?
>
> We are the warriors! Coming on us while we slept, no arms ready,
> the soldiers were brave. Then, when we have only a few rifles in our
> hands, like cowardly coyotes they run away.
>
> These citizen soldiers! Good friends in Bitterroot Valley! Traded
> with us for our gold! Their Lolo peace treaty was a lie! Our words
> were good. They had two tongues. Why should we waste time saving
> his life?[36]

Yellow Wolf adds that when the Nez Perce prisoners were questioned in
Oklahoma Territory as to who killed the *"citizen soldier,"* no one would tell.

At least one wounded soldier left behind during the retreat from the village
was killed by the Indians, though the particulars surrounding his death are
unknown. He was Musician Michael Gallagher who was *"shot through both legs*

---

[35]Duncan McDonald, in *The New North-West*, January 24, 1879; cited in Note 28. The similar
coverage by G. O. Shields in *The Battle Of The Big Hole*, pp. 79-80, appears to have been taken from
McDonald's article.

[36]*Yellow Wolf*, pp. 130-31; cited in Note 5.

and unable to follow the command around in its successive movements. He was found afterward with his throat stabbed in three places. "[37]

McWhorter credits the information obtained from Mitchell with encouraging the Nez Perces to pack up what they could salvage of their possessions and get the families on the road to safety. That may be, though they certainly had no reason to remain longer than to gather and bury their dead. Colonel Gibbon later wrote:

> Few of us will soon forget the wail of mingled grief, rage, and horror which came from the camp four or five hundred yards from us when the Indians returned to it and recognized their slaughtered warriors, women, and children. Above this wail of horror we could hear the passionate appeal of the leaders urging their followers to fight, and the warwhoops in answer which boded us no good.[38]

The work of packing any salvageable possessions, as well as the hasty burial of the dead, was done by the women; but in some families, where there were no women left who were able to work, warriors had to leave the fight to help get the village moving. The wounded who could ride were put on horses (sometimes tied on), while horse-drawn travois were used to carry the seriously injured.[39] The evacuation of the village was managed by Chief Joseph, who had the families moving by late afternoon — protected by a screen of warriors under Chief Looking Glass.

Back at the siege area, some warriors crept through the grass and brush to within fifty feet of the works, and one was mentioned as *"so securely perched behind a dead log that he killed four men in one rifle pit before he himself was picked off . . . [site 34]"*[40]

But it was the fire of Indian marksmen who had found positions behind the large trees up Battle Gulch, and in a brushy pine on the bank of the river opposite the mouth of the gulch, that were particularly galling. The trees on the north side of Battle Gulch were high enough above the trenches to allow a plunging fire at a range estimated at 400 yards, and it was from there that the shots came which mortally wounded Lieut. English and killed at least one other man, as well as wounding a number. Shields states that the sniper was finally dislodged by *"a soldier who crawled up the gulch some distance above the main body and who was equally expert in the use of his rifle."* The soldier managed a crossfire which drove the sniper out, and *"He went down the hill on a run and took refuge in the willows,*

---

[37]"Big Hole Battle Echoes," *The New North-West*, Deer Lodge, M. T., August 24, 1877, p. 3. As mentioned elsewhere, Colonel Gibbon confused Michael with Francis Gallagher when reporting the casualties; an error repeated often in accounts of the battle.

[38]"The Battle of the Big Hole," p. 1235; cited in Note 1.

[39]The travois (from Canadian-French, *travois du train*) was a primitive vehicle made by crossing the small ends of two lodge poles over the withers of a horse, with the butt ends allowed to drag on the ground. Cross pieces lashed to the poles behind the horse carried baggage, children, old people and, in this case, wounded. Also known as a *"pony drag."*

[40]C. S. Wood, "Chief Joseph, The Nez Perce," in *Century Magazine*, May, 1884, p. 139.

but with one arm dangling at his side in a way that left no doubt in the minds of those who saw him that it was broken. "[41]

It is mentioned that several of the marksmen firing into the rifle pits from positions higher up Battle Gulch were sufficiently skilled to understand the necessity of occasionally clearing the powder fouling from their rifles, and bits of rag remaining at their firing positions indicated they had done that. Both Lieutenant Coolidge and Private Coon say that some explosive bullets were used by the Nez Perces [42] (explained as being some sporting ammunition captured by chance in Idaho). In addition to being commercially available, such particularly lethal bullets could be made by boring a hole of the right size to accept a .22 caliber shell in the blunt nose of a large-caliber bullet. The base of the rim-fire .22 cartridge, upon striking something solid, like the bones of a charging grizzly bear, blew up the larger bullet with frightful effect. Without a Geneva Convention to restrict them, the Nez Perces used whatever came to hand.

There is a tendency to confuse the incident of the sniper using one of the large yellow pines which stood on the north wall of Battle Gulch — only one remains — with the *"Twin Trees"* a half mile northeast of the entrenchments. Not only is 850 yards a nearly impossible range for the available firearms, but only the tops of the Twin Trees are visible from the siege area because of the bulge of the intervening terrain. As mentioned earlier the marksman at the Twin Trees menaced soldiers in the village and on the retreat from it.

The marksman at the bushy tree opposite the mouth of Battle Gulch was a particular nuisance because the range was short — a little over 200 yards. Lynde Elliott and Myron Lockwood were in a rifle pit they had prepared in the mouth of Battle Gulch and Tom Sherrill was in an adjacent pit which was barely large enough to shoot from. Tom was watching the willows along the river, trying to spot the sniper who was harassing them, when he heard someone behind him, and

> . . .a soldier plunked himself down in my hole with me, and just as far as he could possibly get in. "Say," I said, "don't you see that there is hardly room for one here, if he is to use his gun?" "Can't help it," he said, "don't try to shoot." "What did you come here for?" I asked. No answer. "Say," I said, "what did you come here for? Didn't you come to fight Indians?" "Yes, but let the other fellows fight. Lay still," he said. We had another volley about this time, and I got up and fired a few shots at the smoke down in the willows, which did no good, as

---

[41]*The Battle Of The Big Hole*, p. 65; cited in Note 16. (Also, Brady's *Northwestern Fights And Fighters*, p. 183). It must be noted here that Pvt. Wilfred Clark, Co. L, of the 2nd Cavalry, received an award of the Congressional Medal of Honor for his *"Conspicuous gallantry, especial skill as a sharpshooter,"* (See, *The Medal Of Honor*, official publication of the Department of the Army, Washington, D.C., 1948). However, since Pvt. Coon has credited Cpl. John Abbott, of Company D, with locating and eliminating the sniper, *"who got about seven of us, including Lieut. English,"* it may be that Clark's award came from a different incident.

[42]Mark Brown, *The Flight of the Nez Perce* (New York: G. P. Putnam's Sons, 1967), p. 267, and, Homer Coon, "The Outbreak of Chief Joseph," n.d., p. 8; Ms. in the Coe Collection, Yale University Library, New Haven, Conn.

there was no one in sight. When I stretched out again my mate said:
"You are a doon [sic] fool to sit up there in plain sight. Some of these
Indians will get you yet; if you don't lie down and stay there."

While this conversation was going on Lind Elliott got shot [site
51]. Soon afterward he was shot the second time and the same bullet
that caused his death wound went through Lockwood and lodged just
under the skin. My neighbor just above me, John Shean [Shinn], said,
"Tom, do you see the water down there?" "Yes," I replied. "Well, we
have been shooting at the smoke just [this] side of that all the time, and
these Indians are still there some place, and pretty close too, and I
believe they are just under the bank on this side of the creek." (He had a
small magazine gun that held twelve cartridges all told). "Now, watch
me. I am going to empty this gun just as fast as I can at that place. I
just want to cut the water over the bank on this side; you watch close,
and if I do say GOOD and I will stop." He took aim and fired and the
shot was a dandy. I said "GOOD". He emptied his gun at that place
and we never had any more shots from it.[43]

During the afternoon the Nez Perces attempted to burn the soldiers out of
their rifle pits. A strong wind was blowing from the west, and, *"taking advantage
of this, the Indians set fire to the grass intending, doubtless, to follow up the fire
and make a dash upon us whilst we were blinded by the dense smoke. But,
fortunately, the grass was too green to burn rapidly . . ."*[44] Evidence of this
ground fire was found northwest of the entrenched area, where a dropped .50-70
commercial cartridge (probably Nez Perce) had exploded with such force that the
primer was blown out and impressions of soil particles were left in the flattened
metal.[45]

Throughout the day the chiefs were heard exhorting their warriors, and their
words *"were interpreted to us, in a low voice, by a half breed, by the name of Pete
Mat . . . "* Despite earlier doubts about Pete, who was a known horse thief with a
price on his head, he stayed with the command to the end of the battle. Tom
Sherrill says that the Bitterroot boys wanted to hold him *"but Gibbon would not let

---

[43]"The Battle of the Big Hole As I Saw It," pp. 11-12; cited in Note 2. When Tom Sherrill was
the USFS caretaker, during the nineteen-twenties, he had a flag set on the river bank, with a sign at the
mouth of Battle Gulch calling attention to it. The text ended with, *"Those Indians fired 75 shots . . . I
counted the shells after the fight."* Bunch Sherrill, in the account cited in Note 10, has a different
version of this incident (indicating that he was in the rifle pit with Elliott and Lockwood when they
were shot, and that he moved from that place, crowding in with his brother and the soldier. See, p.
4).

[44]Gibbon's "Report," p. 11; cited in Note 17.

[45]A. L. Haines, "Report on Research Accomplished at Big Hole National Battlefield During
1965," Big Hole National Battlefield, February 25, 1966. See p. 5.

them, so he got away." For Pete, it was only a brief stay of execution, for he was *"afterwards captured and hung"* (at Pine Hollow, near Stevensville).[46]

For Corporal Loynes, as for the other men of Gibbon's command, August 9th was a very long day; *". . . the sun seemed to stand still, we wanted the night to come that we might get water."*

Unexploded cannon ball found embedded in meadow soil near the south end of the Nez Perce encampment in 1936. Probably fired, unfused, from the 12-pounder Mountain Howitzer before the gun was captured by the Nez Perces. Note the hole drilled in the rusty fuse plug by the finder; very dangerous!

Photo by ALH, 1989

---

[46]Charles N. Loynes, "Battle of the 'Big Hole'," in *Winners of the West*, March, 1925, p. 7. See also, "The Battle of the Big Hole As I Saw It," pp. 3 & 21; cited in Note 2, and Brady's *Northwest Fights And Fighters*, p. 184.

Chapter 6

EBB TIDE OF BATTLE

Night closed upon a scene of destruction and misery. The beautiful meadow called Iskumtselalik Pah — the place of ground squirrels — was littered with the wreckage of the day's conflict: the abandoned poles of lodges from which the covers had been hastily removed standing like isolated skeletons among others overturned or with their covers and contents still smoking from the partially successful attempts to burn them, and scattered throughout, the kettles and pans, the clothing and bedding of the people who had only recently occupied those dwellings. Here and there were the carcasses of horses and dogs, and the bodies of soldiers yet unburied, with evidences of the hasty, and quite inadequate, burial, which was all the grieving Indians could do for their own dead.

In the rifle pits occupied by Gibbon's command there was fear of what the darkness would bring; a fear heightened by extreme fatigue, hunger, thirst and a knowledge that there was not enough ammunition left to repulse the charge of a determined enemy. With their clothing still damp from wading the slough and river, there was that other enemy, the chill of night to crowd emotionally drained men close to the edge of delirium and heighten the shock of suffering wounded. There was raving and crying, and Peo peo Tholekt, a young warrior who crawled close to the trenches in the dark, heard one man shouting, *"Charley! Charley! Hold on there! Hold on! G— d— you, wait!"*[1]

It was during the first part of the night, while the *"yelling and shooting"* of the besieging Nez Perces was the worst, that one of the Bitterroot citizens, William H. *"Billy"* Edwards, volunteered to carry dispatches to Deer Lodge. He *"crawled through the encircling line of Indians, walked forty miles to French's Gulch, obtained a horse and rode forty more, [and] at 10 A.M., Saturday was in the telegraph office at Deer Lodge."* Adjutant Woodruff later called it *"a brave deed and gallantly performed."*[2] Of course, Woodruff had more than an ordinary interest in Edwards' accomplishment because he furnished the boots for that hike, and, most important for the adjutant, personally, he carried a message for Mrs. Woodruff, at Fort Shaw, in addition to Gibbon's dispatches.

That personal message, which went on the telegraph wire at 8:42 a.m., a little earlier than Woodruff recollected, was the first notice the district headquarters had of a battle having been fought. The essential part of the message was this:

> . . . we had a hard fight - took the village but was at last driven with heavy loss we had 17 officers 133 soldiers and 32 citizens Capt Logan

---

[1]L. V. McWhorter, *Yellow Wolf: His Own Story* (Caldwell, Idaho: The Caxton Printers, Ltd., 1986), p. 156n.

and Lieut Bradly [sic] killed Genl Gibbon Lt Coolidge english [sic] and Myself wounded mine are only flesh wounds [2nd page] as is the gen'ls we think english is very dangerous case we are intrenched and all right the Indians are leaving . . .[3]

That information, forwarded from Fort Shaw to General Sheridan's headquarters at Chicago, created some uncertainty, its unofficial nature leading to a fear that the report might be only rumor. But all doubt was soon dispelled when news of the battle — the first to reach the public — appeared under the Deer Lodge *New North-West* date line of *"August 11 - 9 A. M,"* informing that *"W. H. Edwards has just arrived from Big Hole, bringing accounts of a terrible battle . . ."* He carried three dispatches, all addressed to Governor Potts and somewhat repetitious. As presented by the newspaper, they were:

First Dispatch. Big Hole, August 9, 1877. To Governor Potts:
    Had a hard fight with the Nez Perces, killing a number and losing a number of officers and men. We need a doctor and nurses and everything. Send us such relief as you can. John Gibbon, Col. Commanding."

Second Dispatch. Big Hole, August 9, 1877. To Governor Potts:
    We are here near the mouth of Big Hole Pass, with a large number of wounded in want of everything. Food, clothing, medicines and medical attendance. Send us assistance at once. John Gibbon, Col. U. S. Army."

Third Dispatch. To Governor Potts:
    We had a hard fight and took the village, but _____ was driven back with heavy loss. Captain Logan and Lieut. Bradley were killed. General Gibbon and Lieutenants Cooledge [sic], English and Woodruff are wounded — English seriously the others slightly. The troops are entrenched and the Indians leaving. John Gibbon, Col. Commanding.

To that was added, *"When the messenger left, General Gibbon said: 'I want an escort sufficient to protect the wagons which are going in to relieve us. Load the wagons as light as possible. The Indians cut me off from my supplies'. "*
The response those dispatches evoked in the citizens of Montana Territory, and particularly in the towns of Deer Lodge, Butte and Helena, will be covered in Chapter 7; for now, it only remains to clear up a mistake which has long clouded

---

[2]Gen. C. A. Woodruff, "The Battle of the Big Hole," in *Contributions To The Historical Society Of Montana*, Helena, 1910: Vol. 7, pp. 110-11. See also, Woodruff's letter to Amos Buck, September 14, 1908; *Ibid.*, pp. 133-34.
    [3]Telegram, dated "Big Hole 9 1877," sent by *"Charlie"* to *"Mrs. C. A. Woodruff Ft Shaw,"* copy in the Big Hole National Battlefield library. Note: The text published by Edgar Stewart, in "Letters from the Big Hole," *Montana Magazine Of History*, Vol. 2, No. 4 (October, 1952), p. 54, differs in spelling and arrangement, but is accurate.

Billy Edwards' truly remarkable feat. Unfortunately, the record of this incident is confused because the man who *ought* to know got a salient fact wrong. Colonel John Gibbon later wrote in his official report: *"During the night, I sent a runner to the train and two others to Deer Lodge, via French's Gulch, for medical assistance and supplies, fearing our train had been captured."* Four years later, he rephrased that to read this way: *"During the night I sent two runners to Deer Lodge, ninety miles distant, to report our condition. These, a couple of citizens who knew the country, crawled out through the Indians surrounding us and successfully accomplished their mission."*[4]

While Gibbon's two accounts should be the reliable, with regard to how many went for help, there are some good reasons to doubt him. In his epic poem, *"A Vision of the 'Big Hole',"* written only five years after the battle, Gibbon mentions only Edwards:

> *Long years will we with gratitude recall,*
> *How **Edwards** on his midnight mission sped;*
> *How he, in darkness, left our camp to crawl*
> *Towards outside help with perils round his head;*[5]

Amos Buck and John Catlin, both of whom were there, have stated that Billy Edwards went afoot and alone, and the only support for Gibbon's statement — that he sent TWO messengers to Deer Lodge — comes from M. F. *"Bunch"* Sherrill. In 1916, he told A. J. Noyes that Billy Edwards was accompanied by another man *"named Howard,"* who *"played out the next day."*[6] There was no one by that surname, neither soldier nor volunteer, with Gibbon's command, and Sherrill's statement is probably only hearsay. Gibbon did send out a third messenger, but to the miners near present Gibbonsville, warning them that the cavalcade of Indian families was moving in their general direction, and a mental lapse concerning who went where is hardly surprising in a man wounded, sleepless for two days and under the stress of command responsibility. This messenger to the miners was Fred *"Dutch"* Heldt, who managed to get lost in the mountains for three days without food. According to Will Cave, when Fred was asked what he ate, his reply was: *"I yust lived on fried elk tracks."*

The man who took the message to the wagon train is not known definitely; he may have been Sergeant Mildon H. Wilson, but it was one of the volunteers left with the wagons who took the message on. The courier intended to deliver it to General Howard, but missed him on the way and delivered it, instead, to Major Edwin C. Mason, who was bringing the remainder of Howard's cavalry forward —

---

[4]John Gibbon, Colonel, 7th Infantry, Commanding, "Report of battle of Big Hole, M.T., Aug. 9, 1877, with list of killed and wounded," to the Assistant Adjutant General, Department of Dakota, St. Paul, Minn., Sept. 20, 1877, p. 12; See also, Brigadier-General John Gibbon, "The Battle of the Big Hole," in *Harper's Weekly*, Dec. 26, 1895, p. 1236.

[5]Published privately at Fort Snelling, Minn., Aug. 9, 1882. Copy in the Big Hole National Battlefield Library. See p. 20.

[6]Manuscript, SC-739, in the collection of the Montana Historical Society, Helena. See, p. 6.

of which more will be said later. The message, penciled on a small scrap of paper, read:

> General: We surprised the Nez Perce camp at daylight this morning, whipped them out of it, killing a considerable number. But they turned on us, forced us out of it, and compelled us to take the defensive. We are near the mouth of Big Hole Pass, with a number of wounded, and need medical assistance and assistance of all kinds, and hope you will hurry to our relief. Gibbon, Comm'ng Aug. 9, '77[7]

The assistance Gibbon's command so desperately needed was still more than a day away, and, out of sheer necessity, the men did what they could to alleviate their misery. A water detail was organized after dark, but it did *not* result in the death of Alvin Lockwood and a soldier, as Loynes has stated.[8] The water detail consisted of three volunteers from Company G — privates Edward Welsh, Charles Heinze and Homer Coon — who went after water for the wounded. According to Coon:

> . . . it was not entirely because of the wounded that we volunteered — we were so nearly famished ourselves for a drink that we were thinking of ourselves too and that beautiful stream we could see glistening down below. Before we started the rest of our comrades poured volley after volley into the brush lining our side of the stream to drive out any Indians that might be lurking there. Then we collected about four canteens apiece and started crawling down the slope. Although it was only about 100 yards it seemed more like 100 miles to me. We were fortunate in getting there without being seen by the Indians and then proceeded to fill our canteens. I never realized before how much those canteens held; it seemed as though they never would fill up. The shots began to whistle around us and, thirsty as I was, would you believe that I actually forgot in my excitement to get a drink for myself.[9]

The Indians were not unaware of the water detail, but they evidently were puzzled as to what was going on. Yellow Wolf told McWhorter:

> Late in the fore part of the night, we heard noise in the willows under the bluff below the trenches. We heard one talking loud in the trenches. Then we heard him crying! When we heard this, we understood. Must be some young man escaped us to the willows, and the old man could not go. Probably he was wounded. When the

---

[7]Mark Brown, *The Flight of the Nez Perce* (New York: G. P. Putnam's Sons, 1967). p. 261.

[8]Charles W. Loynes, "Battle of the Big Hole," in *Winners of the West* (March, 1925), p. 7. Alvin Lockwood was mortally wounded in the fighting in the river bottom during the retreat and was left there by his brother. See, Earle R. Forrest, "Big Hole Battlefield," in *Frontier Times*, Aug.-Sept., 1965, p. 59.

[9]Homer Coon, "The Outbreak of Chief Joseph," typescript, n.d., Yale University Library, New Haven, Conn.; p. 4. All the water carriers were recruits.

escaping soldiers seemed all returned to the trenches. That was what we thought, hearing such noises.[10]

Hunger was also a problem. The ration of hard bread which the soldiers carried in their haversacks was mostly spoiled by the water during the crossing and recrossing of the river, and the little that remained edible was shared out among comrades and soon gone. Adjutant Woodruff's horse was *"skinned and cut up ready for use in the event of the siege being continued the next day,"* and some was eaten then. Colonel Gibbon, old soldier that he was, laconically noted, *"I ate a piece of it and it tasted very well,"* but Tom Sherrill had a different opinion of that particular horse: *"Once I started for some of him, but he did not look good to me when I got near as it was warm weather, and he was bloated so that his legs were sticking straight out."*[11]

Cold, thirsty, hungry, terribly shaken by their experiences of the past day, and terrified at the thought of the day ahead, some young men deserted that night. Tom Sherrill said:

> I just settled down to digging [site 7] when one of the citizens came to me, and asked me if I wanted to get out of this. It surprised me, and I asked "Why?" "Well," he said, "there are several of us going tonight." I asked if everybody was going, and he said, "No". Then I asked him what would become of the wounded, and he remarked that we would have to let them go. Then I told him that the wounded would have to be taken care of, and that I was not going unless everybody else did. He then turned and left me. There were seven of them deserted that night, and pulled for Bitterroot Valley. It was a cowardly act, and General Gibbons said if he had known it, he would have taken them and had them all shot.[12]

The first knowledge that help was approaching in the form of General O. O. Howard's column, arrived at 6:30 on the morning after the battle — August 10th — when a civilian courier by the name of Nelse McGilliam rode into the works with a dispatch from the general. Having missed the parked wagon train in the darkness, *"This fellow slept in his saddle blankets, about a mile from the breast work. Said he heard shooting occasionally, but could not tell where we were located until daylight. Then he rode into our works and never saw an Indian."* Though stiff and cold, those of the men who were able were up and around, and soon had a fire going. *"But while we were standing around the fire, the Indians turned loose at us again, and we did some quick moving, for the rifle pits. But they only fired one volley at us."*[13]

---

[10]*Yellow Wolf*, p. 156; cited in Note 1.

[11]Tom Sherrill, "The Battle of the Big Hole As I Saw It," as related to A. J. Noyes, n.d. Typescript in the collection of the Montana Historical Society, p. 8.

[12]*Ibid.*, p. 20.

[13]*Ibid.*

Sherrill's guess that that was done to create the illusion they were still surrounded, when actually most of the Indians were already gone, is verified by Yellow Wolf:

> Only eight or nine of us young men who had swift horses remained behind. Only a few of us, we did not try rushing the soldiers. Why get killed? The soldiers were safely corralled. Families a good distance away.
>
> We just settled down to watch those soldiers.
>
> Late in after part of night we heard a white man's voice. He shouted up on the mountain. Might be some soldier lost! Maybe guiding in other soldiers? We did not know what he might be doing up there.
>
> It was almost dawn when we heard the sound of a running horse. Soon a white man came loping through the timber. He was heading for the trenches. We did not try to kill him. Had they wished, some warriors where he passed could have shot him. They said, 'Let him go in! We will then know what news he brings the soldiers!'
>
> When that rider reached the trenches, the soldiers made loud cheering. We understood! Ammunition had arrived or more soldiers were coming. Maybe pack horses of cartridges left in the woods with soldiers guarding? Some of us went back over the trail looking for any horses there. We found none. Had we gone two hundred steps farther, we would have captured their cavalry horses. All their supply train! We did not look in a gulch where concealed. This we learned after the war was quit.
>
> I was watching from south side of hill. When all returned from hunting for pack horses, we assembled south of trenches. There was a short council. Chief Ollokot was our leader. It was thought to quit the watching . . .
>
> We gave those trenched soldiers two volleys as a "Good-bye"! Then we mounted and rode swiftly away.[14]

Sergeant Oliver Sutherland, Company B, 1st Cavalry, who had left Howard's command at Lolo Hot Springs, August 6th, with a dispatch informing Gibbon that General Howard was coming on by forced marches with 200 cavalry, reached the siege area about two hours after McGilliam. Actually, Sutherland had arrived at the wagon train at 11:50 on the morning of the battle — getting there soon after the last of the howitzer crew straggled in. He got off a note to the general, dated *"12 M., Aug. 9, '77,"* containing such information on the battle as he was able to get from the two wounded sergeants, and included his excuse for not arriving sooner — *"Would respectfully state, in explanation of seeming delay on my part, that I was thrown from an unbroken horse . . . and my back severely hurt,"* — and sent it by

---

[14]*Yellow Wolf*, pp. 157-58; cited in Note 1. McWhorter confuses McGilliam's arrival with that of Sergeant Oliver Sutherland (see his Note 15, p. 157), but he is wrong, as will be shown.

Eugene Lent. Sutherland mentioned in the note that he intended *"to take two men from here, and start in five minutes, to endeavor to reach General Gibbon,"*[15] but that did not happen.

There are several possible explanations as to why Sutherland's arrival at the siege area was delayed by nearly a day (a fact Howard was reluctant to admit).[16] The story he got from the members of the howitzer crew who reached the wagon train may have convinced him, on second thought, that Gibbon's whole command was lost, and that it was hopeless to go farther; however, there is a possibility that he did try to reach the siege area, which would account for Yellow Wolf's garbled recollection of chasing ten mounted soldiers back up Trail Creek *after* the howitzer was captured.[17]

The 29 men at the wagon park that afternoon (12 soldiers, Hugh Kirkendall and his 9 wagoners, Joe Blodgett, Anthony Chaffin, Joe Hull, Jerry Wallace, Barnett Wilkerson, S. J. Herron and William Woodcock, proceeded to fortify the train as well as they could. That night William, a black man, took his turn at guard duty — though probably still edgy from his experience with the howitzer crew. He was armed with Lieutenant Jacobs' double-barrelled shotgun, and,

> During the still hours of the night the wagonmaster [Kirkendall] was making the "rounds" to see if the men were on the alert. As he approached William's post the latter called out to him to halt; and without waiting to learn whether his challenge had been heeded, blazed away at the intruder, whom he took to be a prowling redskin. The charge of buck-shot tore up the ground and cut down the brush about

---

[15]O. O. Howard, *Nez Perce Joseph* (Boston: Lee and Shepard Publishers, 1881), p.200. Mark Brown has mistaken *"12 M."* for midnight, when the meaning is 12 Meridian, or *noon*. See, *The Flight Of The Nez Perce*, p. 261; cited in Note 7.

[16]Howard's official report, August 27, 1877, stated *". . . the evening of the 9th — Sergeant Sutherland, Company 'B', 1st Cavalry, whom I sent from Hot Springs, Lolo trail, reached him and reported that I was coming. Colonel Gibbon said this gave him great encouragement and the men cheered."* National Archives, RG-94, Records of the Adjutant General - Dept. of Columbia - Nez Perce War, 1877 (Microfilm 666-336). In an addendum to his report, as it later appeared in *Report Of The Secretary Of War, 1877* (Washington: Government Printing Office, 1877), Vol. I, p. 613, Howard makes this statement:

"Col. Gibbon points out an error in my report made at Henry Lake as to the time of the arrival of Sgt. Sutherland, as follows: 'I received no dispatch from you on the 9th (the day of the battle). First information received was a dispatch by the hands of a citizen courier named McGillen [sic], who reached our position at 6:30 a.m. on the 10th after all hostile operations against us had ceased. A Sgt. of Cavalry came in from our train later in the day, bringing a dispatch of an earlier date, having spent the night previous at the train. This was, I presume, the Sgt. Sutherland you refer to.' Sutherland's report to me, in answer to my reference to him, is as follows: He arrived, as he states, at this supply camp at 11 am. of the day of the battle. Did not reach Col. Gibbon himself till 5 a.m. of the next day (this was the day preceding the Indian's withdrawal at 11 p.m. at night). Surely I am glad to put the matter just in accordance with the facts."

General Howard, who was thoroughly confused, concluded this incident by recommending Sergeant Sutherland for a certificate of merit because, *"His daring attempt to pass the enemy's lines was successfully accomplished."* (See the Appendix to Supplementary Report of January 26, 1878, p. 12; National Archives, Microfilm 666-337).

[17]*Yellow Wolf*, pp. 150-51; cited in Note 1.

the wagonmaster, but fortunately none of them hit him. William showed himself to be a vigilant sentry, but a poor shot, and it is supposed that he will never hear the last of "Who goes there? — bang?"[18]

Returning to General Howard and his command, his effort immediately after sending Sergeant Sutherland off to Colonel Gibbon was hardly what could have been expected of an officer proposing to support an inadequate force in grave danger. Gibbon's courier, Joe Pardee, reached Howard on the afternoon of August 6th at Lolo Hot Springs, informing him of the plan to overtake the Nez Perces and asking for a reinforcement of 100 cavalry. That evening Howard started the two couriers — Sutherland and McGilliam — with word that he was *"making the longest possible marches with my cavalry, and will press it in person bringing him two hundred instead of one."* He should have got his 100 best-mounted men moving early on the 7th; instead, he brought the whole command down to Woodman's Prairie [19 miles] and camped. On the 8th, with time out to critique Rawn's defensive position in Lolo Canyon, and to dictate dispatches at the mouth of Lolo Creek, the command made 34 miles (probably a fair estimate since they were on a good road), and on the 9th, with the horses weakening, they made 20 miles. On the 10th, doing what he should have done earlier, Howard selected 20 of the best-mounted troopers and forged ahead with them and Chief Robbins' 17 Bannock Indian scouts to make what he called 53 miles (but nearer 25). The remaining 15 miles down Trail Creek was made during the forenoon of the 11th.

On the evening of the 10th, just before Howard's party encamped on the head of Trail Creek,

> Robbins and some scouts returned at a trot, with seven citizens on foot. You do not often see this sight — citizens dismounted on a frontier road! In fact, you do not often see any human beings in these mountains.
>
> "Well, my men, what have you to tell us"? One of them replied, "General Gibbon had a fight with the Indians yesterday morning; has lost half his men. It was going hard with him when we left. We haven't had anything to eat for two days." So we invited them to our intended camp, and fed them. General Gibbon and the Indians were not twenty miles from us. As these citizens talked much as men are apt to do who early in the conflict run from the field of battle, it is not fair to the gallant soldiers who remain and fight it out to give their story too much weight.

Howard continued in another paragraph:

---

[18]G. O. Shields, *The Battle Of The Big Hole* (Chicago and New York: Rand, McNally & Company, Publishers, 1889), p. 67. Also, "The Battle of the Big Hole," in Brady's *Northwestern Fights And Fighters* (New York: Doubleday, Page & Company, 1909), pp. 184-85. Woodcock lived for many years in the vicinity of Fort Shaw and at Helena, Montana.

The seven countrymen who dropped in on us the night before were a sorry-looking set. They gave us a graphic account of the fight; of their own part in it; their progress, their escape. One had a brother [who was] desperately wounded [Campbell Mitchell]. The troops had done nobly, but were fearfully outnumbered [not true]. General Gibbon had shown wonderful gallantry, and, with many others, was severely wounded.

They enumerated those who had been killed in the battle; but, even after they had been comforted by a night's rest, and a warm breakfast, they gave us but gloomy views of the final situation at the time they themselves, for dear life, were making their escape to the brush. Now, no offer of favor or money, not even the attraction of a brother wounded and needy, could induce one of those brave men to go back, and guide us to the battle-field.[19]

At the siege area, August 10th was a relatively quiet day. Colonel Gibbon sent a message to General Howard using August K. Gird as a courier (he rode into the works after the Nez Perces gave up pressing the attack on the rifle pits). The young warriors under Chief Ollokot, who remained behind to watch the soldiers — Tom Sherrill thought there were about thirty of them, but Yellow Wolf put their number at half that many — followed Gird for a mile, shooting at him, but he got through unscathed. Like Eugene Lent, he missed Howard's flying column and delivered his message, an urgent request for medical assistance, to Major Mason's cavalry coming on behind.[20] Fortunately, the two doctors, Surgeon C. T.

---

[19]*Nez Perce Joseph*, pp. 197-98; cited in Note 15. Concerning General Howard's estimate of the Indians opposing Colonel Gibbon's command, Jack Williams believes the Nez Perce fighters did not exceed 155 — including several boys and the old men — which is *less* than Gibbon's total of 183; but Private Homer Coon thought the soldiers were outnumbered, *"600 to 170."* In his official report, Colonel Gibbon did not castigate the seven volunteers for their defection, as he did the two soldiers who deserted from the howitzer crew. However, he did not include their names on his list of citizens *"faithful with us to the last."* With regard to the men he listed, Gibbon asked that *"provision may be made by law by which these parties may be placed on the same footing in regard to pay, allowances, pension, etc., as is now provided for soldiers duly mustered into the service of the United States."* The following were listed: John Armstrong (killed), Jacob Baker (wounded), Amos Buck, J. B. Catlin, Anthony Chaffin, Samuel Chaffin, Oscar Clark, I. N. Davis, Samuel Dunham, William Edwards, L. C. Elliott (killed), Charles Hart, Fred Held [Heldt], [George] Hubbard, Joseph Hull, Oscar Judd, Otto Lifer [Leifer] (wounded), Eugene Lent, Almond [Alvin] Lockwood (killed), Myron Lockwood (wounded), Squire [Samuel S.] Madding, Campbell Mitchell (killed), David Morrow (killed), William Ryan (wounded), M. F. Sherrill, Thomas Sherrill, George Waide [Wade], Jerry Wallace, Barnett Wilkinson [Wilkerson], and Michail Wright. See, Letter, Gibbon to Adj. Gen., Dept. of Dakota, September 5, 1877. National Archives, Microfilm 666-338.

[20]Gird stayed with Howard's column, serving first as a courier and later as a scout under S. G. Fisher, who called him *"a brave and good scout,"* and, when Fisher and his Bannock Indians went back to Idaho following the Canyon Creek fight, Gird continued with the army to the end of the campaign. Thereafter, he announced his intention to remain in the Judith Basin and spend the winter *"wolfing."* On November 25th it was reported that a man by the name of *"Gurd, of Deer Lodge County,"* had been murdered by Major Reed at the latter's ranch in the Judith Basin. See, "Personal — Murder in the Judith Basin," in *The New North-West*, Deer Lodge, M. T., December 7, 1877.

Alexander and Assistant-surgeon J. A. FitzGerald, were with the cavalry and left at once for the battlefield, which they reached in ten hours of hard riding.

Two men from the wagon train reached the entrenchments the morning of the 10th — John Miller and Jerry Wallace. The latter had a side of bacon tied to his saddle horn and that was parcelled out among the hungry men. They had been 36 hours without food, except what they cared to take from the adjutant's dead horse. In the afternoon, Gibbon sent Captain Browning and Lieut. Woodbridge with an escort of twenty-five men to bring in the wagon train and the horses, and that was accomplished without interference from the Nez Perces (though getting across the Trail Creek swamp was another matter, as *"the wagons had to be literally carried over some of the worst places"*). With food and blankets available, the men were better off the second night, though they still had no proper medical attention.

The condition of the wounded was very bad. Gibbon's command did not have the services of a surgeon. There was none with the column he brought from Fort Shaw, and Dr. Emil Cooke, the civilian physician listed in the post returns of Fort Missoula in July, did not take the field with the force which left there August 4th in pursuit of the Nez Perces. Instead, 1st Lieutenant Charles A. Coolidge acted in that capacity (he seems to have gained sufficient skill in doctoring to serve briefly as *"acting assistant surgeon"* of the new post at the time of its establishment).[21] But he was severely wounded during the fighting in the village. He had just examined the wound of Private Charles Alberts (shot through the left lung) when he received a shot through both legs above the knees. He became so faint he nearly drowned crossing the river during the retreat and was *"carried to a place of safety by 1st Sergt. Patrick Rogan, to whom Congress awarded a medal for bravery in this engagement."*[22] That, with a crippling wound to one hand and a third in one heel prevented him from doing much for the other wounded during the remainder of the battle.

From the time he was wounded, Lieutenant English lay on the ground inside the works *"suffering dreadfully, and complaining a great deal."* He asked Tom Sherrill, who was nearby [site 15] *"to haul off a boot, and rub his feet. He said his feet were paralyzed."* Tom tried to pull off a boot — gently, of course — but the lieutenant couldn't stand the pain. So Tom took out his pocket knife, and split the boot down to the heel, slipped it off, and rubbed his foot. *"He shook his head, and said, 'It's no use, I am done for this time.'"*[23]

At daylight, Tom and *"Bunch"* Sherrill went back to the mouth of Battle Gulch looking for Myron Lockwood,

---

George F. Weisel, *Men And Trade On The Northwest Frontier* (Missoula: Montana State University Press, 1955), pp. 191-92, agrees that the murdered man was Gird.

[21]See, Post returns, Post near Missoula, M.T., June, 1877 (copy in the Big Hole National Battlefield library).

[22]Lt. A. B. Johnson, "The Seventh Regiment of Infantry," in *The Army Of The United States,* edited in 1896 (New York: Argonaut Press, 1966), p. 509.

[23]"The Battle of the Big Hole As I Saw It," p. 18; cited in Note 11.

. . . expecting to find him dead, but hoping to still find him alive. But we found him alive and resting in the same position as we last saw him . . . He was sitting with his back resting against a wall of rock [site 50]. He had lost considerable blood, and was so cold and stiff he couldn't talk. As we were lightly dressed, we took Elliot's coat off [his] corpse, and put it on Lockwood and got him up to the fire.[24]

There were, in all, 39 wounded — 5 officers (all of them married men), 30 enlisted men and 4 civilian volunteers, reported as follows:

Colonel John Gibbon, Seventh Infantry (left thigh, severe flesh wound)

COMPANY A, Seventh Infantry:
   1st Lt. C. A. Coolidge (both legs above knees, right hand, severe)
   Pvt. James C. Lehman [Lehmer] (right leg, serious)
   Pvt. Charles Alberts (under left breast, serious)
   Pvt. Lorenzo D. Brown (right shoulder, severe)
   Pvt. George Leher (scalp, slight)

COMPANY D, Seventh Infantry:
   Sgt. Patrick C. Daly (scalp, slight)
   Cpl. John D. Murphy (right hip, severe)
   Mus. Timothy Cronan (right shoulder and breast, serious)
   Pvt. James Keys (right foot, severe)

COMPANY E, Seventh Infantry:
   Sgt. William Wright (scalp, slight)
   Sgt. James Bell (right shoulder, severe)

COMPANY F, Seventh Infantry:
   Capt. Constant Williams (right side, severe; and scalp, slight)
   Sgt. William W. Watson (right hip, serious)
   Cpl. Christian Luttman (both legs, severe)
   Mus. John Erickson (left arm, flesh)
   Pvt. Edwin [Edward] D. Hunter (right hand, severe)
   Pvt. George Maurer (through both cheeks, serious)

COMPANY G, Seventh Infantry:
   Sgt. John W. H. Frederics [Frederick] (left shoulder, flesh)
   Sgt. Robert Benzinger [Bensinger] (right breast, flesh)
   Pvt. John J. Connor (right eye, slight)
   Pvt. George Gaughart [Banghart] (right shoulder, thigh & wrist, severe)
   Pvt. James Burk (right breast, serious)
   Pvt. Chas. [Charles] H. [A.] Robbecke (left hip, slight)

---

[24]*Ibid.*, p. 22.

COMPANY I, Seventh Infantry:
  1st Lt. William L. English (through back, serious; scalp, slight)
  Cpl. Richard M. [N.] Cunliffe (shoulder and arm, flesh)
  Pvt. Patrick Fallon (hip and leg, serious)
  Pvt. William Thompson (left shoulder, flesh)
  Pvt. Joseph Devoss (ankle and leg, serious)

COMPANY K, Seventh Infantry:
  2nd Lt. C. A. Woodruff (both legs above knee and left heel, severe)
  Sgt. Howard Clarke [Clark] (heel, severe)
  Pvt. David Heaton (right wrist, severe)
  Pvt. Mathew Devine (fore-arm, serious)
  Pvt. Philo O. Hurlburt (left shoulder, flesh)

COMPANY L, Second Cavalry:
  Pvt. Chas. [Charles] B. Gould (left side, severe)

CITIZEN VOLUNTEERS:
  Myron Lockwood (hips and groin, serious)
  Otto Lyford [Liefer] (foot, severe)
  Jacob Baker (Unknown, slight)
  William Ryan (Groin, slight)[25]

Captain John Catlin adds Fred Heldt to the foregoing list, as also slightly wounded, and he mentions that Otto Liefer's wound resulted from the accidental discharge of a soldier's rifle (this is repeated by Amos Buck in the account he prepared from that source).[26]

The situation was made worse at first by an absence of dressings, and nearly everything from which they could be made. Private Edward D. Hunter's right forearm was shattered and all that could be found to bind it up was a garment sleeve, which did not keep out the flies. He stood his wound quiet well until there was an opportunity to dress it; at which time nearly a cup of maggots were found feasting on the mangled flesh. As disgusting as that was, it may have saved his life by accomplishing the necessary debridement of the tissues. Similar benign neglect appears to have been beneficial in several other cases. Arrival of the wagon train, which was brought to the siege area by Captain Browning's escort about six o'clock in the evening, made dressings available. Also, and nearly as important for men with almost no food for two days, there was *"a full quart of coffee and all*

---

[25]National Archives, 3595 DD 1877; as presented by Merrill D. Beal, *I Will Fight No More Forever* (Seattle: University of Washington Press, 1963), pp. 132- 33.

[26]Amos Buck, "Review of the Battle of the Big Hole," in *Contributions To The Historical Society Of Montana*, Vol.7, 1910, p. 127. Cf. Col. J. B. Catlin, "The Battle of the Big Hole," n.d., Montana Historical Society manuscript SC-52, p. 5. This is also published in *Historian's Annual Report, Society Of Montana Pioneers*, 1927. From context, it appears that Catlin — who died in 1917 — could have written his account as early as 1882.

the hard tack each man could eat. It was mighty good!"[27] A verse in Colonel Gibbon's epic poem hints that the men who came down with the wagon train still felt it necessary to entrench themselves:

> *There, too, the hole Sam Herron dug so well,*
> *And into which he scrambled now and then,*
> *Whenever Indians made the place a hell,*
> *By firing from above us down the glen.*[28]

Thus far, almost nothing has been said about the Nez Perce wounded and how they fared after the Indians left their destroyed village. The cavalcade of families, taking the wounded on horseback or travois, made twelve miles before camping for the night at Swamp Creek — a camp called Takseen (The Willows). There, the care of the wounded was a primary concern, and it is reported that early white visitors to the site found evidences of the dressing of wounds in cast-off dressings and improvised splints littering the area.[29] According to Yellow Wolf, *"Traveling was hard on the wounded. So bad that when we reached more safe places, several of them stopped. Remained scattered and hidden away. A few of them were never afterwards heard of."*[30] At least two wounded who were thus left behind turned up on the Flathead Reservation: Quiloishkish, wounded in the right elbow in the attempt to recover the body of Sarpsis, and White Feather, the Nez Perce girl shot in the shoulder during the fight in the village.

Defense was not neglected at that or subsequent camps. Beal states that, at Swamp Creek, the warriors guarding the families *"prepared a number of stone rifle pits on the edge of a clearing, covering the practical approach to the stopping place."*[31] On a visit to the area in 1943, he found thirty-three intact rifle pits, though earlier visitors spoke of finding 75.

The battle officially ended on the evening of August 10th. Colonel Gibbon wrote in his report that, *"The Indians gave us a parting shower of bullets about 11 o'clock that night and we saw no more of them afterwards."* However, Tom Sherrill puts that parting demonstration earlier:

> Just at dark we saw three bright lights go up, south of us, about a mile away on the bank, in the direction the squaws had taken the wounded. Immediately after we saw the three lights, there were twelve shots fired. The shots reached us, but did no damage, except wounding one horse in the foot, and stampeding all the horses that were not fas-

---

[27]"The Battle of the Big Hole As I Saw It," p. 22; cited in Note 11. Captain John Catlin later thanked Hugh Kirkendall *"for the coffee and bacon that helped make out a meal when we had nothing else but hard tack."*

[28]*A Vision Of The 'Big Hole'*, p. 18; cited in Note 5.

[29]*I Will Fight No More Forever*, p. 130; cited in Note 25.

[30]*Yellow Wolf*, p. 159; cited in Note 1.

[31]*I Will Fight No More Forever*, p. 318; cited in Note 25.

tened. That was the last shot fired at us, and the last of the Indians around there.[32]

---

[32]"The Battle of the Big Hole as I Saw It," p. 22; cited in Note 11. Cf., Gibbon's official report and his 1895 magazine article, both of which are cited in Note 4. Yellow Wolf's account (cited in Note 1), pp. 158-59, tends to support Sherrill, not Gibbon, by putting the departure of the Nez Perce rear guard even earlier.

Chapter 7

THE PIPER'S PAY

As Colonel Gibbon had no way of knowing whether or not Billy Edwards got safely past the Indians and succeeded in reaching Deer Lodge with the original request for help, he decided to send another courier early on the morning of the 11th. Sergeant Mildon H. Wilson, of Company I was selected to go, and, while he prepared for that 80 mile ride, Adjutant Woodruff scratched out a letter to his wife. He wrote from *"Camp on Ruby Creek Aug. 11th 1877"*:

My darling Louie:

I wrote you a note day before yesterday and will write to-day as we send out a courier.

I am getting along well, our train came up last evening and we expect Genl. Howard today. The Indians have all left We had a hard fight lost 2 Officers Killed 10 Soldiers and 6 citizens, Wounded 5 officers 34 soldiers and 2 citizens. "K" Co. Sergt Stortz Private Kleis (the Carpenter) and Mus. Steinbacker [sic] were Killed.

I was shot in the heel of the left foot and in both legs above the knee, fortunately no bones broken. The Genl. and I were the only ones mounted, both our horses were were [sic] shot, I got mine into camp and he was shot again, we ate some of him yesterday.

I left the gun back the night we struck the village it started up at daylight and was attacked, one of the horses was shot and fell on Bennet [sic], lamed him some, and of the three men with the gun one was killed and two wounded.

Our men charged the village in fine shape and the reason we didn't hold it was there was so much brush and high bluffs that we couldn't occupy all the places at once The Indians suffered severely, I think they [sic] loss cannot be less than seventy-five or a hundred. We killed them right and left. Hurlburt of "K" killed the Indian that shot Bradley. Jacobs Killed three. Rawn two Hardin & Woodbridge one each, I didn't get a chance to Kill any of them I was carrying orders &c. The General and I were all over the field and were lucky to come off as well as we did.

The officers and men behaved well and gave the Indians the worst handling they ever seed [?] before.

Bradley and Logan were both Killed dead.

It looked blue for us here on Thursday afternoon [Aug. 9], the Indians set fire to the forest and kept up a fire from the brush and the hills, their idea was to follow up the fire and charge us when it reached us, I began to fear I should never see you again, some of the wounded covered up their heads and expected to be killed, I got my two revolvers said my prayers thought of you and Bertie and determined to kill a few Indians before I died, Our Heavenly Father was on our side and the wind changed and blew away from us.

I didn't know how much I loved you until I thought [we would never] see each other again.

We shall start this afternoon or tomorrow for Deer Lodge, I expect to get home in about ten-days . . .[1]

Sergeant Wilson left before General Howard arrived on the 11th and reached Deer Lodge at 4 p.m. the following day.[2] He was 20 hours in the saddle on that 80 mile ride — an endurance test for both the man and the animal! The dispatches Wilson carried helped to clear up the confusion which the all too brief message carried by Edwards had created in the Army's division and Washington head-quarters. The additional information the editor of the Deer Lodge *New North-West* was able to get from the sergeant was a bonanza for the press. While this ride was spectacular, it would hardly seem to be one of the qualifying parts of the award of the Congressional Medal of Honor, given him the following year. His citation included the statement: *". . . and in carrying dispatches at the imminent risk of his life,"*[3] which would seem to better fit his exploit on the night of August 9th, when he carried Colonel Gibbon's message to the wagon train. Of course, there were other reasons for the award, including saving the life of Lieutenant Jacobs during the fighting.

Back at the siege area, Joe Blodgett and Tom Sherrill took a field glass and went up on Battle Mountain early on the 11th to see if the Nez Perces were safely out of the area. A dust cloud 30 miles to the south, just where the trail along the west side heads the valley, showed in which direction the Indian cavalcade was moving. Satisfied with what they had seen, Blodgett and Sherrill went down to the siege area, saddled their horses, which had been brought there the previous evening with the wagon train, and rode over to the site of the village to assist the burial parties in looking for the bodies of soldiers and volunteers killed in the fighting there.

---

[1]Edgar Stewart includes this in his "Letters from the Big Hole," in *The Montana Magazine Of History*, October, 1952, pp. 55-6.

[2]Mark Brown, *The Flight of the Nez Perce* (New York: G. P. Putnam's Sons, 1967), p. 261. G. O. Shields is wrong in his statement that Wilson *"reached his destination a few hours after Edwards."* See *The Battle Of The Big Hole* (Chicago and New York: Rand, McNally & Company, Publishers, 1889), p. 76, or Brady's *Northwestern Fights And Fighters*, pp. 189-90; he came in 31 hours later. Pvt. Homer Coon also erred in picturing Wilson as a courier to General Howard on the night of the 10th ("The Outbreak of Chief Joseph," Yale Library typescript, n.d., p. 4.); however, he probably took Gibbon's message to the wagon train on the night of the 9th, from whence it was carried on by one of the citizen volunteers.

[3]Department of the Army, *Medal Of Honor* (Washington: Government Printing Office, 1948). Prior to World War I, the criteria for awards of the Congressional Medal of Honor were less strict, and it was sometimes given for acts which would rate a bronze star in this century.

At that time, General Oliver O. Howard's advance party of cavalry, with its screen of Bannock Indian scouts in front, was descending Trail Creek when Chief Robbins signaled from a bare ridge to the left of the track that there was something ahead. While the column waited, Howard rode onto the ridge with his aide-de-camp, Lieutenant C. S. Wood, to see what the scouts had found. Below were soldiers *"going from the smoke there, under the hill, back and forth to the creek."* He was looking down from where the howitzer had been fired during the battle, and could see *"a party bathing in the stream; some dressing, some sitting on the bank, and others moving about, wading in the shallow water."*[4]

Howard reached the siege area just after 10 o'clock in the morning, to find it looking,

> . . . like a hospital at first, though there were lines of rifle-pits, and well soldiers enough to give one the impression of a heavy hospital guard. So many wounded; nearly half lying cheerful, though not able to move; many white bandages about the head and face; some arms in slings; there were roughly constructed shelters from the heat of an unrelenting August sun. Quite on the other side, in the northeast corner of the camp [site 18], reclined the wounded commander.[5]

From down in the meadow Tom Sherrill saw General Howard's Bannock scouts galloping down the ridge toward the siege area. He mistook them for Nez Perces charging the camp, and, having a good horse, made a run for the entrenchments. Upon finding that the Indians wore white plumes in their head dress and were friendly Bannocks, he went back to the meadow and the grim task of recovering bodies.

> Campbell Mitchell was the first citizen found. He was killed among the lodges near the upper part of the Indian camp [stake M-92]. He was lying face down, his arms stretched out full length, with five wounds in his back, stripped of all his clothes. It looked like the squaws had run an iron through him in those five places.[6]

Since two of the volunteers had died in the willows between the village and the siege area,

> John Miller and I rode down into the brush to look for Lockwood's brother [Alvin], who was the first or second man killed [second volunteer; Dave Morrow was first] . . . We found him — he was shot through the head and hips, and his left thumb was shot off. We got two more men, and put him on a saddle blanket and carried him

---

[4]O. O. Howard, *Nez Perce Joseph* (Boston: Lee and Shepard Publishers, 1881), p. 202. Wood mentions, rather inaccurately, that *"Some naked and mutilated bodies of our people were passed, a howitzer wheel was found . . ."* See, "Chief Joseph, The Nez Perce," in *Century Magazine*, May, 1884, p. 139. He saw the body of Corporal Sale, naked but not mutilated.

[5]*Nez Perce Joseph*, p. 203.

out where Mitchell was, and buried them both together. Some of the other boys buried Dave Morrow and John Armstrong.[7]

Meanwhile, *"Bunch"* Sherrill was in the lower end of the village searching for Dave Morrow and there recovered the body of Lieutenant James Bradley.

> . . . the first man killed, being shot through the heart. The day we buried our dead, I found Bradley where the Indians had put him, in the creek. He was stripped clean, lying face down, in about fifteen inches of water. I took his pants that the Indians had left on the bank and got them around him, and pulled him out of the water. He looked very natural, as the cold water had preserved him. The Indians treated our dead good, as none of them were mutilated.[8]

In general, volunteers buried volunteers and soldiers buried soldiers, with Captain Comba in charge of the latter. That must have been a particularly hard assignment for him as Captain Logan was his father-in-law. Mark Brown thinks that all the soldier dead were buried on the bench, just south of the soldier monument, but there is reason to believe that was not done until six weeks later, when Lieutenant Van Orsdale returned to rebury the remains dug up and scattered by wild animals.

Corporal Loynes indicates that they found their *"dead comrades stripped of all their clothing, with their bodies swollen to nearly twice their normal size from the heat of the sun,"* adding that, *"They were buried as best we could at that time . . ."*[9] All they had to work with were the few shovels borrowed from Hugh Kirkendall's freight wagons, and, considering the urgency and the difficulty of transporting bodies in that condition across the swamp, it is likely they did the expedient thing by burying them *"on site"* — as some indirect evidence hints.

P. W. Norris, the Superintendent of Yellowstone Park, visited the Big Hole battlefield in the late Fall of 1878 in the hope of recovering the remains of Lieutenant Bradley for burial at Stryker, Ohio, his former home. He wrote: *". . . alas! the bones of that friend of other days and scenes had been dragged from their*

---

[6]Tom Sherrill, as told to A. J. Noyes, "The Battle of the Big Hole As I Saw It," n.d., typescript in the collection of the Montana Historical Society, p. 23.

[7]*Ibid.*

[8]M. F. *"Bunch"* Sherrill, as told to A. J. Noyes, 1916. Montana Historical Society manuscript SC-739, p. 6. A peculiar error has appeared concerning Bradley's death. One writer has stated, "the bullet passed through a book the young lieutenant happened to be carrying in his breast pocket. The bullet riddled original is on display at the Montana Historical Society, Helena." An inquiry in 1989 located the book in the Society's Bradley collection, and it proved to be a copy of Volume I of *Contributions To The Historical Society Of Montana* (1876), which was presented to Bradley by Granville Stuart, April 19, 1877. When found in a Butte second-hand store, a hole — which may, or may not be a bullet hole — was noticed entirely through the front cover close to the spine, yet the contents were untouched. Such a hole could only have been made by a bullet when the cover was open; the claim that Bradley was carrying the book at the time of his death is otherwise ridiculous from the size of the volume — 7 by 9 inches and rather hefty!

[9]Charles N. Loynes, "Battle of the 'Big Hole,'" in *Winners of the West*, March, 1925, p. 7.

shallow resting-place amid the willows, near where he fell, by ravenous beasts who still haunted the field." And so, he had to return to a grieving father with nothing more than that "*mouldering plate and headboard, carved on the field of gore. By sword of faithful comrade, — His name and date, — no more.*"[10]

In 1964 a remnant of an army boot or shoe was found on the firing line where the men of Captain Sanno paused to fire several volleys into the apex of the Nez Perce camp [see the encampment map]. A metal locator search was made in that vicinity the following summer, and a hot reading was received from under some willow sticks. It came from a sardine tin imbedded in a tan subsoil (the meadow loam at that point is black). Upon retrieving the can — a crudely soldered container and obviously old — there was another signal from beneath the subsoil. It came from two .45-70 Government cartridge cases which were lying on undisturbed meadow soil. Clearing away the dead willow canes exposed a shallow depression three by eight feet in extent from which the subsoil had come. It had the appearance of a grave, so a test transect was made across the center. The indication was that the "*grave ,*" if such it was, had been emptied.

A logical explanation for the apparent absence of remains in the pit, would appear to be that it was a temporary burial site of a soldier killed in the attack on the village (possibly the one killed by Wahlitits or his wife; the location is about right). Removal of the clothing by the Indians, a practice mentioned too frequently to be accidental, would account for the shoe remnant nearby (it has been identified as a Model 1872 military issue), and the subsoil overlaying the cartridge cases indicates the hole was dug *after* the battle. Lt. Van Orsdale returned to the battlefield via Deer Lodge in September 1877, for the particular purpose of reburying the dead reported to have been exposed by wild animals, and may have supplemented the unimaginative army ration of his eight-man detachment with such "*quick foods*" as he could obtain from the stores in Missoula and Deer Lodge. The hand-made sardine tin could have provided part of a grave-side lunch for the men who moved those remains to the burial site in the siege area. Two similar cans have been recovered at the siege area — from a point close to where the mass reburial is supposed to have taken place.[11]

---

[10]Philetus W. Norris, "The Warrior's Grave", in *The Calumet Of The Coteau* (Philadelphia: J. B. Lippincott & Co., 1884), Pp. 123, 198 & 207. There is a monument in the Stryker, Ohio, Cemetery marked "*James H. Bradley Killed At The Battle Of Big Hale [sic] Mont Aug. 9, 1877 Aged 33 Y. 2 M. 14 D.,*" and below that is carved, in fresher lettering, "*Catherine Bradley 1824 - 1914*".

[11]Aubrey L. Haines, "Report on Historical Research Accomplished at Big Hole National Battlefield During 1965," February 25, 1966, p. 7. Big Hole National Battlefield library. The availability of canned sardines at Deer Lodge is confirmed by an item in *The New North-West*, August 17, 1877: p. 4.

According to Colonel Gibbon, *"all [dead] were found, recognized and decently interred,"* with the killed listed as follows:

SEVENTH INFANTRY
Company A
Captain William Logan; Private John B. Smith.
Company B
1st Lieutenant James H. Bradley.
Company D
Corporal William H. Payne; Corporal Jacob Eisenhut; Musician Francis [Michael] Gallagher.
Company E
Private Mathew Butterly.
Company F
Private William D. Pomroy [Pomeroy]; Private James McGuire.
Company G
1st Sergeant Robert L. Edgeworth; Sergeant William H. Martin; Corporal Domminick O'Connor [Dominick O'Conner]; Corporal Robert E. Sale; Private [F.] John O'Brien; Private Gottleib Manz [Mantz].
Company H
Private [G.] McKindra L. Drake.
Company I
Sergeant Michael Hogan; Corporal Daniel McCaffrey [McCafferey]; Private Herman Broetz.
Company K
1st Sergeant Frederick Stortz; Musician Thomas [P.] Stinebaker; Artificer John Kleis.

SECOND CAVALRY
Company L
Sergeant Edward Page.

CITIZEN VOLUNTEERS
John Armstrong; L. [Lynde] C. Elliot [Elliott]; Alvin Lockwood; Campbell Mitchell; David Morrow.

FORT SHAW POST GUIDE
H. O. Bostwick.

The total killed was 29, not including 2 — 1st Lieutenant William L. English, and Sergeant William W. Watson — who died later in the hospital.[12]

---

[12]John Gibbon, "Report of battle of Big Hole, M. T., Aug. 9, 1877, with list of killed and wounded," dated at Fort Shaw, M. T., Sept. 20, 1877, pp. 15-18 (National Archives, RG-94, Doc. 3595 DD 1877). This listing is in error in showing Musician Gallagher as *"Francis"*; it was Michael who was killed. His brother, Francis, was a private in Company F. The inscription on the soldier monument placed in the siege area in 1883 is correct.

No accurate count of the number of Nez Perces killed in the battle is possible for several reasons: the whites did not see all the bodies because some were secretly buried and others were carried from the field mortally wounded to die at some other place, and the Nez Perces relied mainly on memory to preserve the record of their loss. Some idea of the divergent estimates obtained from both white and Nez Perce participants is evident in the following counts:

Colonel John Gibbon reported 83 dead Indians were found by Captain Comba's burial parties, which, with 6 additional dead *"found in a ravine some distance from the battlefield"* made a total of 89.[13] It remains the best estimate by a white participant in the battle.

1st Lieutenant John Van Orsdale, who returned to the battlefield in the latter part of September for the purpose of reburying those dead soldiers reported to have been exposed by animals and Indians, also made a count of Nez Perce remains, finding *"more than eighty (80) scattered from a point one mile below where the lower end of their Camp rested at the time of the battle to a point opposite the rifle pits . . . Said number included those visible or partially so. "*[14]

There are no other estimates by white participants or observers of the battlefield with sufficient standing to be worth repeating. However, for some time after the battle the public press carried estimates from various sources — often no more than hearsay — putting the Nez Perce loss as high as 125; but it is unlikely any of those figures were based on systematic counts.

A number of counts of the Indian dead obtained from Nez Perce sources have been summarized by McWhorter: Wottolen's count is the smallest — 43, and Peopeo Tholekt's is only a little larger at 50, though he contradicted that at another place by saying *"near one hundred. "* Wounded Head, who tallied the deaths on his buffalo drinking horn, could account for 63, and Yellow Bull remembered 74, including 33 men. When Duncan McDonald visited White Bird's band in Canada the following year, a count of 78 was obtained (tallied with bits of sticks). Chief Joseph, in his own story, as published in the *North American Review* in 1879, put the Nez Perce loss at *"fifty women and children and thirty warriors"* for a total of 80. Out of those widely divergent figures, McWhorter could only presume that there was an actual loss of somewhere between 60 and 90 lives.[15]

Upon his arrival at the siege area at 10 a.m., General Howard was invited to lunch with Colonel Gibbon, who had *"bread and to spare"* after getting his wagons down to the siege area. Howard described the meal as *"good enough for a soldier, "* and afterward, though Gibbon found the saddle painful, they rode over to the village for a look around.

Very little effort was expended by the burial parties in covering those of the Nez Perce dead inadequately buried by their relatives. J. W. Redington, later one

---

[13]*Ibid.*, p. 13. The basis of this estimate was a count of 40 bodies found on half the battlefield.

[14]Lieut. J. L. Van Orsdale, Letter to the Post Adjutant, Post Near Missoula, M. T., from Deer Lodge, M. T., Sept. 29th, 1877. Copy in Big Hole National Battlefield library.

[15]L. V. McWhorter, *Hear Me, My Chiefs!*, Ruth Bordin, ed. (Caldwell, Idaho: Caxton Printers, 1983), pp. 393, 402-03.

of General Howard's white scouts, confused this matter in after-years, when he told an interviewer:

> After the fight at the Big Hole, the soldiers laid out about eighty Nez Perce bodies alongside the river and caved the bank in on them. That was the way we buried them. After they were buried some of the Bannocks rooted around in the loose earth until they found a head, then they scalped it, but they didn't actually take any tool and dig the bodies out. That would have been too much work for an Indian, besides they didn't have any shovels. They only used their hands to push the dirt aside.[16]

Of course, Redington, who did not join General Howard's command until much later, had no first-hand knowledge of the work of the burial parties; he merely assumed that Gibbon's men put the dead Nez Perces under the river bank from what he saw at the battlefield as he passed hurriedly by on his way to join Howard's command, but it is more likely they were buried that way by the Nez Perces prior to leaving the village on the 9th. Their hasty and inadequate effort is what Howard referred to when he stated: *"We found, just under the river bank, a part of the Indians unburied, and fresh marks of the hasty burial of others."* The General indicates that some of his people attempted to decently cover the exposed bodies, and that futile effort is recounted in this romantic style:

> See these women's bodies disinterred by our own ferocious Bannock scouts! See how they pierce and dishonor their poor, harmless forms, and carry off their scalps! Our officers sadly look upon the scene, and then, as by a common impulse, deepen their beds, and cover them with earth. Poor Jack Carleton hardly dared own his motive for his hard work in the burying of so many people, with poor instruments, and too little help. "Oh, general," he says, "let us bury them; the settlers on the Big Hole below will desert their ranches if we leave 'em here."[17]

Amos Buck seems to be responsible for a story, concerning the first Nez Perce killed, which is definitely not true. He wrote: *"Strange to say, when the Nez Perces buried their dead, they would not touch their medicine man. He was left on the trail unburied. When Howard's scouts were taken to him they jumped off their horses and each gave a kick, saying, 'No good medicine man.'"*[18] But when L. C. McWhorter took that up with Yellow Wolf, the old warrior stated very positively:

---

[16]Arthur Woodward, "A Brief Account of the Services of J. W. Redington in the Nez Perce Campaign of 1877," p. 10. Typescript in the history file of Yellowstone National Park (1934). Mark Brown has much to say about this brash and inept youngster in *The Flight Of The Nez Perce*, p. 272; cited in Note 2.

[17]*Nez Perce Joseph*, pp. 204 & 210-11; cited in Note 4.

[18]Amos Buck, "Review of the Battle of the Big Hole," in *Contributions To The Historical Society Of Montana*, Vol. 7, 1910, pp. 127-28.

Natalekin [Wetistokaith], killed when going to look after his horses in early morning — first Indian killed — was not a medicine man. Was just a common man, too old to engage in fighting. He could not see very well. He was not buried, because there was no time to bury those killed outside the main battlefield.[19]

Medical assistance for Colonel Gibbon's wounded reached the battlefield during the forenoon of August 12th. Major Charles T. Alexander (surgeon) and Captain Jenkins A. FitzGerald (assistant-surgeon) had, by hard riding, managed to gain five hours on Major Mason's cavalry from whence they came with a mule load of medical supplies. Though weary and hungry, they went right to work dressing wounds and soon had the smell of *"ether"* mingling with the odor of wood smoke in the siege area.[20]

According to Dr. FitzGerald, *"We found a horrible state of affairs. There were 39 wounded men without Surgeons or dressings, and many of them suffering intensely. "*[21] All the doctors were able to do at that time was to probe and dress the wounds, and prepare the men for transportation.

The remainder of General Howard's cavalry having arrived on the 12th, his pursuit of the fleeing Nez Perces was resumed the following day. The column was strengthened by the addition of fifty of Gibbon's men, who volunteered to go as far as the stage road under Captain Browning and lieutenants Van Orsdale and Wright. Colonel Gibbon dismissed the civilian volunteers, and, with the remainder of his command in Hugh Kirkendall's rough freight wagons, or carried on travois, began the journey to Deer Lodge.

Corporal Loynes has this to say about the travois: *". . . skinning the dead ponies lying around, we cut the hides into strips and braiding them over the poles, improvised what is termed a travois, upon which we laid our wounded, the other end dragging upon the ground, where a soldier walked for the purpose of lifting it while crossing streams or when the ground was too rough. "*[22]

A. J. Noyes, who was driving a Concord wagon in the relief party that came out from Butte in response to Gibbon's plea for help recalled that they *"met Gen. Gibbon and his wounded at the point of the "hog-back" between the north and south forks of the Big Hole . . . "*

He was sitting by a bunch of willows when Major Clark and I walked up to see him. Clark introduced himself and said: "You had a hard fight, General." "I tell you, Major Clark, that we hadn't been in that fight but a short time when I thought it would be another Custer massacre, and to tell the truth there is only one reason, in my mind, why it was not. When we left Missoula we had trowel bayonets issued to us; these were used . . . to dig holes into which we got for protec-

---

[19] *Yellow Wolf* (Caldwell, Idaho: The Caxton Printers, 1986), p. 127.

[20] "Battle of the Big Hole," p. 7; cited in Note 9. See also, "Report of Brigadier-General O. O. Howard . . .," August 27, 1877 (National Archives, RG-94; Microfilm 666-336).

[21] *The Flight Of The Nez Perce*, p. 263; cited in Note 2.

tion. If it hadn't been for them, none of us, in my opinion, would have lived to tell the tale."[23]

The relief operation launched by the people of Deer Lodge, Helena and Butte was a generous response to the plea for help carried by Billy Edwards. The news of the Big Hole disaster reached Helena by telegraph at 9 o'clock on Saturday morning, the 11th. Concerned citizens immediately organized an ambulance which left Helena early in the afternoon with doctors Thomas Reece and William L. Steele, accompanied by hospital attendants Pope, Millrun and Stipe, and another vehicle left at nearly the same time with Father Palladino and two Sisters of Charity.

The people of Deer Lodge, mindful of Gibbon's request for an armed guard, mustered Captain Stewart's militia company and were in the Big Hole with Dr. Armistead H. Mitchell and 20 ambulances and spring wagons by noon the next day. Editor Mills noted that the Chinese of the city contributed liberally toward assisting the wounded, *"and do it cheerfully."*[24]

At Butte, Major William A. Clark also called out the militia, though not all were willing to go again (many having marched that way before to no good purpose), and contributions amounting to $412 were gathered for the purchase of medicines and other supplies. The Butte company reached French Gulch Sunday night, adding 42 men, five vehicles, two surgeons — doctors James Wheelock and O'Dillon B. Whitford — and commissary stores for 20 days to the gathering expedition.

The hospital supplies provided the corps of five doctors included 4 gallons of brandy, 2 gallons of whiskey, 50 yards of bleached muslin for bandages, some lint, 2 cases of surgical instruments, $75 worth of medicines, and a case each of strawberries, peaches, oysters and sardines.[25]

Monday morning, the 13th, the rescuers met a courier about 15 miles north of the battlefield,[26] informing them that Gibbon had started with his wounded, and soon his train of heavy freight wagons and nearly as rough Indian-style travois with the serious cases appeared. The wounded were then transferred to the easier-riding spring wagons and Concords for the remainder of the journey to Deer Lodge.

Alva Noyes states that *"Gen. Gibbon and his son-in-law, Lt. Jacobs, were furnished a team and buggy and left at once for Deer Lodge,"* where he arrived on the 15th. Captain Rawn was left in charge of the slow moving hospital train,

---

[22]"Battle of the Big Hole," p. 8; cited in Note 9.

[23]Alva J. Noyes, *The Story Of Ajax* (New York: Buffalo Head Press, 1966), p. 33.

[24]"Local Brevities," in *The New North-West*, Deer Lodge, M. T., August 17, 1877.

[25]"To the Rescue," *Ibid.*

[26]"Lost in the Mountains," *Ibid.*, August 31, 1877. J. W. Redington, who was then passing himself off as a correspondent for a Salt Lake City newspaper, left the concourse of rescuers where they waited for Gibbon's wounded, and proceeded alone to the battlefield and then along the track of Howard's command until he became thoroughly lost, reappearing several adventures later as a scout for General Howard. Mark Brown considers his tale *"windy."*

which made only five miles before camping for the night at Doolittle Creek (*"it was early in the afternoon but the wounded needed attention"*). That was Noyes first experience with wounded men; *"Frank and I had a sergeant, Watson by name, who was shot through the hips, also calf of one leg. The wagon behind us had Lieut. Wm. English. "*[27]

The *"Personal"* column in *The New North-West* of August 17 noted that *"At camping time, when all others went for the commissary stores, the surgeons went to work, satisfied with a bite of hardtack and bacon when the work was done;"* and another item mentioned a *"Mr. William, who acted as surgeon for the wounded soldiers until the arrival of the relief party,"* noting, also, that *"The boys speak highly of him. "* Could this have been William Woodcock, the man-servant of Lieutenant Jacobs? It seems quite likely, in view of the fact that Gibbon referred to Woodcock only by his first name in mentioning his part in the howitzer incident.

The wagon train stopped for the second night on Seymour Creek, and for the third on Mill Creek, near the fine brick home of Mr. and Mrs. Morgan Evans, and there, the women of the household tore up bed sheets made from Irish linen to make dressings for the wounded.[28] On the last day, as the slow procession approached Deer Lodge, the wife of Lieutenant English met them. Noyes says, *"Her's must have been a stout heart, or she had been told to be very cheerful on her husband's account. She climbed into the wagon, saying in a cheerful voice: 'How are you, Willie?' She stayed with him through the balance of that ride to town. "* [29]

The wounded arrived in Deer Lodge at mid-day on the 16th after three and a half days travel averaging nearly 26 miles per day. Uncomfortable at best, it was an excruciatingly painful journey for some. A vacant building had been prepared to serve as a hospital for the men with relatively minor wounds, and the others were taken to St. Joseph's Hospital — the first hospital in Montana Territory designed for surgical and medical treatment. Only recently completed by the Sisters of Charity, it was a two-story, frame building with twelve rooms for patients.[30]

Colonel Gibbon spoke for all in the statement he gave the local paper the afternoon of the 17th (too late for inclusion in that issue of what was then a weekly):

> I desire to return the heartfelt thanks of myself and my command
> to the citizens of Deer Lodge, Helena and Butte, for the prompt liberal
> assistance forwarded to us in the Big Hole Bason [sic]. By the speedy
> help sent us and the sympathy and care shown the wounded since their

---

[27]*The Story Of Ajax*, p. 34; cited in Note 23.

[28]F. Quinn, "Big Hole Battle . . .," in *The Montana Standard*, Butte, August 10, 1958, Sec. B, p. 1 (See the text which provides a caption for the photograph of the Evans house.)

[29]*The Story Of Ajax*, pp. 34-5; cited in Note 23. Mrs. English was the former Kate Murray of Jacksonville, Illinois — married only four months and also pregnant!

arrival in Deer Lodge, the people of this section have endeared themselves to us in a way that can never be forgotten. I wish especially to
acknowledge our obligations to Doctors Mitchell, Steele, Reece,
Wheelock and Whitford, and their assistants, and the Sisters of Charity
who met us on the road and did so much to alleviate our sufferings. As
also to the ladies of Deer Lodge who, since our arrival, have taken the
care of the wounded entirely out of our hands. John Gibbon, Colonel,
7th Infantry, Commanding.[31]

Though in good hands at last, not all the wounded were home free. First
Lieutenant William Lewis English died on *"Monday, August 20, 1877, of wounds
received in the battle of Big Hole,"* and he was given a Masonic burial, with
military honors. Called the finest funeral seen in Montana Territory up to that
time, Editor Mills supplied a requiescat from Sir Walter Scott's *"The Lady of the
Lake"* (xxxi):

> *Soldier rest! thy warfare o'er,*
> *Sleep the sleep that knows not breaking;*
> *Dream of battlefields no more,*
> *Days of danger, nights of waking.*

The lieutenant's body was later removed to Jacksonville, Indiana, where he
now rests with his faithful Kate beside him; she never remarried.

On Thursday, the 29th, the flags were flown at half-mast in memory of *"Sgt.
William Watson, Company F, Seventh Infantry, who had his left hip shattered in
the fight with the Nez Perces on Big Hole, [and who] died at the Sister's Hospital
at Deer Lodge on Wednesday at one o'clock p.m. "*[32]

Those were the only post-battle deaths, but some of the wounded were a long
time healing. Three months later, when Colonel Gibbon sent ambulances to take
the convalescents back to Fort Shaw, three soldiers remained behind for further
treatment: Private Charles Alberts, wounded by a ball which shattered a rib and
passed through the lower lobe of the right lung, remained behind for further
operations to remove bone fragments; Private James C. Lehmer, wounded by a ball
which struck the sole of his foot and passed up the leg to the knee, had twice
undergone amputation and religature, and was still in no condition to travel; while
Private Joseph Devoss, with an ankle completely shattered by a ball, remained in
the hospital with amputation probable in the near future.

Among those who were able to return to Fort Shaw on November 18th were
several whose recovery verged on the miraculous. No small part of that miracle
could be credited to Doctor Steele, whose deft trauma surgery was perfected
patching-up construction workers injured in the building of several western

---

[30]Paul C. Phillips, *Medicine In The Making Of Montana* (Missoula: Montana State University
Press, 1962), p. 173.
[31]"Local News," in *The New North-West*, Deer Lodge, M. T., August 24, 1877.
[32]"Local Brevities," *Ibid.*, August 31, 1877.

railways. His most famous surgery, which gained him a flattering reputation, occurred enroute to the hospital. Working on into the night by kerosene lantern, the chloroform and ether were soon exhausted; but the operating went on with wagonmaster Hugh Kirkendall holding the patients for the surgeon.[33]

In addition to the three soldiers remaining at St. Joseph's Hospital in November, there was Myron Lockwood, who was financially ruined as well as desperately wounded. General of the Army William T. Sherman visited the men hospitalized at Deer Lodge on September 1st, and noted:

> . . . one citizen badly wounded through the hip and groin, Lockwood, deserves special mention, for he was a pure volunteer, lost his brother in battle, and had his farm pillaged by the Indians, and his stock, mostly if not all, used by the pursuing troops. Genl Gibbon speaks of him in high terms of his courage, and services, and will do all that is possible to secure him pay for what he has lost, and meantime will pay his charges at the hospital during convalescence, which may be slow and leave him a cripple for life.[34]

The Deer Lodge and Butte militiamen who accompanied the ambulances into the Big Hole found they were not needed as a guard, and, not having had their fill of Indian fighting, most elected to go with Major Clark in an attempt to join General Howard's column less than a day ahead. That they did, but found service under the general not to their liking and returned along the stage road, ending the participation of Montana volunteers in that Indian war.

Al Noyes, who was on the way to rejoin the militiamen after driving the Concord wagon containing Sergeant Watson to Deer Lodge, met the stage and was hailed by Major Clark, who was on the box with the driver.

> "Hello, Al, where are you going?" "After Indians." He began to laugh and said: "I guess you had better go home, as the Indian war is over, so far as we are concerned. We overtook Gen. Howard on Horse Prairie, camped one night with him and were pulling out independently the next morning, when he informed us we were under him if we went to the front. I explained that I was independent — under no one. He replied that I must go with him or go back, so we left his command and started for Butte. You will soon meet the boys as they are but a short distance behind."[35]

Not all the Montana volunteers who declined to serve under General Howard went home by the stage road. *"Five or six of the party wishing to see the scene of Gibbon's famous fight left their comrades at Bannack and proceeded up Grasshopper Creek and across the range to Big Hole."* They were unable to

---

[33]*Medicine In The Making Of Montana*, p. 88; cited in Note 30.

[34]Letter, Sherman, to Geo. W. McCrary, Secretary of War, September 3, 1877 (National Archives, 3464 AGO 1877; Microfilm 666-339).

[35]*The Story Of Ajax*, p. 35; cited in Note 23.

examine the battlefield proper because of the overpowering stench of putrefying corpses, but they did see several dead Nez Perces in the river below the site of the village, and, more important from their viewpoint, they were able to gather up seventeen abandoned Indian horses. The editor of the Butte newspaper in commenting on their "good fortune," remarked (with a smile, I am sure) that *"Travellers who have visited the Nez Perces on their reservation declare they have in their band full blooded Arabian horses, and that some are worth as much as $40,000. The horses captured by our boys are full blooded cayuses and are believed by competent judges to be worth something less than $40,000 apiece. "* [36]

When Gibbon dismissed the Bitterroot volunteers following the battle, some went with General Howard's column, and some started home. Tom Sherrill was among the latter and they had gone about ten miles when they met some settlers from the valley, *"with a wagon load of everything that was good to eat, which had been prepared by the settler's wives, and with many articles for the wounded. "* Since they had had nothing but hardtack and coffee for some time, they stopped for a feast, and, with no one remaining at the battlefield, the grub wagon turned around and all continued toward the Bitterroot Valley. Near the Continental Divide, they met some more settlers who wanted to see the battlefield and also catch up with the wounded, so Tom went back with them.

> After we had a bite to eat, we all went down and looked over the field until the boys were satisfied. Then we went to the camp, spread down our blankets, and went to sleep. The only thing left to break the stillness of the night was a lone Indian dog, whose master had been killed. Every little while the dog would put up a howl. Poor fellow! He was master of the ground, [which] three days before was the [scene] of a desperate and bloody struggle.[37]

When they left the following day, the Nez Perce dog still guarded the lonely battlefield.

---

[36]"To The Rescue," in *The Butte Miner*, August 14, 1877. Shields adds that a *"citizen volunteer"* picked up 32 buffalo robes, several of which were *"badly stained with blood,"* and sold them at Helena as relics of the battle (see, *The Battle Of The Big Hole*, pp. 80-81; cited in Note 2.

[37]"The Battle of the Big Hole As I Saw It," p. 26; cited in Note 6.

Chapter 8

AFTERMATH OF BATTLE

In one way a battle is a moment in time, existing briefly on its own bloody field for some great national purpose — at least there *ought* to be a such a purpose behind it; but the *New York Times*, in its editorial, "A Lesson from the Nez Perces," was quick to demolish that idea:

> Now that the Nez Perce War has ended in victory, thanks to the energy and courage of our much enduring Army, it is worth while before it passes out of mind to ask why it was fought. We freely express the opinion that the Nez Perce War was, on the part of our government, an unpardonable and frightful blunder. A crime whose victims are alike hundreds of our gallant officers and men who fell prey to Nez Perce bullets, and the peaceful bands who were goaded by injustice and wrong to take the war path. It is greatly to be regretted that the immediate responsibility for the occurrence was so obscurely distributed that it is difficult to bring anybody to account for it at the bar of public opinion . . . Joseph, who held back for months, and to the last from a resort to which the peaceful Nez Perce were repugnant, at length counseling with his brother non-treaty chiefs, and seeing soldiers assembling to drive him from his home, desperately plunged into war; a war which, on our part, was in its origin and motive, nothing short of a gigantic blunder and a crime.[1]

But in another way, a battle is also an epicenter, generating shock waves felt both to a distance and over many years — influencing group fortunes, of course, but also deranging individual lives and setting in motion events to bless or trouble their futures. In its own very small way, the Battle of the Big Hole was such a happening. Its influence on the lives of many white survivors was great; but, for the non-treaty Nez Perces, it was universally calamitous, both as a group and individually, though the lack of written records and accounts tends to obscure its effect on the lives and fortunes of individuals. Also, for the Indians it was but an incident in a war of broader scope, so that it is mostly unclear how much of their individual misfortune can be charged directly to the battle; but, for most white participants, it *was* the war, with a clear-cut relationship to the futures of many.

The only blessing which can be attributed to the battle was its effect on the military careers of surviving officers and some enlisted men. In his official report, Colonel Gibbon stated:

> For the officers engaged in this sharp little affair, I have nothing to ask, and am unable to persuade myself to ask for that next to nothing,

---

[1]*New York Times*, October 15, 1877.

a brevet. But I earnestly urge that the authorities may ask Congress the enactment of a special law giving officers below the grade of Field officer and soldiers wounded in battle the same increase of pay as they are now entitled to for every five years of service; the law to go into effect from the commencement of the present fiscal year.[2]

As far as the officers were concerned, they had to be content with *"that next to nothing,"* the brevet (an honorary promotion without increase in pay or authority), which, in this case, came too late to be much of an honor. By the time the brevets *"for gallant service in action against Indians at Big Hole, Mont., 9 Aug. 1877"* were allowed — February 27, 1890 — three of the officers who survived the battle were dead and all but five of the others had gained an equivalent or higher rank before the honor was bestowed. Two of the five who were so fortunate as to receive a brevet rank above their service rank were in that position only because they had each been breveted three times during the Civil War and had profited from the accumulation of honors. The lucky ones were Captains Sanno and Coolidge, who could embellish their signatures with *"Brevet Major,"* if they chose to, while Captain Jackson and Major Comba could likewise use *"Brevet Lieutenant-Colonel."*

It can be added that career officers could look forward to a retirement which was only genteel poverty, and their widows to even less. Captain Constant Williams served in the Civil War, was twice wounded in the Big Hole battle, and retired May 25, 1907, with the rank of brigadier general; yet, upon his death in 1922, after devoting *"practically his entire life to the military service of the United States,"* his wife, Cornelia, was left to subsist on a pension of $30 per month. A bill for her relief stated that *"on account of age and physical disabilities the claimant is unable to perform any manual labor,"* and,

> In view of all the facts, it is believed that Congress should grant the claimant a substantial increase of pension in appreciation of the long and faithful service of her husband. The allowance of increase of pension to the rate of $50 per month is fully warranted and it is so recommended.[3]

Six enlisted men received awards of the Congressional Medal of Honor: Private Lorenzo D. Brown, Company A, 7th Infantry, a 25 year old recruit from North Carolina, who *"continued to do duty in a most courageous manner, after having been severely wounded in the right shoulder,"* Private Wilfred Clark, Company L, 2nd Cavalry, from Philadelphia, Penn., who showed *"conspicuous gallantry, especial skill as a sharpshooter;"* Sergeant William D. Edwards, Company F, 7th Infantry, a Brooklyn lad mentioned for *"outstanding bravery in action"*; Musician John McLennon, Company A, 7th Infantry, a Fort Belknap

---

[2] John Gibbon, "Report of the battle of Big Hole, M.T., Aug. 9, 1877, with list of killed and wounded," Headquarters, District of Montana, Fort Shaw, Sept. 20, 1877. (National Archives, RG-94, Doc. 3595 DD 1877).

[3] File of Captain Constant Williams, Big Hole National Battlefield.

Texan who was cited for *"verifying and reporting the company while subjected to a galling fire from the enemy;"* First Sergeant Patrick Rogan, Company A, 7th Infantry, an immigrant Irishman who *"verified and reported the company while subjected to a galling fire from the enemy,"* and Sergeant Mildon H. Wilson, Company I, 7th Infantry, whose citation included *"gallantry in forming company from line of skirmishers and deploying again under a galling fire,"* as well as the courier service mentioned elsewhere.[4]

Sergeant Wilson was what can only be called an anomaly in the ranks — an overachiever. According to Corporal Loynes, he was not well liked by the men, but his eagerness at Big Hole, and the award it brought him, became the basis of a very long military career. On July 14, 1897, Ordnance Sergeant Mildon H. Wilson was placed on the retired list after 30 years of service, but he did not take his retirement, but remained on active duty. In 1912 he was refused a pension for his Civil War service because he was still in the Army, and he died on February 6, 1924, near his last duty station, Fort Sheridan, Illinois. It seems likely that the army was all he had.[5]

Beyond those few examples, it is hard to find any blessings attributable to the Big Hole battle; but there are more than enough troubled lives that can be traced to it.

In the weeks following Gibbon's fight, the battlefield was visited by many curious people from the Bitterroot Valley and elsewhere. Among those visitors was *"Brother Van"* — Reverend W. W. Van Orsdel, a Methodist minister of the circuit-rider type — who passed by the battlefield in mid-September on his way from Bannack to the Bitterrroot Valley. He was appalled at the sight of *"the bodies of dead soldiers and citizens . . . dug up and dragged, some almost limbless over the field"* by wild animals.[6] As a result, the people of the Valley sent over a party to prepare the citizen dead for removal to cemeteries in the Bitterroot Valley, and Captain Rawn sent Lieutenant John T. Van Orsdale with an 8-man detail to rebury the soldier dead.

The burial detail left Fort Missoula on September 20th, going by way of Deer Lodge, and was back at Deer Lodge on the 29th, from whence the lieutenant reported that he had found fourteen burials disinterred, including those of the officers — Lieutenant Bradley and Captain Logan. The latter being his father-in-law, those remains were brought to Deer Lodge for temporary burial in the local

---

[4]See Chapter 6. The source of the foregoing information is, Department of the Army, *Medal Of Honor* (Washington: Government Printing Office, 1948).

[5]"Biography of Mildon H. Wilson," Big Hole National Battlefield library. An incident related in that file may explain Wilson's single-minded interest in the army. He served the Union two years in the Civil War, then married Miss Sarah Carr in 1866 and returned to the life of an Indiana farmer. But that was not a satisfactory relationship and they separated, with Mildon enlisting at Toledo, Ohio, for a five-year hitch in Company I, 7th Infantry. In 1877, Mrs. Wilson tried to claim a widow's pension from the government on the basis of her husband's presumed death in action against the Sioux during the Yellowstone Campaign of the previous year. Upon learning that he was a very live soldier, and with her credibility shattered, Mildon's *"wife"* disappeared from the record. He never married again.

[6][Letter to the Editor], in *The Weekly Missoulian*, September 21, 1877, p. 3.

cemetery.[7] Exactly where the others were reburied was not stated, but it seems, from several clues, to have been on the edge of the bluff below the siege area (between the Soldier Monument and Battle Gulch).

The best reason for believing that all the burials were finally located there is that statement in Colonel Gibbon's epic poem, written four years after the battle, in which he says,

> *There is the very spot where **English** fell,*
> *Close by the spot where our dead soldiers sleep,*[8]

which, of course, places the graves in the lower end of the siege area (the place where Lieutenant English was mortally wounded is known; site 22).

That surmise is supported by the fact that human remains have been found in the area on several occasions. In 1962, Earle R. Forrest of San Marino, California, who had been employed by the Forest Service on pine beetle control work in that vicinity in 1913, supplied Big Hole National Battlefield with a manuscript he had prepared concerning the battle. In it he had this to say about the burials:

> Along the edge of the battlefield, at the top of the slope down to the river, a row of mounds marked where those fighting men were buried on the field where they had fought . . .   There was something pathetic about those graves of 'Unknown Soldiers' on this wilderness battlefield, for with the exception of officers no record had been made of the men buried in each grave.
>
> As proof of this, a few days before my visit Ranger Keyes [Arthur Keas] had found the skull of a soldier lying beside a grave; but whose it was he never knew for the graves were unmarked. It had been dug up by a pair of badgers that had preempted a homestead on the battlefield; but their young lives were cut short by the ranger's rifle. Keyes thought that the skull might be that of Captain Logan . . .   However, Logan's body had long before been removed to the Custer Battlefield National Cemetery. Keyes later buried the skull in the grave from which it had been unearthed.[9]

Mr. Forrest visited the battlefield on August 8, 1965, and, while there, he took me to the place where he remembered the graves to be (on the point on the

---

[7]Lieut. J. [T] Van Orsdale, Letter to the Post Adjutant, Missoula, M.T., September 29, 1877. Copy in the Big Hole National Battlefield library. Captain Logan's remains were moved to the Custer Battlefield National Cemetery in 1892 and reburied with those of Van Orsdale's wife and infant son in Sec. A, Grave-745.

[8]John Gibbon, *A Vision Of The 'Big Hole,'* privately printed, compliments of Captains J. W. Jacobs and C. A. Woodruff, n. p., [1882], p. 18.

[9]Earle R. Forrest, "The Big Hole Battlefield," 1962, manuscript in the Big Hole National Battlefield Library, pp. 19-20. This material appeared in nearly the same form, and under the same title, in *Frontier Times*, August-September, 1965, pp. 6-9, 56-59. The statement that Ranger Keas *"later buried the skull in the grave from which it had been unearthed,"* does not appear in the magazine article.

right side of Battle Gulch and near the prospect pit; site 48), and he was quite sure the place was right. He also allowed me to copy a photograph he made of the skull in 1913.

Ten days later, Mrs. Arthur (Frances) Keas, of Las Vegas, Nevada, the wife of the former ranger, visited the battlefield during my absence. Seasonal Historian Walter L. Bailey interviewed her, recording, among other things, this information concerning the finding of *two* skulls:

> She found the two skulls, one of which she believed to be the skull of a white man, the other that of an Indian [offering no information as to what criteria she used to determine the race of either skull]. She gave them to her husband and for a long time they were kept and displayed in the Keas' home [the old Battlefield Ranger Station].
>
> After the birth of their baby daughter, the Keas hired a house keeper/nurse who felt very uncomfortable with the skulls in the house. Mr. Keas, therefore, placed the skulls in a bag and stored them in the barn.
>
> One day, while searching for eggs in the barn, Mrs. Keas noticed a hen 'jump' out of the hay loft. She climbed to the loft to recover any eggs that may have been left there. She found the nesting place and after reaching into the crevice, she touched, grabbed, and pulled forth the bag containing the skulls.
>
> To avoid any future encounters with these gruesome relics, Mr. Keas sent the skulls to a museum. (Which museum was unknown to Mrs. Keas.)[10]

Mrs. Keas also remembered that the area in which the skulls were found contained several graves — she was not sure how many — on a point overlooking the North Fork of Big Hole River *"quite close to the soldier monument."* She did not remember any graves on the far (south) side of Battle Gulch.

The appearance, or appearances, of skeletal remains in the siege area after the Battlefield Ranger Station was built in 1912 is not the earliest mention of the finding of human remains in that area. There are two references to earlier *"finds,"* of which the following is the most reliable observation:

> Sunday, the 16th [September, 1901], we visited Big Hole battleground. The thrilling story of that historic event is so well told by the editor of **Recreation** in his book that every reader should have a copy. Just previous to our arrival, a badger had dug into one of the graves on the point and a skull and bones lay exposed to view, thus rudely disturbed after more than 20 years' peaceful rest. Whether white

---

[10]Walter L. Bailey, Memorandum to File H 22, Personal Interview with Mrs. Arthur Keas, August 18, 1965, Big Hole National Battlefield. Mrs. Keas was described as *"a very strong, hardy, and active woman despite her seventy plus years . . . [with] a clear, resonant, almost professional sounding voice, nearly as deep in pitch as a man's. "*

or Indian we could not determine. The monument is much defaced. The badger and the vandal are on the same level of ignorance.[11]

The other report, involving the finding of three skulls by early campers in the siege area, came to light 57 years after the discovery in the course of a conversation Historian Kermit Edmonds had with Selman P. Eldridge, of Victor, Montana. This is what was learned from him:

> Mr. Eldridge came to BHNB in 1907. He camped there with a friend from Minnesota. Sometime during the early evening, while the young companion was dozing, Mr. Eldridge walked down to the foot of the rise on which the Siege Area is found, and stumbled onto three skulls. He said that the ground was swampy and covered with tall grass, underneath which the skulls were encountered, Mr. Eldridge kicking one to the surface accidentally with his foot. The remaining two were found after a brief search by the interested discoverer. He soon brought them up to the camp area and set them at the feet of his sleeping companion, who woke up . . .[12]

It can also be added that an official metal-locator survey in 1964 found a brass suspender clasp adjacent to the Chief Joseph Memorial placed in 1939. Such a regulation clothing item could have been exposed in the course of digging the foundation for the memorial. If it *was* from the clothing of a buried soldier, the implication is that the graves occupied much of the area from the Chief Joseph Memorial [site 12], northward past the memorial to the Indian noncombatant dead [site 13], toward the large battlefield monument, which may have been located with reference to the graves. Unfortunately, we really don't know.

There is an interesting story behind the placing of the little memorial to the Indian noncombatants killed in the battle, and, though it is a digression, it is too good to leave untold. Superintendent Jack Williams sent me a copy of an unsigned letter which he received August 30, 1959, to which he had added a notation in the upper right hand corner, *"I do not have White's permission to use this letter. Hold it confidential."* Since Thain White himself gave the story to the newspapers two years later, it violates no confidence to publish his letter:

Dear Sir:

> Very early Aug. 9 [1951] a good friend and I put the marker in place. We had studied it over for 2 or 3 years . . . The rock came from Kilowatt pass . . . We wanted to put it in the day before 75 years but

---

[11]Westly Jones, "On the Nez Perces Trail," in *Recreation*, July, 1902, pp. 3-10. The large granite monument, weighing six tons, was placed at the battlefield in 1883. It was cut in Concord, New Hampshire, and shipped by rail to Dillon, Montana, from whence it was hauled eighty miles on an ox wagon to the battleground. The original road into the siege area [see siege area map] was built for that particular purpose. General of the Army, William T. Sherman, visited the battlefield that fall to inspect the emplaced monument.

[12]K. Edmonds, Note "per conversation with Mr. Selman P. Eldridge, Victor, Montana," July, 1964. Big Hole National Battlefield library.

found out there probably wouldn't be any [celebration for the 75th anniversary] . . . so we put it on the grounds 1 year before . . .

We assembled a dog goned tin wheel barrow at switch back [on the old road] and it sure made a lot of racket in the dark. It was getting sorta lite and we wheeled the barrow up the hill plus sand, cement, rock, plaque already mounted, gravel, hoe, shovel and a couple of buckets. Mixed the material while my good friend went after water for cement it was dark down in the brush [&] he fell in slough below big monument. While he was doing this I went to Rangers spring and put a yellow pine cone in the inlet. I had thot about this for a couple of years on how to keep the blumin ranger out of there. It took me only a very short time to do it and afterwards after my friend got dry, he made contact with ranger and (maybe it was you was it?). Any way this stopped his water but he told my friend that it was frogs or toads . . .

It only took us ten minutes to get it all done. But I don't think the ranger found out until the afternoon. It was fun . . .

Hope someday NP Service can do a real bang up job at Big Hole. It sort of makes my heart ache . . .

Someday I'll give them Josephs Powder horn that he traded for milk at Stevensville to give to some little Indian children two of them killed at Big Hole.

Be sure to put the Indian side of it in **please . . . a friend**.[13]

Returning to Lieutenant Van Orsdale's reburial party, it had been noted previously that the Nez Perces had not mutilated the soldier dead, as the Sioux had at the Custer Battlefield the previous summer; and in most cases they had not been robbed. Private Coon stated: *". . . even the jewelry on the body of my 1st Sgt. [Robert L. Edgeworth, Company G] and Corporal O'Conner was found by 2nd Lt. Van Orsdale who conducted the burial."*[14] But there was an exception — the little finger of Captain Logan's left hand was gone, evidently in order to remove two rings he habitually wore.

Captain William Logan belonged to a family of Scots who could trace their lineage back to Robert the Bruce, and when he emigrated to America his father gave him a seal ring which had been in the family for many generations. It had *"a dark blue stone setting, with a heart pierced by an arrow engraved thereon, surrounded by the inscription, 'hoc majoram virtus.'"*[15] How that unusual device became the crest of the Logans is an interesting story.

---

[13]Thain White, letter to Superintendent Jack R. Williams, received at Big Hole National Battlefield, August 30, 1959. Copy in the author's file. See also, "Unauthorized Marker Testimony to Death of Indian Women, Children," in *The Great Falls Tribune*, August 10, 1961, p. 17, and "Thain White Admits Putting Monument at Big Hole Battlefield," in *The Flathead Courier*, August 17, 1961.

[14]Homer Coon, "The Outbreak of Chief Joseph," p.5; original manuscript in Coe Collection, Beineke Library, Yale University, New Haven, Conn. Among many Indian peoples mutilation was a favorite method of dishonoring an enemy, since it consigned him to an afterlife in a crippled condition. The Nez Perces did not subscribe to that belief.

[15]"Can They Be Found?," in *The Avant-Courier*, Bozeman, M. T., July 31, 1879.

It was the ambition of Robert the Bruce to make a pilgrimage to the Holy Land, but he was unable to go. Upon his death in 1329, King Robert asked his faithful retainer, Lord James Douglas — the *"Black Douglas"* of border legend — to take his heart to the scene of the crucifixion of Jesus. That dying request was fulfilled. The heart was placed in a silver casket, and, according to legend, in one furious battle with the Saracens, Douglas threw the casket into the thick of the fight, crying: *"Go first, brave heart, in battle, as thou were wont to do, and Douglas will follow thee."* Recovered at last, the casket and heart were found transfixed by an enemy's spear, creating the *"bleeding heart"* so precious to Scottish tradition.

There were two brothers named Logan in that fight; one was killed and the other returned to Scotland where he married the granddaughter of Robert the Bruce, founding a family which took for its crest *"a heart pierced by a passion nail surrounded by a belt bearing the inscription 'Hoc majorum virtus',"* and it was from that illustrious line that Captain Logan was descended.

The other ring which was on Logan's finger was *"a plain band covered with Masonic emblems in enamel."* It was presented to him in Florida where he had been a worshipful master of the Masonic Lodge during his post-Civil War duty there. It was not an heirloom, as the seal ring was, but it, too was important to Captain Logan's family; so, his wife, Odelia, put advertisements seeking recovery of the rings in the *Army And Navy Journal* and in various territorial newspapers. The rings were finally recovered in this manner:

> . . . some three years after the Battle of the Big Hole, a Nez Perce killed by Blackfeet near the Canadian border, wore the seal ring. It passed from hand to hand among the Blackfeet until it finally came into the possession of a trapper. One day when the latter was in Fort Benton, Billy Todd, who knew the story of the rings and was an old friend of Captain Logan, saw the seal band on the trapper's finger, and bought it. Then he sent it to the commanding officer of Cantonment Badlands on the Missouri River (North Dakota), with the request that it be sent to Mrs. Logan. The C. O. [sent] the missing ring to Mrs. Logan in Helena.
>
> For twenty-three years all trace of the Masonic ring was lost until one day in 1900, William R. Logan, a son of Captain Logan, noticed a band ring on a finger of a Piegan squaw who came into his office at the Blackfoot Agency to lodge a complaint. Always on the lookout for his father's ring, Logan recognized the badly worn outlines of Masonic emblems when he examined it. He purchased the ring and turned it over to his mother.
>
> The squaw told him how it came into her possession. Some time after the Battle of the Big Hole, a Piegan hunting party met a band of Nez Perces and several Indians of both tribes were killed in the ensuing battle. A dead Nez Perce wore the Masonic ring, which a Piegan warrior cut from his finger. The Piegan wore the ring until his death,

and then the squaw from whom Logan purchased it, inherited it. She was probably his wife.[16]

It was mentioned earlier that the other officer killed in the Big Hole battle — 1st Lieutenant James H. Bradley — is remembered by a monument in the cemetery at Stryker, Ohio; but it is a virtual certainty that he is not buried there (though his mother may be). Word of Bradley's death reached Fort Shaw by way of the telegraph on the morning of August 11, and it appears that his widow left Fort Shaw hastily; so much so that a news item of the 24th mentioned her arrival on the steamboat *Benton* at Bismarck, Dakota Territory,[17] bound for the home of her father, Dr. Beech, in Atlanta, Georgia. Six years earlier she had arrived in Montana as a bride, with a husband so ill his life was despaired of. He had an infectious malady, probably typhoid fever or Asiatic cholera, for both were common along the Missouri River at that time and more likely to kill than not. So, Mary was urged to leave the doctoring to the hospital stewards. Instead, she bravely nursed her lieutenant through that dangerous illness. *"She could die, she said, but she would not in life separate from him who was her husband, her all . . . "*[18] But death was something else; she took her two daughters and a few clothes and fled from it. The editor could only wish for *". . . consolation to her wounded heart in this her sorest hour of trial. "*

Five years later, the Bozeman newspaper was able to close this particular facet of the after shock of battle, with an announcement: *"The widow of Lieut. Bradley, 7th Infantry, was married recently at Atlanta, Georgia, and is now Mrs. Allen. "*[19]

Concerning the receipt of that first notice of the battle to reach Fort Shaw by telegraph following the arrival of Billy Edwards at Deer Lodge, Mrs. Woodruff, by her own admission, nearly dropped the baby she was carrying in her arms at the shock it created.[20] Somehow, the *Helena Herald* attributed that incident to Mrs. Bradley, and, though the rival *Independent* denied the story (even quoting the messenger to the contrary), its romantic appeal created an enduring myth.

Myron Lockwood, the civilian volunteer who was so grievously wounded during the fighting in the siege area, was left a cripple and unable to return to the ranching which had provided a living for his family. That prospect was even harder to bear from knowing that his wife and five children were left destitute by the damage done to their ranch and personal property by some young men of Chief Toohoolhoolzote's band. Fortunately, the people of Deer Lodge had the solution for his problem, as he acknowledged in an open letter:

---

[16]"The Big Hole Battlefield," p. 58; cited in Note 9.

[17]"Personal," in *The Tri-Weekly Tribune*, Bismarck, D. T., August 24, 1877.

[18]"Lieut. James H. Bradley," in *Helena Daily Herald*, August 13, 1877, p.2.

[19]*The Avant Courier*, March 31, 1882, p.3.

[20]Edgar Stewart, "Letters from the Big Hole," in *The Montana Magazine Of History*, Vol. 2, No. 4 (Oct., 1952), p. 54. See also, Mark Brown, *The Flight of the Nez Perce* (New York: G. P. Putnam's Sons, 1967), pp. 266-67.

To the citizens of Deer Lodge County: . . . alarmed by a possible
hungry and destitute wife and five children, I accepted your generous
offer to send for and maintain my family during my confinement. This
has been handsomely done; they live in Deer Lodge convenient to the
hospital, fully provided with every comfort possible to our peculiar
situation. I am not one who enjoys the receiving of charity, but yield to
what has proven a necessity. I thank you with a gratitude beyond
anything I can put in words and in a couple of months will be on hand
and as active in my duties as a man and citizen as before.[21]

As noted in Chapter 7, General of the Army William T. Sherman visited the
wounded men at St. Joseph's Hospital in September, and took an interest in
Lockwood's case; probably encouraging him to submit a claim for his losses to the
Secretary of War. His letter of October 30, submitted through military channels,
sought a total reimbursement of $1,600 dollars, consisting of $200 for loss of
stock, $300 for loss of forage (trampled wheat and oats), $600 for damage to house
and furnishings, and $500 for miscellaneous expense. Sherman's endorsement
noted, *"I think Lockwood ought to be paid somehow − but in this form it is
impossible. Just two things could be accounted for 'beef & forage'."* He did
suggest, as an expedient, that they could *". . . make vouchers of 'purchases' and
vouchers of 'issues' or expenditures for the first two items of Lockwood's Bill, [and
then] have Lockwood petition Congress for Relief for the other items."*[22]

Under date of December 8, 1877, the foregoing came to Colonel Gibbon with
the comment that *"The Secretary of War concurs in the views of General Sherman
and decides that upon presentation of proper vouchers the amounts due Mr.
Lockwood may be allowed."* But that honest old warrior could not, in good con-
science, do what had been suggested, as his reply indicates:

I have every disposition to assist Mr. Lockwood who has not only
suffered pecuniary loss by Indian depredations, but was badly wounded
in the battle of Big Hole, and is now a great sufferer from his wounds.

But his claim belongs to a large class of similar ones for settling
which, proper vouchers must be furnished.

Unfortunately I know nothing which would enable me to certify to
his loss of stock and forage. They were not used by my troops and of
course could not be certified as "issued". I regret it is not in my power
to put Mr. Lockwood's papers in such shape as to pass the scrutiny of
the Treasury Department and see no other way for this meritorious,
deserving claimant to obtain indemnity for his losses except thr'o an Act
of Congress.[23]

[21]"A Card to the Public," in *The New North-West*, Deer Lodge, M. T., Sept. 14, 1877.
[22]Myron M. Lockwood, St. Jo's Hosp., Deer Lodge, M.T., Oct. 30, 1877, to The Hon. Sec. of
War, Washington, D.C. (thro Hd. Qtrs., Fort Shaw, M.T.). National Archives, Microfilm 666-339.
[23]John Gibbon, Colonel, 7th Infantry, Comdg. District, to Adjutant General, U.S.A. (Thr'o
Headqrs., Dept. of Dakota), Washington, D.C., Dec. 28, 1877. National Archives, Microfilm 666-339.

The Secretary of War did forward a recommendation for the relief of Lockwood, with particulars, to the Speaker of the House, which resulted in House Report No. 804, 45th Cong., 2d Sess., and eventuated in House Bill 4798, Feb. 16, 1878. But there had been no useful result by October 2nd, when his further inquiries were answered by the War Department's Judge Advocate to the effect that the Secretary had, *"at the last session on several occasions recommended Congress to make you some reparation; a copy of one of his letters is herewith enclosed . . . It is to be hoped that Congress will yet take the matter into favorable consideration. "*[24]

A more immediate relief came to Lockwood in June, 1879, with appointment to a position of guard at the United States Territorial Penitentiary at Deer Lodge, where he served a number of years.

William H. *"Billy"* Edwards, the Englishman who carried Gibbon's message to Deer Lodge and thus alerted the people of Montana Territory to the fact that a battle had been fought, was a recognized hero; yet, he did not prosper with the years. He was prospecting in the Big Hole in 1885 when *"Old Man"* Lane (Henry Lane, a prospector who had been chasing golden mirages since 1850) made his strike two miles up Trail Creek from the battlefield. That touched off a *"rush"* which got the usual extravagant comment in the press:

> A Salt Lake company with $25,000 capital as a starter have secured about 1,000 acres across Ruby creek and are preparing for extensive hydraulic mining early in the spring. The country is full of gold . . . Two hundred claims have been taken . . . A town has been laid out by P. H. Poindexter and prominent partners in Dillon . . . a store has been built . . . The town is named Monumental City. It is situated one mile above the well known monument on Gibbon's battlefield.[25]

Billy Edwards signed on as foreman for the mining company, but the *"Mormon diggings,"* as they have since been known, proved unprofitable through inability to separate the gold dust from the bentonitic clay of the Ruby Bench. From there on Billy's future faded away to that day when he sat down on the bank of Bitterroot River, below the Grantsdale bridge, with his pint of whiskey laced with blackberry brandy — and was clubbed to death by an unknown person for an unknown reason.[26]

---

[24]Henry Goodfellow, letter to Myron Lockwood, Stevensville, M.T., Oct. 2, 1878. National Archives, Microfilm 666-340.

[25]"The Big Hole Placer Mines," in *The Livingston Enterprise*, December 26, 1885. The site of Monumental City — a number of foundations and associated debris just west of the present battlefield entrance — was cleaned up in 1965 by construction crews building the new road to the Siege Area.

[26]"The Edwards Case," in *Missoula Gazette*, August 22, 1890. Billy Edwards is buried in the Grantsdale Cemetery, opposite Hamilton, Montana, where his grave has at last been appropriately marked. See, John Barrows, "New Stone Marks Pioneer Hero's Grave," in *The Ravalli Republic*, Hamilton, Mont., July 12, 1979.

The pension records provide some insight into the effect of the Big Hole battle upon the lives of enlisted men who suffered disabilities, and upon the lives of their dependents. However, it is unlikely that the 22 cases which are a matter of record are the full measure of the hardships attributable to the battle.

Ten of the wounded received medical discharges as soon as they were able to travel. The following excerpts from pension and other records available at Big Hole National Battlefield gives some idea of how these men fared:

Private **Charles Alberts**, a 31-year-old recruit from San Francisco, came though better than most. He was shot through the right lung during the fighting in the village and asked Adjutant Woodruff, *"Do you think I will live Lieutenant?"* He was told, *"Alberts you have a severe wound, but there is no need of your dying if you have got the nerve to keep your courage up."* Two years later, on Woodruff's arrival at the St. Paul station, he was surprised when *"Alberts, a hotel runner, rushed up to me, grasped my hand and luggage and said, 'You see, I had the nerve, Lt.'"*[27] Alberts married in 1881, raised three children and lived to 1910; he was a lucky one.

Private **James Burk**, a 25-year-old recruit from Ireland, was not so lucky. The ball which passed through his right shoulder damaged the joint so that he had little use of the arm. Receiving a medical discharge at Fort Ellis, he settled at Painesville, Ohio, where he applied for a pension because he was unable to work as a farmer. On February 5, 1891, he asked for an increased Invalid Pension, at which time his arm was said to be *"much worse than when last examined and is now entirely useless and paralyzed. Can do no work with it. Circulation is very deficient and can bear no weight on the shoulder — not even a heavy overcoat."* He entered the U. S. Soldier's Home in Washington, D.C., that year and probably died in the latter part of 1908.

Another Irish immigrant soldier spent his last years in an old soldier's home in Virginia — after a military career which was both unusual and quite pointless. Musician **Timothy Cronan** was shot through the right shoulder and lung in the Big Hole battle, receiving a medical discharge in December of 1877. Five and a half years later he enlisted in the 23rd Infantry under the name of Thomas Cronin, but deserted from Fort Union, New Mexico, less than a year later. Then, in August 1884, he enlisted in the 5th Cavalry — as Thomas C. Shehan — deserting from Fort McKinney, Wyoming, six weeks later. In October of the same year he enlisted in the 17th Infantry, as Timothy J. Cronin, but deserted from Fort D. A. Russell, Wyoming, and was apprehended two days later, March 12, 1887. Tried for desertion, he received a dishonorable discharge and five months in the military prison at Leavenworth, Kansas. Even so, he was able to get a pension for the wound he received at Big Hole ten years earlier and was cared for at public expense until his death June 10, 1898.

---

[27]Gen. C. A. Woodruff, "The Battle of the Big Hole," in *Contributions To The Historical Society Of Montana*, Vol. 7 (1910), p. 112. In that day *"runners"* were employed to frequent the depots, soliciting business.

Private **Joseph Devoss** had seen prior service, enlisting the first time in the 7th Cavalry, in 1866, by exaggerating his age (then only 17). Completing his five-year hitch, he went back to Ohio and life as a farmer until Lt. Col. Custer led Devoss' old outfit, Company L of the 7th, to defeat on the Little Bighorn River in June, 1876. Three weeks later Joseph Devoss reenlisted; this time with Company I, 7th Infantry. His ankle was shattered by a ball in the Big Hole battle, resulting in amputation of his left foot. Following his discharge from the army, he married Sara Pickens at Chillicoth, Ohio, where he died late in 1886, leaving three children and a widow who blamed his military service for the lung condition which killed him.

Private **Patrick Fallon** was an Irish immigrant but no recruit. He had seen service in the Civil War and was in his fourth enlistment, all in the 7th Infantry and all as a private. He was also a married man, and his first child was born the same month he was wounded in the Big Hole battle. The bullet which disabled Fallon entered his left thigh, passed through the scrotum and severed the urethra, then coursed through the right thigh to come out above the knee. He received a medical discharge in April 1878 and fathered another child in October of the following year. He died of cancer nine years later.

Private **Edward D. Hunter**, a 29-year-old printer from Columbus, Ohio, had nearly completed his five-year hitch when he was wounded in the Big Hole battle. A ball shattered the bones of his right forearm, rendering his hand useless. He received a medical discharge December 7, 1877, and returned to Columbus. He was married twice but had no children, dying in 1923 in the old soldier's home at Hillyard, Washington.

Private **James C. Lehmer** was one of the older enlisted men in the Seventh Infantry, and an *"old soldier"* in that other sense of having seen service in the Civil War (as a sergeant-major in the 2nd California Volunteer Cavalry). He returned to military life following the death of his wife in 1875, and was so seriously wounded in the Big Hole battle that his leg had to be amputated twice. Upon receiving a medical discharge, he applied for a disability pension and died in the care of the U. S. Soldier's Home on July 24, 1899.

Another *"old soldier"* was Corporal **Christian Luttman**, a German immigrant. He served throughout the Civil War, in which he was wounded; but afterward, he was unable to adjust to civil life. With brief interludes *"outside,"* he reenlisted with the regulars — in the 16th Infantry, 8th Cavalry and then the 7th Infantry. It was with the latter, in the Big Hole battle, that he was again seriously wounded by a bullet which passed through both thighs. He was disabled to the extent that he was given a medical discharge. Admitted to the U. S. Soldier's Home in 1907, he died there three years later.

Private **George Maurer**, a 28-year-old recruit from Germany, was wounded in the dawn attack on the village. A ball struck him in the face carrying away ten teeth and most of his upper jaw. He received a medical discharge March 28, 1878, with the post surgeon at Fort Benton noting, *"the upper front half of his mouth is*

gone entirely, and the man is unfit for duty by reason of impediment in speech. "
He went to Bellingham, Washington, married, and lived there to age 86.

Private **William Thompson**, a 23-year-old recruit from Pennsylvania, was
wounded in the left shoulder in the Big Hole battle and received a medical
discharge. A year later he reenlisted in the 7th Cavalry, and, on completion of that
five-year hitch, he applied for a pension on account of the wound received in 1877.
It was allowed, as was an increase in 1902, at which time he claimed to be
suffering from pulmonary tuberculosis believed to be a result of the gunshot
wound. He died on October 19, 1903.

There were a number of soldiers who were later pensioned for conditions
other than wounds attributable to their service in the Big Hole battle. Two,
privates Antoine Schohn and Philo O. Hurlburt, later claimed a disability due to
rheumatism resulting from service at Big Hole. Schohn's was certified by the
surgeon at Fort Douglas, Utah, in 1880, and Hurlburt's case developed gradually
in his wounded left shoulder. Two other cases are less definitely associated with
the battle: Private Benjamin F. Woodward obtained his pension because he *"had
to wade cold mountain streams, sleep in wet clothes exposed in the snow in the
mountains and exposure brought on rheumatism,"* which sounds like the march
from Fort Shaw to Missoula, while 1st Sergeant Thomas McLaughlin was
pensioned in 1879 for a heart condition attributed to exposure during the
campaign.

There was one disability claim, submitted by William Stillwell in 1911 —
many years after that single enlistment which included the Big Hole battle, which
was not approved. He had managed as a farmer during the intervening years, but
his declaration of May 8, 1911, states, as a basis for the claim: *"Claimant alleges
that at the Battle of Big Hole Pass, Montana, about August 9, 1877, he became
nervous and has continuously grown worse, until now he is not able to get about,
[it] also affecting his hearing . . . "*[28] The Pension Bureau didn't believe him.

Private Thomas Bundy, a tough, boisterous fellow who later tried to get a
pension for injuries sustained in drunken brawls during his one enlistment in the
Seventh Infantry, did *not* claim the one certifiable disability he got at the Big Hole
battle — a case of piles!

It was not just the disabled whose lives were seriously affected by the Big
Hole battle; one way or another, it blighted the lives of dependents (already noted
in the case of several officers). Though enlisted men were not supposed to have
dependents in that day, some did, and there were hardship cases that were
recognized by the Pension Bureau. 1st Sergeant Robert L. Edgeworth, killed
during the fighting in the village, had aged parents and an adolescent sister in
Ireland, and, from the time he entered our military service as an immigrant soldier
in 1870, it was his habit to send part of his pay to them. It took over a year for his
mother, Annie Edgeworth, to get on the pension roles — for the twelve dollars she
received each month until her death in 1890. Likewise, the mother of Private

---

[28]Excerpt from William Stillwell's file; copy, Big Hole Battlefield library.

Gottlieb Mantz, also killed early in the battle, received a pension from 1884, when her husband died, until her death in 1896.

The case of Corporal Robert E. Sale, killed beside the mountain howitzer he was serving, was a most unusual one. Both his parents died in the mid-1870s, leaving two minor children to be supported by those of the family who could manage something. After Robert's death, his brother-in-law, Thomas Thackery, was appointed legal guardian of the minor children and he applied for pension benefits for them based on the military service of Robert Sale. During the investigation it was established that, though Robert *"ran with fast women, drank to excess and was generally a reckless person,"* he had helped support the parentless children. The claim was allowed, and backdated to be effective August 10, 1877 — the day following his death.

The casualties suffered by the troops in the Big Hole fight had the effect of putting a crimp in the temperance movement at two army posts where it was very much needed — Fort Shaw and Fort Ellis. Worst hit was the latter, where Lincoln Lodge No. 10 of the Independent Order of Good Templars lost all its officers and became inactive until reconstituted three months later by an officer from the Grand Lodge.[29]

The Nez Perce side of the aftermath of battle, though less well known, was undoubtedly more disruptive because whole families were so often involved. Of the many tragic consequences, only a few have been recorded — most slipped almost unnoticed into oblivion with the passing of those generations that remembered the battle.

Historian L. V. McWhorter has left a vivid impression of the immediate effect on a Nez Perce family. *Husis Owyeen* (Shot in Head) took his rifle and ammunition belt and went out to defend the village as soon as he heard the alarm, leaving his wife and two-year-old child at their tipi. He said:

> Day drawing on, I went back to camp. Many of the tepees were ashes, some of the blackened poles still standing. I inquired for my wife and little child. The bad news came about them. When I reached the tepee, escaped from the burning, standing at the end [stake M-4] my wife and baby had both been shot.[30]

The toddler, left in the care of an aunt, strayed toward the soldiers — probably toward the Bradley firing line — and was shot in the hip. The mother,

---

[29]Massena Bullard, *Proceedings Of The Grand Lodge Of Montana, I.O.G.T.*, at the Tenth Annual Session, Butte City, October 10, 11 and 12, 1877; p. 11. If the idea of a temperance organization at a frontier military post seems a bit odd, the following excerpt from the 1874 *Proceedings*, following organization of a lodge at Fort Shaw, may help: *"Since the organization of this Lodge changes have occurred at Fort Shaw as though a magician's wand had been brought into requisition. Drunkenness is now the exception where formerly it was the rule. Pay-day is no longer the occasion for a general debauch; bank accounts now take the place of whisky scores, and decency and good order prevail. Resort is now had to the Lodge room instead of the saloon, and the guard-house is fast losing its terrors."*

[30]Luculius V. McWhorter, *Hear Me, My Chiefs!* (Caldwell, Idaho: The Caxton Printers, 1983), p. 373.

catching sight of him too late, gathered up the baby and was shot in the back as she returned with him. *Husis Owyeen* continued:

> During the day when the fight came on again [at the siege area], I did not leave the tepee. I had to care for my wounded wife and child . . . I did not want to attend the battle further. When the camp moved, I went with it. Kept going with the tribe, camping instead with the women until I got over this feeling . . . Four days and my little child died. It was shot in the hip. My wife was shot in the back, just about the waste. The bullet came out through the breast.[31]

The care of the many suffering wounded following the battle slowed the movement of the Nez Perce cavalcade southward along the west side of the Big Hole. The camping places were littered with bloody bandages, and the great need for dressings was partly satisfied by the advance scouts, who, when pillaging ranch houses on Horse Prairie, took even the bed ticks. Among the grievously wounded were the wives of Chief's Joseph and White Bird, while *Aihits Palojami* (Fair Land), the wife of Joseph's brother, died at the *Takseen* camp the first evening — before *Ollokot* came in with the rear guard.

White Feather, the Nez Perce maiden who was shot in the shoulder during the attack on the upper end of the village — and then smashed in the face with a rifle butt — travelled with the column, bumping along on a dusty pony drag, as did her mortally wounded father. Gray Eagle died at the third camp and was buried as inconspicuously as possible, but the daughter was soon after sent north to the Flathead Reservation to recover (as at least one other of the wounded — *Weweetsa* — was).

While living among the Pend d'Oreille Indians, White Feather received a new name, *In-who-lise* (Broken Tooth), from the damage done to her mouth by the soldier's rifle butt, and she met and married a trapper by the name of Andrew Garcia, beginning a migratory life with him which soon led to her death at the hands of Piegan Indians. Garcia's tender account of their return to the battlefield two years after the Big Hole fight, in search of the graves of the sister and father lost there, is a revealing narrative of the emotional scarring of that battle.[32]

Other Nez Perce wounded, in addition to those spirited off to sanctuary among the Flatheads and Pend d'Oreilles (which was not entirely safe, as *Weweetsa*, after recovering from his wound, died there in a squabble with his hosts), were left to recover in secluded places along the line of travel — and it is said that some were never heard from again.

In addition, a number of sick and exhausted old people were left behind at camping places, at their own request and out of consideration for the well-being of the whole band, to be killed and scalped by General Howard's merciless Bannock scouts. The loss of these elders added another dimension of grief to the Nez Perce flight.

---

[31] Ibid., p.374.
[32] Andrew Garcia, "Graves and Grizzlies," in *American Heritage*, 18/4 (June, 1967), p. 36.

In quite another sense the losses suffered by the Nez Perces appear to have changed the futures of at least some Indian families. Both Chief Joseph and his brother, Ollocot, lost wives, and that may have contributed to the fact that Joseph's line ran out with the death of his daughter, Kap-kap Ponmi, and that Ollocot's line has continued only through a daughter. It seems likely there were other long-term effects of this type, but they are obscured by the lack of available records.

As soon as the battle was obviously over, Colonel John Gibbon issued *"Regimental Orders, No. 27"* from his uncomfortable corner of the entrenchment which was, on August 11, 1877, *"Headquarters Seventh Infantry, Battle-Field of the Big Hole, Montana Territory."* In it he implied a victory in these words:

> The regimental commander congratulates the regiment upon the result of the conflict here with hostile Nez Perces on the 9th and 10th inst. While mourning for the dead, Capt. William Logan and First Lieut. James H. Bradley and the twenty-one enlisted men, who fell gallantly doing a soldier's duty, we can not but congratulate ourselves that after a stern chase of over 250 miles, during which we twice crossed the rugged divide of the Rocky Mountains, we inflicted upon a more numerous enemy a heavier loss than our own, and held our ground until it gave up the field. In respect to the memory of the gallant dead, the officers of the regiment will wear the usual badge of mourning for thirty days.
>
> *JOHN GIBBON*
> *Colonel Seventh Infantry, Commanding.*[33]

However, there was in *that* several half-truths. It may not have been immediately apparent that they had not faced a numerically superior enemy, but one of about the same strength, taken by surprise and not fully armed; but it should have been abundantly evident that the advantage claimed in regard to the body count came from noncombatant deaths, and also, that they had not really held their ground, but had been driven from their objective, to a defensive position where they could have been exterminated, had the Nez Perces cared to pay the price. That did not add up to victory for the troops, and neither the high command nor the press made any extravagant claims immediately after the fight.

As Mark Brown has pointed out, *"In the weeks to come, there were some, including Colonel Gibbon, who tried to stretch the results into a' victory — or, at least, a victory of sorts. But among the members of the 'cloth,' it was recognized as 'a very bad defeat'."*[34] With the passage of time, opinions concerning the outcome of the battle became increasingly negative; varying from a feeling that the lives of soldiers had been unduly hazarded by attacking an enemy with an insufficient force, to Duncan McDonald's bitter denunciation: *"The gallant Seventh Infantry! It should be called the Cursed Seventh! They were not satisfied*

---

[33]G. O. Shields, *The Battle Of The Big Hole* (Chicago and New York; Rand, McNally & Company, Publishers, 1889), pp. 106-07.

[34]*The Flight Of The Nez Perce*, p. 267; cited in Note 20.

in killing Indians whom they found asleep. They must kill women and children too. "[35]

Even G. O. Shields, he whose bias in favor of the troops was so evident in all he wrote about the battle; he who called it, *"a glorious achievement, a victory dearly bought but gallantly won, and the grand old Seventh Infantry has no brighter page in its history . . ."* — even he, admitted *"the fight was not a complete victory for our troops, it was nevertheless a most stinging blow to the Nez Perces."* [36]

From the Nez Perce viewpoint, what happened at the Big Hole was much more than a *"most stinging blow."* Though they drove off their attackers, saved their horse herd, salvaged some of their property, and were able to continue their hegira, *"In any case, the battle losses were disastrous to the Nez Perces. Before the Battle of the Big Hole, their losses were insignificant, thereafter, nearly every family was disrupted."* [37] The specter of ultimate defeat was raised before them; they had won the victory they could not afford.

It should be obvious now that there were no winners in the battle of the Big Hole; rather, it cost everyone involved more than it was worth. The Nez Perces who were there in 1877 tended to shun the battleground in later years as a place where memory was just too painful, and most white participants in that fight remained apologetic about it. A letter to the editor of the *Missoulian* many years later made that point rather well:

> The writer recalls some years ago when Colonel J. B. Catlin, of Missoula, a Civil War veteran who organized a company and was captain of it at the Big Hole battle, was called upon by a committee from the Big Hole. They were arranging an anniversary celebration of the Big Hole fight [probably 1915], they explained, and wanted him present. "Celebration, did you say," said the Colonel, "Celebration. I don't Know what we'd celebrate. The Indians licked hell out of us." [38]

The celebration of the 38th anniversary of the battle was held on Sunday, August 8, 1915, *"attracting nearly 500 people"* from various towns in western Montana (90 vehicles from Darby, Hamilton and Missoula crossed Gibbon's Pass on the road completed by the Forest Service that spring, and half as many came from Wisdom, Jackson and Dillon). There was a barbecue, *"consisting of a whole beef and several sheep with all the trimmings, and pot after pot of honest to goodness coffee, steaming hot . . ."* followed by the speeches of such important persons as the head of the Stockman's Association, former Lieutenant-Governor W. R. Allen, Judge R. Lee McCullough of Hamilton, Dr. Owens of the Hamilton

---

[35]"The Nez Perces War of 1877. The Inside History from Indian Sources," in *The New North-West*, Deer Lodge, M. T., January 24, 1879.

[36]*The Battle Of The Big Hole*, pp. 83 & 97; cited in Note 33.

[37]Merrill D. Beal, *I Will Fight No More Forever* (Seattle: University of Washington Press, 1963), p.129.

[38]Algonquin, "An Underdog View," in *The Missoulian*, n.d., Missoula Public Library clipping file.

Chamber of Commerce, the Butte postmaster and several of its citizens; *but*, there was only one veteran of the fight present among the throng that ate, listened and then prowled the trenches for souvenirs. He was Sam Chaffin, of Stevensville, *"and he refused to make a talk from the platform."*[39] "Colonel" Catlin was not there, nor were a half-dozen other surviving battle participants living in and near the Bitterroot Valley.

---

[39]"In Memory of the Men Who Fought At the Big Hole," in *The Anaconda Standard*, September 15, 1915.

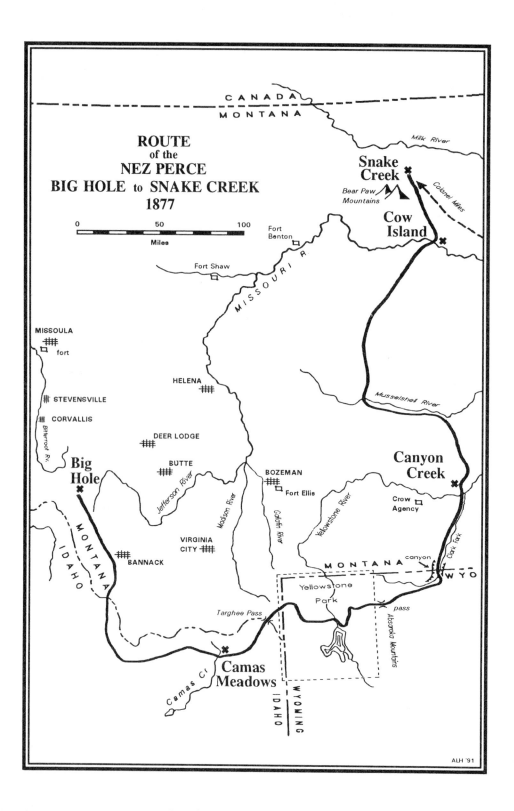

ROUTE
of the
NEZ PERCE
BIG HOLE to SNAKE CREEK
1877

0   50   100
Miles

CANADA
MONTANA

Milk River

Snake
Creek

Bear Paw
Mountains

Colonel Miles

Cow
Island

Fort
Benton

Fort Shaw

MISSOURI R.

MISSOULA
fort

HELENA

Musselshell River

STEVENSVILLE

CORVALLIS

DEER LODGE

Bitterroot Rv.

BUTTE

Big
Hole

Jefferson River

BOZEMAN

Fort Ellis

Canyon
Creek

Crow
Agency

Clark Fork

Madison River

Gallatin River

Yellowstone River

VIRGINIA
CITY

MONTANA   canyon

BANNACK

MONTANA
IDAHO

Crow
Agency

MONTANA   WYO

Yellowstone
Park

pass

Targhee Pass

Absaroka Mountains

Camas
Meadows

Camas Cr.

IDAHO   WYOMING

ALH '91

EPILOGUE

The Big Hole battle was a turning point for the Nez Perces: their early successes had not been costly in terms of lives lost and there was reason to believe they might escape further warfare, but the crippling losses of this fight raised the specter of ultimate defeat.

The sad and dismayed people buried their dead as best they could along the river bank and moved on with the property they were able to salvage. Stopping some twelve miles to the south at a camp they called *Takseen* (Willows), the wounded were attended to and some who had died enroute were properly buried. It was there that Ollokot's wife, Fair Land, died the next morning just before he and the others of the rear guard caught up. That was the only place anyone ever saw that great man cry.

After the battle, Chief Looking Glass was removed from the position of leadership, and Hototo, (Lean Elk), who knew the country well, took over that responsibility. While the Nez Perces had a three-day start on General Howard, their progress was painfully slow because of the wounded, and they were only about fifty miles ahead of their pursuers. The attitude of the warriors toward settlers had changed; they began raiding for livestock and there were some killings along the way.

The course of the Nez Perces from the Big Hole basin was south and east — back into Idaho's Lemhi country. However, many of the young men, angry about the Big Hole disaster, became nearly uncontrollable, so that raiding and killing occured on Horse Prairie and at Birch Creek. Chief Tendoy and his Lemhi Shoshoni would not join the hostiles, but urged them to leave quickly. They did so, taking an easterly direction, toward Yellowstone Park, for the chiefs wanted no trouble.

General Howard, following on a more direct line with his command, intended to trap the Indians between a cavalry detachment sent to occupy Targhee Pass and his main force which swung in behind them where they crossed the Montana stage road. His Bannock scouts reported that the Nez Perces were camped at Camas Meadows on August 18, only fifteen miles ahead, and Howard was able to reach Camas Creek the following evening — with his quarry still leading by about the same distance.

The Nez Perces knew Howard's location and decided to delay him by capturing his horses and mules. Through the carelessness of one of the warriors who went back to Howard's camp on that mission, they got the mules but not the cavalry horses, so that there was a pursuit and a brief skirmish which recovered some mules at the cost of a dozen casualties.

The next day Howard was able to move his command up to Henrys Lake with the help of a civilian wagon train, and the troops waited there for additional supplies and transportation. Meanwhile, the Nez Perces had crossed Targhee Pass without hindrance because the cavalry sent to block their way had not stayed in place. The route from the pass was up the Madison River with the intention of crossing Yellowstone National Park to the country of the Crows — still under the illusion they would be safe there.

A rear guard was maintained to insure against a surprise attack by the army, and small scouting parties moved ahead and on the flanks of the Indian cavalcade. These groups destroyed some property and killed several tourists in the park, and probably some prospectors in the mountains on its eastern rim.

The route of the main body of Indians through the Park was up Nez Perce Creek, across Mary Mountain and down Trout Creek into Hayden Valley, where the Yellowstone River was crossed above the Mud Volcano. At that point, some tourists captured in the Lower Geyser Basin were released. On the evening of the twenty seventh — the day Howard's troops renewed the pursuit — the Nez Perces were camped in the valley of Pelican Creek, four miles above Yellowstone Lake.

General Howard knew the Nez Perces were heading for the Crow country, so he sent two troops of cavalry to the Crow Agency, by way of Fort Ellis and the Yellowstone Valley, to intercept them. In the Park the Indian trail was easy to follow, but the country was heavily timbered, so that the command had to lay over several days while a wagon road was cut across Mary Mountain; a slow and painful march because so much labor was required to get the wagons through. Upon reaching Yellowstone River, Howard abandoned the track of the Nez Perces, turning northward to the Baronett Bridge, near Tower Fall, where he arrived on September 5th.

The Nez Perces had gone up Pelican Creek, over the Mirror Plateau and down Lamar River to Cache Creek, where they killed a settler's cattle and dried the meat for their journey across the Absaroka range. As they were leaving Cache Creek on September 4, Captain Fisher's few remaining Bannock Indian scouts came upon their rear guard. A lot of shouting and shooting ensued but the only casualty was a horse of one of the scouts. The Bannock scouts withdrew with the coming of darkness.

On September 6, after two weeks in the Yellowstone wonderland, the Nez Perces were over the dividing range and moving down Crandall Creek toward the Clark Fork of Yellowstone River, while General Howard's command was only leaving Baronett's bridge.

The wagons were abandoned at the bridge, which had been partially burned by the Indians, but, with some hasty repairs, the soldiers and their pack train crossed the Yellowstone River to continue eastward up the Lamar River, and Soda Butte Creek to Cooke City, then over Colter Pass and down the Clark Fork.

The Yellowstone River runs generally north through the Park and turns west near Tower Fall to begin a huge arc northward and eastward, ever broadening as it flows toward the Missouri. The Clark Fork is an important tributary which enters the Yellowstone from the south about 160 miles east of Fort Ellis, and 25 miles east of the Crow Indian Agency. Both Fort Ellis and the agency were supply depots for the Army in 1877, and a military telegraph line connected them with garrisons farther down the Yellowstone River. The one thing the valiant band of Nez Perces could not elude was the *"talking wire."* Troops had been alerted far in

advance. Therefore, in addition to Howard on their heels, five more commands
lay in wait ahead.

Things began to happen quite rapidly for the Nez Perces. Their scouts kept
the chiefs informed concerning the whereabouts of the troops in their immediate
vicinity, and the deadly game of cat-and-mouse intensified as they moved down the
Clark Fork to its deep and nearly impassable canyon. There they climbed up and
around Dead Indian Hill. A detachment of the Seventh Cavalry (six troops under
Colonel Samuel D. Sturgis) was positioned to block exit from Clark Fork;
however, those troops were decoyed southward some twenty miles by a small party
of Nez Perces. The ruse allowed the main body of Indians to move down the
narrow, wooded defile of Dead Indian Creek to the river and out of the mountains
onto the plains — an incredible feat for a caravan as encumbered as theirs was.

At this time, the objective was sanctuary with the Crow Indians, so it is
difficult to imagine the disappointment of the Nez Perces, who had lived with the
Crows and helped fight off their arch enemy, the Sioux, when both clans of the
Crows rejected them. This was not their fight, they said, but the Nez Perces could
pass through without harm. That proved to be untrue as many Crows scouted for
the Army and soon fought their old friends. The only haven left to the Nez Perces
was the Grandmother's country — Canada. So they continued northward.

Two miles downstream from the mouth of Clark Fork was the Brockaway
ranch, where stagecoaches crossed Yellowstone River. The appearance of the
Indians coincided with arrival of the daily coach, which was promptly abandoned
with driver and passengers seeking shelter in the brush. Several young Nez Perce
warriors decided to have some fun; tying their ponies on behind, they climbed
aboard and went for a joy ride on the prairie, scattering the contents of mail bags
in the sagebrush. Tiring of such sport, they left the stagecoach undamaged and
went on their way whooping and laughing.

Small parties of warriors flanking the main column at the Yellowstone
crossing raided nearby ranches for horses and supplies, and several occupants were
killed. All white men were now considered enemies.

Soon after the nearly 600 Nez Perces had crossed the Yellowstone, they were
sighted near the mouth of Canyon Creek by the cavalry of Colonel Sturgis (sent
forward by General Howard because his own horses were worn out). That began a
desperate race; the Indians hastening toward a rocky defile, where the cavalry
could not reach them, and the Army in hot pursuit in an effort to cut them off
before they reached that shelter. About three miles up the canyon, the soldiers ran
into a rear guard of sharpshooters under Chief Looking Glass and a lively skirmish
developed. That and some tactical errors on the part of the troopers allowed the
retreating Nez Perces to escape under cover of darkness and travel a distance into
the hills beyond Canyon Creek.

Sturgis pulled back, to camp his command at the mouth of the creek. The
brief battle of Canyon Creek was over, with three soldiers dead, eleven wounded
and forty-one horses lost. The Colonel later claimed he had killed sixteen Indians
and picked up 900 ponies, but Yellow Wolf said three Nez Perce were wounded,

and that the Army's Crow scouts managed to run off about forty horses the next day, in addition to the many worn-out animals they had abandoned.

The pursuit was resumed at dawn on the 14th. After several days of brutal travel (covering 150 miles), Sturgis managed to reach Musselshell River where he called it quits. Both horses and men were exhausted and supplies were low; also, most of his Crow scouts had left him.

General Howard had managed to regroup and resupply at the Canyon Creek camp and he was able to join Sturgis on the Musselshell with much needed supplies on September 20. While on that stream, Howard received word that a telegraphed message to Colonel Nelson A. Miles at Tongue River, requesting assistance, had been received, and that Miles had entered the campaign on the morning of the 18th, heading northwest.

Of course the fleeing Nez Perces did not know about Colonel Miles as they continued north through the Judith Gap and into the lush Judith Basin. As they hurried past Big Spring Creek, near present Lewistown, Montana, and along the foothills of the Snowy Mountains to Dog Creek, then down to the Missouri River, the seriously ill, the tired and the elderly were left by the wayside. By covering seventy miles in thirty-six hours, the remaining Nez Perces arrived at Cow Island Crossing during the morning of September 23rd.

Cow Island Landing was on the north bank of the Missouri. It served as a depot for steamboat freight when low water prevented the boats from going on to Fort Benton. When the Nez Perces arrived they found a large amount of military and other freight stacked there. Twenty warriors went ahead, crossing first as a protective shield. They were unopposed and the families followed safely.

Cow Creek comes into the Missouri River near the landing, and the Indians proceeded several miles up it to make camp. The warriors remaining behind to watch the small detachment of soldiers guarding the depot tried to buy supplies. Their peaceful offer was refused; then someone fired a shot and a fight was on. One warrior and two civilians were wounded during the night-long exchange of shots which served to protect other Indians — men and women — as they raided the stockpiles. At dawn the Nez Perces were gone.

The twenty-fourth was a busy day. A detachment of volunteers from Fort Benton arrived at Cow Island and immediately took up the chase. They came upon the rear guard of the Nez Perces just as they were burning a train of freight wagons they had looted after killing three teamsters. A few shots were fired and a volunteer was killed before the detachment retreated to Cow Island.

By noon of the twenty-ninth, the Nez Perces had caught up with their vanguard on Snake Creek where it meanders through a prairie northeast of the Bear Paw Mountains. The Indians knew General Howard was at least two days behind them, and that Canada was still two days —about 40 miles — away. Some thought they should keep moving, but Chief Looking Glass decided to camp there where they had water and grass for the horse herd and buffalo meat for the people.

Looking Glass did not know that his real antagonist was Colonel Nelson A. Miles, at that time probably this nation's most successful Indian fighter and also the Indian's champion. This man, though much maligned by history, was a very efficient military commander. With great skill and some luck he moved his force of mounted infantry, cavalry, scouts and a Hotchkiss gun, rapidly in a northwesterly direction in order to cut the Nez Perces off from Canada. The maneuver was successful; on the morning of September 30, he reached and attacked the Nez Perce camp established on the east side of Snake Creek in a highly vulnerable position — crowded between the stream and a low bench to the east.

The initial assault against a ridge-line defense south of the camp cost Miles dearly. Fifty-three of 115 men of the Seventh Cavalry were either killed or wounded by a handful of courageous and determined warriors. Two additional assaults were repelled by the Indian's deadly marksmanship; that, with the temporary loss of the Hotchkiss gun (a small, rapid-firing cannon) shortly after noon, forced Miles into a reluctant siege of the Nez Perce camp.

Several of the great warriors were killed that day in what is erroneously called the Battle of the Bears Paw. Joseph's brother, Ollokot, Poker Joe, old Chief Toohoolhoolzote died, along with nineteen other men, women and children. Those Nez Perces who had not escaped from the battle area were forced to seek shelter in the ravines or in pits dug with butcher knives, camas digging tools and the trowel bayonets captured at the Big Hole.

The loss among the troops was very heavy; two officers and twenty-two enlisted men killed, with four officers and thirty-eight men wounded the first day. The next morning left little hope for a quick victory as five inches of snow had fallen and the weather had turned bitterly cold.

Colonel Miles decided his best course of action was to encourage the Nez Perces to surrender. Negotiations were opened but things were at an impasse when General Howard arrived the night of October 4 (a great relief to Miles as the Custer fight with its heavy toll of life weighed on his mind with Sitting Bull so close in Canada).

A council of Chiefs was held and Joseph voted for surrender to end the suffering of his people. Chiefs Looking Glass and White Bird were against it.

Those who did not wish to surrender were morally free to escape if they could; that was the custom.

The council had just broken up when Looking Glass was killed by a civilian scout's long, lucky shot. White Bird would not surrender and escaped to Canada to be killed by one of his own five years later.

Although there is some doubt if the famous surrender speech which ended with, *"From where the sun now stands, I will fight no more forever,"* correctly represents Joseph's words, as the only major chief left alive at the battlefield he spoke for the survivors, and that enhanced the myth that had been building concerning his great military prowess.[1]

---

[1] Chief Joseph did little actual fighting during the War of 1877. He left that to others more experienced in war. His role was that of a guardian of the people. He was a spiritual leader and mediator. His eloquence, compassion and nobility would have made him a great man in any culture. Joseph had nine children but none survived to produce descendants, but the blood line has survived through the descendants of his brother, Ollokot.

At two o'clock that afternoon of October 5 Joseph, with five followers on foot, rode out through a light snow storm, on a borrowed black horse, to surrender his rifle to General Howard, who waved him on to Colonel Miles. Thus ended a truly heroic Indian resistance to white *"Manifest Destiny."*

After the surrender the Nez Perces were assured there would be no more bloodshed and life would be good again. They were told they and their possessions would be returned to Idaho after spending the winter at Fort Keogh. So, over 400 people turned in the few firearms they had and received the first hot food in six days, which improved both their physical condition and mental outlook.

On October 7 the Army began the 200 mile journey to Fort Keogh with its Nez Perce prisoners. Due to bad weather it took six days to reach the Missouri River where the wounded and sick were loaded on steamboats. The remainder continued overland and arrived at the fort on October 23 where Col. Miles command was given a military welcome complete with a band and cannon salute.

General Phillip H. Sheridan, commanding the Military Division of Missouri, refused to let the Nez Perces winter at Fort Keogh, and, in November, ordered them moved to Fort Leavenworth. The move was accomplished by flatboat and horseback. From November 27 until the following July of 1878 — the most miserable period of their exile — the prisoners lived in a swamp about four miles from Fort Leavenworth, with 21 dying from malaria.

In July the Army released the Nez Perces to the Bureau of Indian Affairs and they were moved by railroad, in stifling heat, 200 miles south to the Quapaw Reservation. There, at what they called *"Eeikish Pah"* (The Hot Place) the prisoners spent another miserable year, and Forty-seven more died.

In January 1879 Chief Joseph journeyed to Washington to plead his case but Congress would not approve a return of the Nez Perces to Idaho. On June 6 the exiles moved again 180 miles by wagon to the Ponca Reservation where they had gardens and 100 head of cattle, and thus fared somewhat better for a time.

But then the situation deteriorated; a continuing drought spoiled their farming and neighbors stole their cattle, and the indifference of their agents (four in three years) left them without redress. Their only help came from Lapwai, Idaho, in the form of three Christian Indians who opened a day school at Ponca and acted as interpreters the people could believe.

In May of 1883 twenty-nine people, mostly widows and orphans, were allowed to return to Idaho. By 1884 only 282 Nez Perces survived in the Indian Territory, which created a ground swell of sympathy with 14 petitions to the Congress to let those people go home. So, on May 22, 1885, 268 Nez Perces were allowed to board a train at Arkansas City and begin the 1200 mile journey home.

While Chief Joseph remained adamant that he and his group should be allowed to return to the lovely Wallowa, that was not to be. One hundred eighteen were sent to Lapwai and the remainder, including Joseph, were sent to the Colville Reservation in Washington State — where neither the Indian agent nor the other Indian tribes wanted them.

In 1887 the Allotment Act, intended to provide the Indians on various reservations with particular parcels of land, became law, and by 1892 the Nez Perce Reservation at Lapwai, Idaho, had been surveyed for that purpose. Joseph could have taken land there but he refused an allotment, insisting that the Wallowa Valley in Oregon was his land.

Joseph even offered to buy land in the Wallowa, but the settlers told him there was none for sale. A final visit to his old home in 1900 with Inspector General James McLaughlin of the Indian Bureau made him realize he was defeated when they were bluntly told by the citizens that they did not want the Indians back, period! A downcast Joseph went to see his father's grave for the last time.

Chief Joseph returned to Nespelem, Washington, where he died September 21, 1904. The Colville Agency physician, Dr. Lathan, later said he felt Joseph *"died of a broken heart,"* thereby ending a long journey into sorrow.

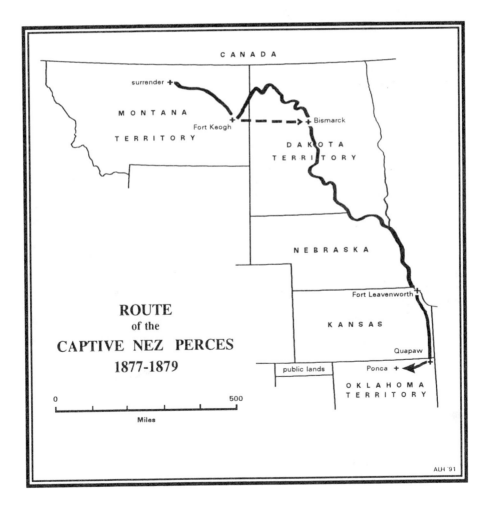

BATTLE MEMORIALS

Chief Joseph memorial designed by sculptor Alonzo Lewis and placed in the Siege area by L. V. McWhorter and Nez Perces in July 1928. NPS Photo.

Unofficial memorial to the Nez Perce noncombatants killed during the battle. Placed in the Siege area by Thain White, August 9, 1951. Photo by ALH, 1965.

The six-ton granite Soldier Monument placed in the Siege area in 1883 by the Army. As it appeared in 1920 when photographed by E. S. Ship for the U.S. Forest Service.

APPENDIX A - NEZ PERCES

This appendix lists the names of Nez Perces who were recorded as being present at the Battle of the Big Hole by L. V. McWhorter, E. S. Curtiss, R. Pinkham and others. The names of less than one quarter of the Nez Perce participants are known.

There are up to three name entries per individual: his/her Nez Perce name, appearing in bold type (i.e. **Alla-Lem-Yah-Takanin**); the English translation, in italic type (i.e. *A Vision*); and a "white" name, in sans-serifs type (i.e. Chief Looking Glass).

About Asleep; see Eelahweemah
Aihits Palojami[F] (*Fair Land*)
Alahoos[OM]
Alla-Lem-Yah-Takanin[M] (*A Vision*); Chief Looking Glass
Allezyakon[OM]; Lazzykoon

Bad Boy Grizzly Bear; see Hohots Elotoht
Big Noise; see Too-Hool-Hool-Zote
Bird Alighting; see Peopeo Tholekt
Black Eagle[YM]
Black Hair
Black Owl
Black Tail Eagle
Black Trail; see Iskatpoo Tismooktismook
Bull Bait; see Gosawyiennight
Burning Coals; see Waptastamana

Calf-of-leg; see Pitpillooheen
Chapowits[M] (*Plenty Coyotes*)
Chellooyeen[M] (*Bow and Arrow Case*); Phillip Evans
Chee-Nah[F]; Martha Joseph
Chi-mih
Chtwiweyunaw[M]
Chuslum Hahlap Kanoot[M] (*Naked-footed Bull*)
Chuslum Moxmox[M] (*Yellow Bull*) & Weyatanatoo Wahyakt (*Sun Necklace*)

Coals-of-fire; see, Waptastamana
Dawn-of-Day; see Halpawinmi
Dropping-from-a-Cliff; see Tenahtahka

Earth Blanket; see Wattes Kunnin
Eeahlokoon[M]
Eelahweemah[YM] (*About Asleep*); David Williams
Elaskolatat[M] (*Animals Entering a Hole*); Joe Albert
Ell-is-ya-kon
Eloosykasit[YM] *Standing-on-a-Point*)
Espowyes[M] (*Light-in-the-mountain*) Old Yellow Wolf

Fair Land; see Aihits Palojami
Five Fogs; see Pahka Patahank
Five Lightnings[M]
Five Wounds; see Pahkatos Owyeen

Gosawyiennight[M] (*Bull Bait*)
Gray Hawk[M]
Grizzly Bear Youth

Ha-hots Tof-nu-kuns
Hair Cut Upward; see Witlayah Palakin
Hah-tale-kin[M] [Chief] & Taktsoukt Ilppilp (*Red Echo*)
Halahtookit[OM] (*Daytime Smoke*) [son of William Clark]
Half Moon[M]
Halpawinmi[M] (*Dawn*)

[I] Infant. [Y] Young. [O] Old. [M] Male. [F] Female.

Heinmot Tosinlikt[M]; Henry Tabador
He-Mene-Mox-Mox[M] (*Yellow Wolf*);
    Yellow Wolf
    also Heinmot Hihih (*White
    Thunder*)
He Meen Ilppilp[M] (*Red Wolf*)
Heyoom Pishkish[M] also Uwhee
    Tommoset; Lame John
Heyoom Tamalikinma[M]
He-Yoom-Yoykt
He-yum-ta-nan-mi
Hill, Tom[M]
Hin-Mut-Too-Yah-Lat-Kekht[M]
    (*Thunder Rolling in the
    Mountains*); Chief Joseph
Hohots Elotoht[M] (*Bad Boy Grizzly
    Bear*)
Horn Hide Dresser; see Tepsus
Hototo [Chief]; see Wahwookya
    Wasaaw
Hoyt, Johnson[M]
Husis-Husis-Kute[M] [Chief](*Naked
    Head, Bald Head*)
Husis Owyeen[M] (*Wounded Head, Shot
    in Head*)

I-at-Tu-Ton-My[F] [Wife of Looking
    Glass]
I Block Up; see Tumokult
Illatsats[YM]
Iltolk[F] [granddaughter of William
    Clark]
In-who-lise[F] (*Broken Tooth*) also
    White Feather; Susie
Ip-nan-ye-ta-ma
Iskatpoo Tismooktismook[M] (*Black
    Trail*)
Iskiloom[M]
Itsiyiyi Opseen[M] (*Coyote with Flints*)

Jee-noh
Jekunkun[M] (*Dog*); John Dog
Joseph [Chief] see Hin-Mut-Too-
    Yah-Lat-Kekht

John Dog; see Jekunkun

Kap-Kap-Ponmi[YF] (*Noise of Running
    Feet*); Sarah Moses
Kahpots[OM] also Kapoochas
Kahwitkahwit[M] (*Dry-land Crane*)
Kalotus[M]
Ketalkpoosmin[M] (*Stripes-turned-
    down*)
Kilkilchuslum
Kinikinik Squalsac (*Little Tobacco*);
    see Wahwookya Wasaaw
Kip-kip Owyeen (*Wounded Breast*)
Kosooyeen[M] (*Traveling Alone, Going
    Alone*); Luke Andrews
Kosooyeen Ipsewahk[M] (*Lone Bird*)
Kowtoliks (*Scattered Human Bones*);
    Charley Kowtoliks

Lakochets Kunnin[M] (*Rattle on
    Blanket*)
Lahpeealoot[M] (*Two Flocks on Water*);
    Phillip Williams
Lazzykoon; see Allezyakon
Lean Elk; see Wah-Woo-Tya-Wasaaw
Left Hand[M]
Lepeet Hessemdooks (*Two Moons*)
Li-kin-ma[M] (*Last in a row*)
Lindsay, Thomas[M]
Lindsley, Lillie[F]
Lone Bird; see Kosooyeen Ipsewahk
Looking Glass [Chief]; see All-Lem-
    Yah-Takanin
Lucy[F]

Many Wounds[YM]; Sam Lot
Minthon[YM]
Moore, Albert; see Tu-Ta-Mal-Way-
    uom
Mulkamkam[M]; John Mulkamkam
Muscles in Back Thigh; see
    Pitpilooheen

Na-tal-e-kin; see Wetistokaith
No Feet; see Itskimze Kin

[I] Infant. [Y] Young. [O] Old. [M] Male. [F] Female.

No Heart; see Zhaya Timenna

Old Yellow Wolf; see Espowyes
Ol-lo-cot[M] [Chief](*Frog*)
Otskai[M] (*Going Out, Go Out*)
Otstotpoo[M]
Owhi[M] (a Yakima Indian)
Owyeen[F] (*Wounded*)

Pahit Palikt[YM]
Pahka Alyanakt[M] (*Five Snows*)
Pahka Pahtahank[M] (*Five Fogs*)
Pahkatos Owyeen[M] (*Five Wounds*)
Passing Overhead; see Watyo Chekoon
Pa-tsa-kon-mi[OF]
Penahwenonmi[OF] (*Helping Another*)
Peopeo Ipsewahk[M] (*Lone Bird*)
Peopeo Tholekt[M] (*Bird Alighting*)
Pitpillooheen[M] (*Calf of Leg*)
Poker Joe; see Wahwookya Wasaaw

Quiel-spo[M] (*Red Heart*)
Quiloishkish[M]

Rainbow; see Wahchumyus
Red Cloud
Red Elk[YM]
Red-Headed Woodpecker
Red Heart; see Temme Ilppilp and see
    Quiel-spo
Red Moccasin Tops; see Sarpsis Ilppilp
Red Spy; see Seeyakoon Ilppilp
Red Star
Red Wolf, Josiah[YM]

Sahm Keen[YM] (*Shirt On*); Sam Tilden
Sarpsis Ilppilp[M] (*Red Moccasin Tops*)
Seeyakoon Ilppilp[M] (*Red Spy*)
Sewattis-Hih-Hih[M] (*White Cloud*)
Shore Crossing; see Wahlitits
Shot-in-Head; see Husis-Owyeen
Silooyam[M]
Springtime; see Toma-Alwa-Win-Me
Strong Eagle; see Tipyahlahnah
    Kapskaps
Stuart, Mrs. James[F]

Sundown, Jackson; see Waaya-Tonah-
    Toesits-Kahn
Sun Tied; see Weyatanatoo Latpat
Sun Necklace; see Chuslum Moxmox
Swan Necklace; see Wet-Yet-Mas-
    Way-Aykt
Swans Alighting On Water; see Yoyek-
    Wasum

Tababo (also Tabador); see Heinmot
    Tosinlikt
Tah-kin-pal-loo
Tahomchits Humkon[M]
Tahwis Tokaitat[M] (*Bighorn Bow*)
Ta-Mah-Utah-Likt
Tap-sis-il-pilp[M]
Teeto Hoonnad[M]
Teeweeyownah[M] (*Over the Point*)
Tememah Ilppilp[M] (*Red Heart II*)
Temetiki[M]
Temme Ilppilp[M] (*Red Heart*)
Tenahtahkah Weyun[M] (*Dropping
    from a Cliff*)
Tepsus[M] (*Horn Hide Dresser*)
Teweeyownah[M]
Tewetakis[IM]
Tewit Toitoi[M]
Tim-lih-poos-min
Tipyahlahnah Elassanin[M] (*Roaring
    Eagle*); George Comedown
Tipyahlahnah Kapskaps[M] (*Strong
    Eagle*)
Tissaikpee[OF] (*Granite or Crystal*)
Tok-ka-lik-si-mai[M] [Chief]
Tok-ta-we-ti-sha
Toohoolhoolzote[M] [Chief](*Sound*)
Towassis[M] (*Bowstring*)
To-wit-Toi-toi
Tsi-a-yah
Tumokult[F] (*I Block Up*)
Tul-Ta-Mal-Way-Uom

Ugly Grizzly Bear Boy[M]
Um-til-ilp-cown[M]

Uwhee Tommoset; see Heyoom
    Pishkish

Waaya-Tonah-Toesits-Kahn[YM];
    Jackson Sundown
Wahchumyus[M] (*Rainbow*)
Wahkukunah Ilppilp[M] (*Woodpecker*)
Wah-Lit-Its[M] (*Shore Crossing*)
Wah-nis-tas Aswet-tesk[OM]
Wahwookya Wasaaw[M] (*Lean Elk*) &
    [Chief] Hototo; Poker Joe
Wai-nat-ta-ka-kan
Waptastamana[OM] (*Blacktail Eagle;*
    also Burning Coals)
Watyahtsakon[M]
Wat-et-mas
Watyo Chekoon[M] (*Passing Overhead*)
Wa-Win-Te-Pi-Ksat
Welehewot[YM]
Wetatonmi[F]; Susie Conville
Wetistokaith[OM]; also Natalekin
Wetwhowees[F]; Lucy Ellenwood
Wetyetmas[M] Likleinen & Wat-yet-
    mas-lik-li-nin (*Circling Swan*)
Weweetsa[M] (*Log*)
Weyatanatoo[M] Latpat (*Sun Tied*)
Weyatanatoo Wahyakt; see Chuslum
    Moxmox
White Bird; see Peopeo Hihhih
White Bird II[YM]
White Bull[M]
White Eagle
White Feather; see In-who-lise
White Hawk
Whylimlex (*Black Feather*)
Witlayah Palakin[M] (Hair Cut Upward)
Woodpecker; see Wookawkaw
Wookawkaw[M] (*Woodpecker*)
Wot-to-len[M] (*Hair Combed Over Eyes*)

Yellow Bull [Chief]; see Chuslum
    Mox-Mox
Yellow Hair
Yellow Wolf; see He-Mene-Mox-Mox
    & Heinmot Hihih
Yettahtapnat Alwum[M] (*Shooting
    Thunder*)
Yiyik Wasumwah[OF]

Zhaya Timenna[M] (*No Heart*)

[I] Infant. [Y] Young. [O] Old. [M] Male. [F] Female.

NEZ PERCE BATTLE PARTICIPANTS

1

2

3

4

5

1. Peopeo Tholekt (Bird Alighting) — Idaho Historical Society.
2. Chuslum Mox-mox (Chief Yellow Bull); 1912 — NAA 2952.
3. Hin-Mut-Too-Yah-Lat-Kekht (Chief Joseph); earliest photo — NAA 2905.
4. He-Mene-Mox-Mox (Yellow Wolf); 1908 — warrior and chronicler — McWhorter.
5. Josiah Red Wolf; 1967 — last survivor of the battle — NPS

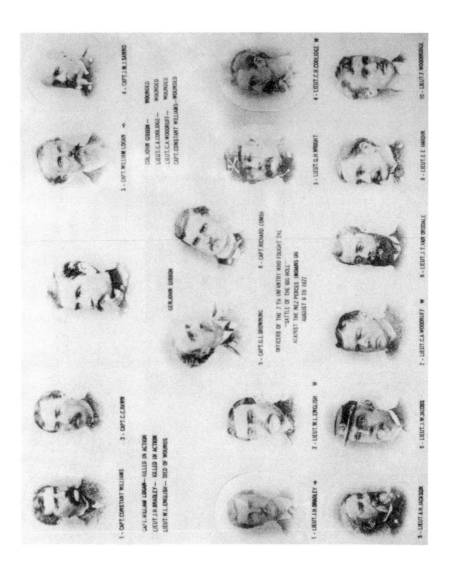

APPENDIX B - OFFICERS

Name	age	birthplace	unit	notes
Bradley, 1 Lt. James H	33	Ohio	7 "B"	C k
Browning, Capt. George L		New York	7 "G"	C
Comba, Capt. Richard		Ireland	7 "D"	C
Coolidge, 1 Lt. Charles A	32	Massachusetts	7 "A"	C w
English, 1 Lt. William L	37	Illinois	7 "I"	C k
Gibbon, Col. John	49	Pennsylvania	7 COM	A,M,C,w
Hardin, 2 Lt. Edwin E		Kentucky	7 "F"	A
Jackson, 1 Lt. Allan H	42	New York	7	C
Jacobs, 1 Lt. Joshua W	34	Kentucky	7 QM	C
Logan, Capt. William	47	Ireland	7 "A"	M,C k
Rawn, Capt. Charles C	40	Pennsylvania	7 "I"	C
Sanno, Capt. James M W	37	New Jersey	7 "G"	A,C
Van Orsdale, 2 Lt. John T	27	New York	7 "D"	A
Williams, Capt. Constant		Pennsylvania	7 "F"	C w
Woodbridge, 2 Lt. Francis	24	Michigan	7 "A"	
Woodruff, 1 Lt. Charles A		Vermont	7 "K"	C w
Wright, 1 Lt. George H		Wisconsin	7 "G"	C

A Military Academy.   M Mexican War.   C Civil War.   k Killed.   W Wounded.

Officers, 7th United States Infantry*
Present at the Battle of the Big Hole
(opposite page)

*This montage hung in the Fort Missoula day room until that structure was destroyed by fire. Though rescued, it was seriously damaged, and was not suitable for reproduction; instead, a copy was made from the July 27, 1960, edition of the Missoulian - Sentinel (Sec. A, p. 26).

Cpl. Charles N. Loynes
Co. I, 7th U.S. Infantry
Writer of an account of the Battle of the Big Hole.
Photo courtesy of Washington State University Archives
Pullman, Washington

APPENDIX C - SOLDIERS

Name	age	birthplace	unit	notes	
Abbott, Cpl. John	26	Switzerland,	7 D	1	w
Alberts, Pvt. Charles	36	San Francisco, CA	7 A	0	w
Andrews, Mus. Peter	19	Ireland	7 K	0	
Banghart, Pvt. George	23	Patterson, NJ	7 G	0	w
Bell, Sgt. James 2nd	35	Ireland	7 E*	2	w
Bender, Pvt. August W	25	Germany	7 K	0	
Bennet, Pvt. John	56	Masalus, NY	7 B	7	M A
Bensinger, Sgt. Robert	28	Germany	7 G	1	w
Brandt, Sgt. Frank	32	Germany	7 D	0	
Brietenstein, Cpl. August	32	France	7 E*	0	
Broetz, Pvt. Herman	23	Germany	7 I	0	k
Brown, Pvt. Lorenzo D	25	Davidson Co, NY	7 A	0	h w
Bundy, Pvt. Thomas	30	New Harmony, IN	7 F	0	c
Burk, Pvt. James	25	Ireland	7 G	0	w
Burke, Sgt. Joseph	25	Natick, MA	7 K	0	
Burns, Cpl. John	29	Dover, OH	7 E*	0	w
Butterly, Pvt. Mathew	36	Ireland	7 E*	1	k
Buty, Sgt. William	28	Germany	7 F	1	
Carpenter, Mus. Robert L	30	New York, NY	7 H	0	
Carson, Pvt. William	27	Franklin, IN	7 I	0	
Clark, Sgt. Howard	27	Charleston, WV	7 K	0	
Clark, Pvt. Wilfred	?	Philadelphia, PA	2 L	?	h
Clark, Pvt. Washington	30	Washington, DC	7 I	1	w
Clarke, Pvt. George	23	Troy, NY	7 I	1	
Collins, Pvt. Thomas	29	Ireland	7 I	0	
Connor, Pvt. John J	24	New York, NY	7 G	0	w
Coon, Pvt. Holmes L	26	Cleveland, OH	7 G	0	
Crogan, Pvt. James	30	Ireland	7 D	0	
Cronan, Mus. Timothy	29	Ireland	7 D	0	w
Cumminskey, Pvt. Joseph	24	Bucks Co, PA	7 F	0	
Cunliffe, Cpl. Richard N	24	Lakers, NY	7 I	0	w
Daly, Sgt. Patrick C	44	Ireland	7 D	3	w
Dauth, Pvt. Adolph	24	Germany	7 G	0	
Devine, Pvt. Mathew	23	Carell Co, VA	7 K	0	w

* Attached to Co."D". 0-7 Number of prior enlistments in 7th Infantry. M Mexican War veteran.
A Civil War (Army). N Civil War (Navy). h Awarded Congressional Medal of Honor.
c Awarded Certificate of Merit. d Deserted Aug. 9, 1877. k Killed. w Wounded.

Name	age	birthplace	unit	notes	
Devoss, Pvt. Joseph	30	Waverly, OH	7 I	1	w
Drake, Pvt. McKindra L	23	Choseakton Co, OH	7 H	0	k
Drummon, Cpl. Socrates	28	Ross Co, OH	7 K	2	A
Edgeworth, 1 Sgt. Robert L	29	Ireland	7 G	1	k
Edwards, 1 Sgt. William D	26	Brooklyn, NY	7 F	1	h
Eisenhut, Cpl. Jacob	31	Switzerland	7 D	2	k
Elmore, Pvt. James	27	Philadelphia, PA	7 F	0	
Erickson, Mus. John	19	Hudson City, NJ	7 F	0	w
Evans, Pvt. James	32	Manchester, NH	7 I	0	
Fallon, Pvt. Patrick	43	Ireland	7 I	2	A w
Ferris, Pvt. Charles	28	Fairfax Ct Hs, VA	7 F	1	
Frankenfield, Pvt. Isaac	27	Doylestown, PA	7 D	1	
Frederick, Sgt. John W H	30	Cincinnati, OH	7 G	1	N w
Frost, Pvt. Peter M	32	Hamilton Co, OH	7 K	2	N
Gallagher, Pvt. Francis	30	Philadelphia, PA	7 F	0	
Gallagher, Mus. Michael	25	New York, NY	7 D	0	k
Geant, Pvt. Eugene	24	Germany	7 H	0	
Goale, Pvt. John H	26	Cincinnati, OH	7 G	0	d
Goff, Pvt. Peter	26	Canada	7 A	0	
Goldberg, Pvt. Jacob	25	Germany	7 K	0	
Gould, Pvt. Charles B	?	?	2 F	?	w
Grace, Pvt. Gerald J	25	Munroe Co, OH	7 G	0	
Groff, Pvt. Henry S	28	Cincinnati, OH	7 H	1	
Hamilton, Pvt. Price	25	Bath, VA	7 F	0	
Harryman, Pvt. Byron	26	Morgan Co, IN	7 K	2	
Heaton, Pvt. Davis	27	Ireland	7 K	1	A w
Heider, Cpl. Levi	28	Germany	7 A	1	
Heinze, Pvt. Charles	29	Germany	7 G	0	
Heinzman, Cpl. Adolph	36	Germany	7 A	1	
Herdmerton, Pvt. Carl	29	Germany	7 G	0	
Hexter, Pvt. Nehm	25	Cleveland, OH	7 F	0	
Hogan, Sgt. Michael	25	Ireland	7 I	0	k
Hunter, Pvt. Edward D	29	Columbus, IN	7 F	0	w
Hurlburt, Pvt. Philo O	24	Allegheney Co, NY	7 K	0	w
Jacklin, Pvt. George	24	Ann Arbor, MI	7 G	0	
Johnson, Pvt. Oliver	28	Walworth Co, WI	7 F	1	

* Attatched to Co."D". [0-7] Number of prior enlistments in 7th Infantry. [M] Mexican War veteran.
[A] Civil War (Army). [N] Civil War (Navy). [h] Awarded Congressional Medal of Honor.
[c] Awarded Certificate of Merit. [d] Deserted Aug. 9, 1877. [k] Killed. [w] Wounded.

Name	age	birthplace	unit	notes	
Keys, Pvt. James	25	Elkhart, IN	7 D	0	w
King, Pvt. Edward C	27	Baltimore, MD	7 G	0	
King, Pvt. Habern R	30	Milford, IA	7 G	0	
Kleis, Art. John	28	Germany	7 K	0	k
Lane, Sgt. Riley R	39	Paxensia, OH	7 D	1	A
Lay, Pvt. John	?	?	2 L	?	
Lefferty, Pvt. Thomas	?	?	2 L	?	
Lehmer, Pvt. James C	36	Rome, NY	7 A	0	A w
Leher, Pvt. George	27	Germany	7 A	1	w
Loveland, Pvt. Seth D	32	New York, NY	7 G	0	
Loynes, Cpl. Charles N	24	Pittsfield, MA	7 I	0	
Ludke, Pvt. Charles	24	Buffalo, NY	7 E*	0	
Luttman, Cpl. Christian	39	Germany	7 F	2	A w
Malley, Pvt. James E	30	Ireland	7 F	0	
Mantz, Pvt. Gottlieb	23	Germany	7 G	0	k
Martin, Sgt. William H	33	Trenton, NJ	7 G	1	k
Matthews, Pvt. William W	38	Jefferson Co, IN	7 G	1	A
Maurer, Pvt. George	28	Germany	7 F	0	w
McCafferey, Cpl. Daniel	24	Canada	7 I	0	k
McCaffery, Sgt. Francis Jr	29	Scotland	7 D	2	
McGregor, Pvt. Malcolm	31	Scotland	7 G	1	d
McGuire, Pvt. James	37	Ireland	7 F	0	k
McHenry, Pvt. John	?	?	7 K	?	
McLaughlin, 1 Sgt. Thomas	27	Canada	7 D	2	
McLennon, Mus. John W	25	Ft. Bellknap, TX	7 A	1	h
Meinart, Pvt. Charles	47	Germany	7 I	3	
Molloy, Pvt. James	25	Bedford Co, TN	7 K	0	
Monaghan, Sgt. Thomas	35	Ireland	7 G	2	
Moore, Pvt. John G	?	?	2 L	?	
Moran, Pvt. William	37	Ireland	7 H	1	A
Morton, Pvt. David B	27	Gibson Co, IN	7 G	0	
Murphy, Pvt. Frank	23	Providence, RI	7 K	0	
Murphy, Pvt. John A	24	Boston, MA	7 D	0	
Murphy, Cpl. John D	23	Ireland	7 D	2	
Murphy, Pvt. Nicholas	23	Ireland	7 I	0	
O'Brien, Pvt. F. John	?	?	7 G	1	k
O'Connor, Cpl. Dominick	29	Ireland	7 G	1	k
Page, Sgt. Edward	?	?	2 L	?	k
Payne, Cpl. William H	27	Scotland	7 D	1	k

Name	age	birthplace	unit	notes	
Pomeroy, Cpl. Noah G	23	Winston, NJ	7 K	0	
Pomeroy, Pvt. William D	36	England	7 F	2	k
Raferty, Sgt. John	37	Ft. Hamilton, NY	7 A	3	
Renz, Pvt. George	31	Germany	7 D	1	
Robbecke, Pvt. Charles A	25	Germany	7 G	0	w
Rodgers, Pvt. Seldom M	22	Yontville, IN	7 I	0	
Rogan, 1 Sgt. Patrick	30	Ireland	7 A	2	h
Sale, Cpl. Robert E	29	Nashville, TN	7 G	0	k
Sanderer, Pvt. George	29	Pittsburgh, PA	7 G	0	
Sanford, Pvt. Joseph	28	Canada	7 K	0	A
Schairer, Pvt. Albert	28	Switzerland	7 F	0	
Schlept, Pvt. George	?	?	2 L	?	
Schohn, Pvt. Antoine	34	France	7 D	1	
Sipfel, Cpl. Christian W	37	Germany	7 A	1	
Smith, Pvt. Alexander A	?	?	2 L	?	
Smith, Pvt. Calvin	34	Lancaster, PA	7 I	0	
Smith, Pvt. George	31	Germany	7 K	1	
Smith, Pvt. John B	?	?	7 A	?	k
Spayd, Cpl. Isaac H	26	Lebanon, PA	7 G	0	
Stillwell, Pvt. William	24	Conneautville, PA	7 D	0	
Stinebaker, Mus. George W	19	New York, NY	7 G	0	
Stinebaker, Mus. Thomas P	?	New York, NY	7 K	0	k
Stortz, 1 Sgt. Frederick	26	Rochester, NY	7 K	1	k
Stretten, Cpl. Michael	?	?	7 K	?	
Stumpf, Pvt. Edward	30	Germany	7 A	0	
Sullivan, Pvt. Martin	24	Milwaukee, WI	7 G	0	
Thompson, Pvt. William	23	Pittsburgh, PA	7 I	0	w
Wachtel, Pvt. Daniel V	26	Frederick Co, MD	7 F	0	
Watson, Sgt. William W	?	?	7 F	?	k
Welch, Pvt. Edward	25	England	7 G	0	
Whalen, Sgt. Patrick	43	Ireland	7 F	2	A
Williams, Pvt. Robert F	31	Greene Co, NY	7 D	0	
Wilson, Sgt. Mildon H	30	Huron Co, OH	7 I	1	A h
Woodward, Pvt. Benjamin F	36	Spencer Co, IN	7 D	0	
Wright, Sgt. William	34	Richmond, VA	7 E*	0	w

---

* Attatched to Co."D". 0-7 Number of prior enlistments in 7th Infantry. M Mexican War veteran.
A Civil War (Army). N Civil War (Navy). h Awarded Congressional Medal of Honor.
c Awarded Certificate of Merit. d Deserted Aug. 9, 1877. k Killed. w Wounded.

Skull (probably of a soldier) found in the Siege area prior to 1912. Photo by Earle Forrest, an early
U.S. Forest Service employee.

Citizen volunteers present at the Battle of the Big Hole: Samuel O. Chaffin (upper left); Samuel S. Madding (upper right); Myron M Lockwood (center); Millard F. Sherril (lower left); and, Thomas C. Sherrill (lower right). From *Contributions to the Historical Society of Montana*, Vol. VII, p. 123.

APPENDIX D - CIVILIANS

Name	age	status	location	ref
Armstrong[k], John		Volunteer	In the attack	1,2,3,4
Baker[w], Jacob		Volunteer	In the attack	1,2,3,4
Bear, Jack		Volunteer	?	4
Blodgett, Joseph	42	Local guide	With howitzer	2,4
Bostwick[k], Henry S.		Army guide	In the attack	3,4
Buck, Amos		Volunteer	In the attack	1,2,3,4
Burch, Vincent		Volunteer	?	2,3,4
Catlin, John B.	40	Volunteer	In the attack	1,2,3,4
Chaffin, Anthony	54	Volunteer	With wagons	1,2,3,4
Chaffin, John S.		Volunteer	?	3,4
Chaffin, Newton J.	29	Volunteer	In the attack	2,3,4
Chaffin, Samuel O.	18	Volunteer	In the attack	1,2,3,4
Chaffin, William		Volunteer	?	2,4
Clark, Oscar	43	Volunteer	In the attack	1,2,3,4
Cooper, Riley B.		Volunteer	In the attack	3,4
Davis, Isaac N.		Volunteer	In the attack	1,2,4
Dunham, Samuel		Volunteer	In the attack	1,3,4
Edwards, William H.		Volunteer	In the attack	1,2,3,4
Elliott[k], Lynde C.		Volunteer	In the attack	1,2,3,4
Gird, August K.		Courier	At siege area	3,4
Hart, Charles B.	34	Volunteer	In the attack	1,2,3,4
Heldt, Fred		Volunteer	In the attack	1,2,3,4
Herron, Samuel J.		Unofficial	With wagons	4
Hubbard, George		Volunteer	In the attack	1,2
Hull, Joseph G.	42	Volunteer	With wagons	1,2,3,4
Johnson, Luther		Volunteer	In the attack	3,4
Judd, Oscar		Volunteer	In the attack	1,4

[k] Killed. [w] Wounded.

[1] Volunteers from Captain Catlin's Company No. 2, listed by Col. John Gibbon as "Faithful with us to the last" (see letter, Gibbon to Adj. Gen'l., Dept. of Dakota, Sept. 5, 1877; NA, 3464 AGO 1877).

[2] Leeson's *History Of Montana* (1881), p. 146.

[3] Amos Buck, "Review of the Battle of the Big Hole," in *Contributions* (1910), p. 122.

[4] Other.

Name	age	status	location	ref
Kirkendall, Hugh		Wagonmaster	With wagons	3,4
Leifer[w], Otto	37	Volunteer	In the attack	1,2,3,4
Lent, Eugene		Volunteer	With wagons	1,2,3,4
Lockwood[k], Alvin		Volunteer	In the attack	1,2,3,4
Lockwood[w], Myron	36	Volunteer	In the attack	1,2,3,4
Madding, Samuel S.		Volunteer	In the attack	1,2,3,4
Matt, Pete		Interpreter	At siege area	4
McGilliam, Nelse		Courier	At siege area	4
Miller, John		Wagoner ?	At siege area	4
Mitchell, Alexander E.	21	Volunteer	In the attack	2,3,4
Mitchell[k], Campbell	29	Volunteer	In the attack	1,2,3,4
Morrow[k], David		Volunteer	In the attack	1,2,3,4
Ryan[w], William		Volunteer	In the attack	1,2,3,4
Sherrill, Millard F.	24	Volunteer	In the attack	1,2,3,4
Sherrill, Thomas C.		Volunteer	In the attack	1,2,3,4
Shinn, John		Volunteer	?	3,4
Wade, George		Volunteer	In the attack	1,3,4
Wallace, Jerry		Volunteer	With wagons	1,2,3,4
Wilkerson, Barnett H.	18	Volunteer	With wagons	1,4
Woodcock, William		Servant	With howitzer	4
Wilson, Harrison		Volunteer	?	2,3,4
Wright, Mike		Volunteer	In the attack	1,3,4

[k] Killed. [w] Wounded.

[1] Volunteers from Captain Catlin's Company No. 2, listed by Col. John Gibbon as "Faithful with us to the last" (see letter, Gibbon to Adj. Gen'l., Dept. of Dakota, Sept. 5, 1877; NA, 3464 AGO 1877).

[2] Leeson's *History Of Montana* (1881), p. 146.

[3] Amos Buck, "Review of the Battle of the Big Hole," in *Contributions* (1910), p. 122.

[4] Other.

Pvt. Homer Coon's Map, n. d.
(opposite page)

Copy in Big Hole National Battlefield collection, cat. 91, acc. 46.

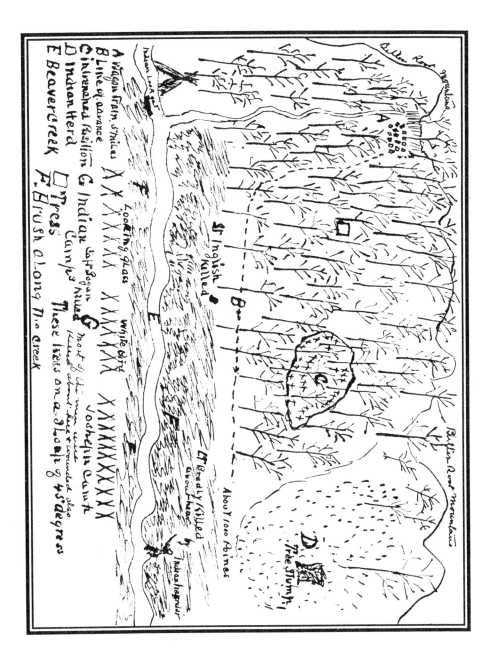

A Wagon train 3 Miles
B Line of advance
C Intrenched Position G Indian lift began
D Indian Herd
E Beaver creek

F. Brush along the creek

□ Trees

Looking Glass

White Bird

Josephs Camp

These trees on a Slant of 45 degrees

St Inglish Killed

B

Ct Deadly Killed Arowhead

About 1000 Poines

G most of the men were killed about that wounded also

by Indian hagreler

Indian Lodges

D Tree Stump

Bitter Root mountains

A

Bitter Root mountains

164

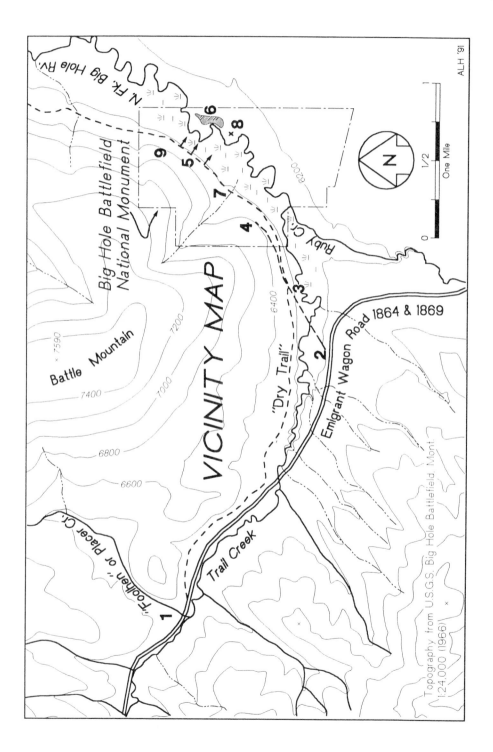

VICINITY MAP

Big Hole Battlefield National Monument

Battle Mountain

N. Fk. Big Hole Rv.

"Foolhen" or Placer Cr.

Trail Creek

"Dry Trail"

Emigrant Wagon Road 1864 & 1869

Ruby Cr.

7590

7400

7200

7000

6800

6600

6400

6200

ALH '91

N

One Mile

0   1/2   1

Topography from USGS, Big Hole Battlefield Mont.
1:24,000 (1966)

VICINITY MAP

1   Wagon park at "Foolhen," or present Placer Creek, where Hugh Kirkendall corralled his freight vehicles and guarded the horses and mules.

2   Approximate point on the old emigrant road (2 miles from Placer Creek) where the howitzer crossed Trail Creek through a brushy meadow; probably the same crossing used by Capt. Browning when he brought Kirkendall's wagons forward following the battle (they had to be taken apart and manhandled over the stream). The meadow crossing is about one-half mile.

3   Foot of Battle Mountain, up which the howitzer was hauled another half mile over the open hillside (diagonally across the contours on a ten percent grade; the sideslope of the ridge measures 30 to 40 percent) to the "Howitzer Pit" location.

4   "Howitzer Pit" where the gun was put in battery to fire on the Indian encampment 1,200 yards distant. From there it commanded the encampment, which would not have been possible in the timber lower down.

5   Indian trail at the foot of Battle Mountain, along which Col. Gibbon's soldiers and civilian volunteers formed their line-of-battle prior to the dawn attack on the Indian encampment. This was the "Dry Trail" of the approach march, so-called by the civilians in contradistinction to the emigrant road which was boggy in early summer from the many small drainages crossing it near the mouth of Trail Creek.

6   The Indian encampment in the dry meadow east of the North Fork of Big Hole River. West of the river, to the foot of Battle Mountain, the ground was a wet meadow cut by old meanders and obstructed by large patches of willow brush. A large swamp around the juction of Ruby and Trail creeks extended up the latter nearly to the brushy meadow where the cannon and wagons were crossed over.

7   Siege area, where Col. Gibbon's men fortified and stood off the Indians in a "point of timber" on the alluvial fan at the mouth of "Battle Gulch," a dry draw descending from the southeast slope of Battle Mountain.

8   Where the cannon ball was found embedded in meadow soil near the south end of the Indian encampment. This shell, fired unfused, had failed to explode.

9   "Twin Trees" sniper position from which an Indian marksman was able to harrass soldiers and civilian volunteers retreating from the Indian encampment.

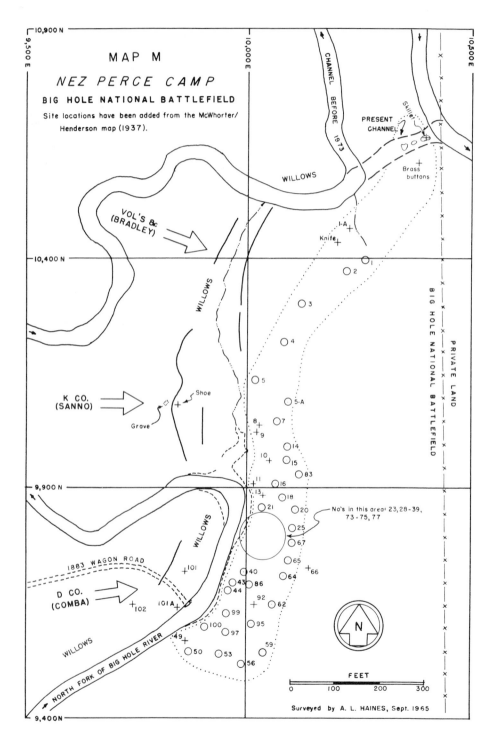

MAP M

NEZ PERCE CAMP

BIG HOLE NATIONAL BATTLEFIELD

Site locations have been added from the McWhorter/
Henderson map (1937).

Surveyed by A. L. HAINES, Sept. 1965

CAMP AREA MAP

1	Tipi of Wo-to-len; NE limit of the camp, according to McWhorter.	52	Tipi of Coals of Fire (old man; owned fast horses).
1A	Two soldiers killed here (Bradley & Morrow?). Some brush remained along the this drain in 1965.	53	Tipi of Red Cloud (too old to fight).
		54	Tipi of Red Spy (warrior).
2	Tipi where Yellow Wolf slept unarmed on the night of the attack.	55	SE corner of the camp.
		56	Tipi of Lean Elk, or "Poker Joe."
3	Tipi where Rattle-on-Blanket slept unarmed that night.	57	Tipi where Kit-tel-poos-man (warior) slept unarmed.
4	Tipi of Shot-in-head.	58	Tipi of Che-mih (aged warrior) killed in the fight.
5	Maternity tipi (mother, nurse and new born baby killed).	59	Eastern edge of the camp.
5A	Tipi in which two children and a woman were killed.	60	Same.
6	Je-kam-kun (warrior), wounded.	61	Tipi of Tah-kin-pal-loo (warrior, past 40 snows) killed in battle.
6A	Red Heart (young warrior) mortally wounded.	62	Tipi of Black Owl; killed in battle.
7	Tipi of warrior Li-kin-ma.	63	Dead woman and child in a depression.
8	Washout where the wife of Li-kin-ma and four other women were killed.	64	Tipi where He-yum-ta-nan-mi (young woman) was killed.
		65	Tipi of Ell-is-ya-kon; killed in battle.
9	Soldier killed by Li-kin-ma.	66	Sink where ex-slave "No Feet" (not a Nez Perce) sheltered.
9A	Soldier killed by Wah-li-tits.		
10	Wah-li-tits and wife killed.	67	Tipi of Tim-lih-poos-min (warrior) killed in battle.
11	Soldier who killed Wah-li-tits killed by his wife.	68	Ip-nan-ye-ta-ma Lil-pith (young sister of Yellow Wolf) killed.
12	Black Tail (warrior) wounded.		
13	Dead soldier; described by Indians as wearing braid and ornaments (Capt. Logan?).	69	Tok-ta-we-ti-sha (woman) mortally wounded; died two days later.
14	Tipi of Ugly Grizzly Bear Boy.	70	Pit-like depression where children took shelter.
15	Tipi of Chief White Bird.	71	Tsi-a-yah (boy) killed.
16	Tipi of Chief Too-hool-hool-zote.	72	No-heart (boy) killed.
17	Tipi of John Dog (wounded early in the fight).	73	Tipi burned; child died in bedding.
18	Tipi of Two Moons (older warrior).	74	Tipi burned; two little boys — Red Thunder & a son of Peo-peo-Tholekt — survived under blankets and a buffalo robe.
19	Tipi of Lone Bird (warrior).		
20	Tipi of Na-tal-le-kin (first killed — while going for horses).		
		75	Pa-tsa-kon-mi (aged woman) killed.
21	Tipi of Wah-li-tits.	76	Wife of Wat-yet-mas-lik-li-nin killed.
22	Wat-yet-mas Lik-lei-nen killed fighting in front of his tipi (wife killed also).	77	Tipi set afire by a soldier.
		78	Dead Indian (half-dressed and unarmed).
23	Te-wit-Toi-toi (warrior) killed at his tipi.	79	Dead Indian (aged man; unarmed).
24	Wah-nis-tas Aswet-tesk shot many times while smoking at his tipi.	80	Dead Indian, with lifeless child in his arms.
		81	Mortally wounded Indian boy; died later on the trail.
25	Tipi of Chief Looking Glass.	82	Gray Eagle (White Feather' father) mortally wounded; died at 2nd camp.
26	Tipi of White Bull.		
27	Tipi of Chief Nah-tal-e-kin.	83	Tipi of Ha-hots Tof-nu-kuns, or No Tail Grizzly Bear (warrior).
28	Dead Indian boy.		
29	1st Sgt. Frederick Stortz killed (found sitting upright in willows).	84	Tipi burned; mother and two children escaped to river.
		85A	Tipi of buffalo hides; would not burn — wrecked by pulling over.
30	Cpl. Daniel McCaffry killed.		
31	Sgt. Michael Hogan killed.	85	Tipi partly burned.
32	Cpl. Dominic O'Connor killed.	86	Tipi wrecked; body of a young Indian girl underneath.
33	Pvt. Herman Broetz killed.	87	Tipi of Wai-nat-ta-ka-kan; killed later in Canada.
34	Pvt. Gottleib Mantz killed.	88	Dead soldier.
35	Dead Indian woman with live baby (one hand nearly severed).	89	Aged Indian man killed.
		90	Half grown Indian girl, wounded and helpless; died on the retreat.
36	Capt. William Logan killed.		
37	White Feather (young woman) shot in shoulder & clubbed in mouth.	91	Indian and soldier died fighting each other.
		92	Captive volunteer killed by Ots-kai.
38	Dead Indian (old man).	93	Dead Indian baby and young boy.
39	Dead Indian girl (child).	94	Dead Indian (old man; not a warrior).
40	Burned tipi.	95	Tipi containing five dead women and children.
41	Dead Indian boy (half grown), at water's edge to the west.	96	Tipi burned.
		97	Tipi wrecked; dead soldier underneath.
42	Wrecked and partly burned tipi.	98	Tipi of White Eagle, wounded in battle.
43	Tipi of Chief Joseph.	99	Tipi of Rainbow; killed in battle.
44	Tipi of Chief Ol-lo-kot.	99A	Tipi of Strong Eagle.
45	Tipi of Light-in-the-mountain.	99B	Tipi of parents of Red-headed Woodpecker (young warrior killed in battle).
46	Tipi of Black Tail Eagle.		
47	Unnamed Indian killed.	100	Tipi of Chief Tok-ka-lik-si-mai (escaped to Canada with White Bird).
48	Dead Indian boy (half dressed).		
49	Five Fogs killed (fighting with a bow and arrows).	101	Soldier killed by Yellow Wolf.
50	Tipi of Five Fogs.	101A	Dead Indian and soldier.
51	Tipi of White Eagle (warrior; wounded, he died 5 days later).	102	Dead Indian.

168

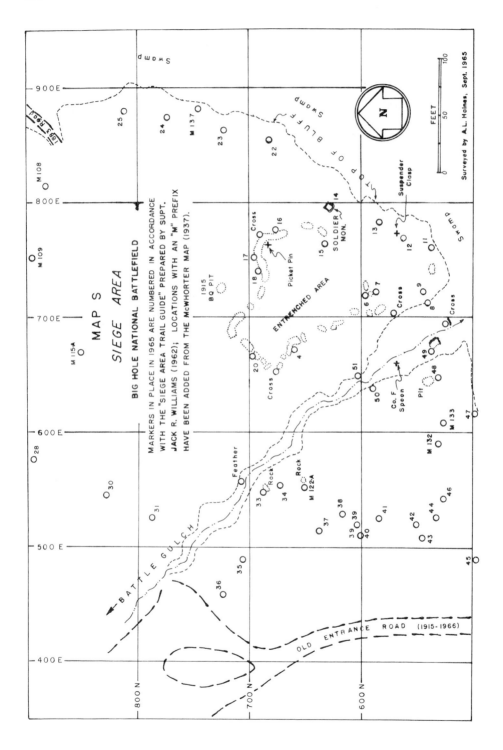

MAP S

SIEGE AREA

BIG HOLE NATIONAL BATTLEFIELD

MARKERS IN PLACE IN 1965 ARE NUMBERED IN ACCORDANCE
WITH THE "SIEGE AREA TRAIL GUIDE" PREPARED BY SUPT.
JACK R. WILLIAMS (1962); LOCATIONS WITH AN "M" PREFIX
HAVE BEEN ADDED FROM THE McWHORTER MAP (1937).

Surveyed by A.L. Holmes, Sept. 1965

FEET
0   50   100

SIEGE AREA MAP

4   Rifle pit held by Captain John B. Catlin (volunteer officer).

6   Rifle pit occupied by two citizen volunteers.

7   Rifle pit dug by M. F. and T. C. Sherrill, night of Aug. 9 & 10.

8   Where Pakatos (Five Wounds) was killed.

9   A citizen volunteer was slightly wounded here.

11   Where Tom Sherrill received a bullet through his hat.

12   Location of the Nez Perce memorial made by sculpter Alonzo Lewis and placed in July, 1928, by L. V. McWhorter and Nez Perce survivors.

13   Location of the memorial to Nez Perce noncombatant dead placed by Thain White and a friend at dawn on Aug. 9, 1951.

14   Location of the six-ton memorial placed by the U. S. Army in 1883 to honor the soliers and civilian volunteers who fought here.

15   Where T. C. Sherrill cut the boot from the foot of Lt. English.

16   Rifle pit dug by a soldier after he was shot through the breast.

17   Rifle pit of W. H. "Billy" Edwards, who went to Deer Lodge for help.

18   Col. John Gibbon's command post.

20   Rifle pit from which Otto Leifer was reputed to have "killed the Indian who sang his own death chant" (at No. 33); not true.

22   Where Lt. W. L. English was mortally wounded.

23   Where Sgt. Edward Page, Co. L, 2nd Cav., was killed.

24   Swan Necklace fought from behind a tree at this point (the only one of the three Salmon River murderers to survive this battle).

25   Ten Owl fought from this point; he escaped to Canada from the last battle (Bear Paw) and returned to Lapwai, Idaho.

28   A tree at this point sheltered a shrpshooter, Kool-kool Kah-lou, who was also a "medicine man."

30   Lean Elk, better known as Poker Joe, fought here. He led the retreat from Big Hole to Cow Island, and died in the Bear Paw battle.

31   A tree at this point sheltered Peo-peo Tholekt, a battle survivor who helped McWhorter locate significant sites in 1928.

33   Tims-poos-man fought from behind this boulder, chanting to his Wyakin for help (he was not killed — see No. 20).

34   Wot-to-len (Hair Combed Over Eyes) fought from behind a log here. He was not made a "good Indian," as claimed, but died in 1928 — age 109.

35   Where the right elbow of Quilo-ish-kish was shattered in the attempt to rescue the body of Sarp-sis; he escaped to Canada.

36   Where We-weet-sa, or Log, was wounded in the left collarbone in the attempt to rescue the body of Sarp-sis.

37   A stump at this point sheltered Bald Head (lost his hair to a cannon shot in earlier fighting); he surrendered with Chief Joseph.

38   Where Peo-peo Tholekt and Sarp-sis fought behind a tree barricaded with timber until the latter received his death wound.

39   Red Spy did sharpshooting from a tree at this point following capture of the howitzer, where he killed Cpl. Sale.

40   Where Strong Eagle was wounded while attempting to carry Sarp-sis out of danger. He participated in every battle and escaped to Canada.

41   Bighorn Bow, a strong and brave young man, dragged the body of Sarp-sis to this point, from which it could be taken away.

42   Another place where Raven Spy fought.

43   Bow and Arrow Case fought here. He died at Nespelem in the thirties.

44   A tree which is no longer here sheltered Going Alone.

45   Chief Ol-lo-kot, Joseph's younger brother and leader of the young men, fought from behind a tree that stood here.

46   Two Flocks Lighting on Water, the only member of Joseph's band to take part in the Salmon River forays, fought from a tree at this place.

47   Two Moons sheltered under the lip of the bench here; he escaped to Canada and joined Sitting Bull, later returning to Idaho.

48   As a miner, Luther Johnson dug this prospect hole ten years before the battle; he and two others sheltered in it during the fight.

49   A citizen volunteer and several soldiers held this position,

50   Myron Lockwood, a citizen volunteer, was seriously wounded in the hip behind a rock barricade in this draw.

51   Lynde Elliott, another citizen volunteer, was killed in that place at the same time, and was buried temporarily at the cross down the draw.

M-108, M-109, 115-A, M-132, M-133 & M137,

Trees sheltering unknown Nez Perce marksmen.

M-122:

A, small boulder from which an unknown Nez Perce fought.

INDEX

Y